THE JOB SEEKER & THE COACH

HOW TO RESCUE AND FAST-TRACK YOUR JOB SEARCH IN NO TIME.

WRITTEN BY

HAMZA ZAOUALI

ISBN: 978-9948-36-350-7 (Printed Book)
ISBN: 978-9948-36-351-4 (E-Book)

Portions of this book are works of nonfiction.
Certain names and identifying characteristics have been changed.

Portions of this book are works of fiction. Any references to historical events, real people, or real places are used fictitiously. Other names, characters, places and events are products of the author's imagination, and any resemblance to actual events or places or persons, living or dead, is entirely coincidental.

Edited by Taylor Williams
Re-edited for the American version by Clare Levijoki
Book design by Zvonimir Bulaja
Cover design and illustrations by Nina

First printing edition 2019.

Hamza Zaouali

help@nameyourcareer.com

www.nameyourcareer.com
www.thejobseekerandthecoach.com

Acknowledgements

All thanks and praises to God.

This book has been written in memory of my parents, Habiba Nabli & Béchir Zaouali, for their unwavering sacrifice, wisdom, love, patience and support throughout these years.

Also in memory of Salvatore Cali, my teenage-years math tutor and engineer by profession, who could no longer bear the burden of unemployment.
This book wouldn't have been written without you.

And finally, my deepest thanks to my wife, Aurore Robinot, whose support and encouragement were instrumental.
I love you.

Special thanks to Taylor Williams, my amazing editor, that helped me critique and improve this book as if it were her own.

Preface

The story recorded in this book is based on true events, experienced by real professionals. They are job seekers from all walks of life, job sectors, industries, seniority, and countries that I have had the honor to serve and guide during a vulnerable time in their career journey, whether through my live seminars, video programs, or individual coaching.

As a career coach, international recruiter, and entrepreneur/employer, I've sat at the crossroads between job seekers and employers since 2003. I have studied countless books on the topic of job searching, as my thirst for designing simpler and more effective job search tools and methods for my clients grew.

I have enjoyed reading and learning from many top authors and coaches, but something was missing: I was never able to find a book that truly reflected the beautiful but difficult journey of a job seeker, transforming through coaching and experience while confronting the emotional ups and downs that a job search inevitably brings about.

I chose to write this book as a story to narrate the step-by-step transformation that my simple system has allowed so many job seekers from all over the world to achieve. It is thanks to them that this book was born, and from them that it was inspired. Although the story is set in Dubai, please make no mistake: the tools, techniques, methods, templates, and scripts are universal.

Many of these tools have not made it into mainstream career books.

Looking at the career book market, I knew I had to solve this problem. So within these pages, you will find little-known tools and techniques for using search engines and other websites to find job opportunities and hacks to get the attention of corporate decision-makers. You will also discover my three-step method to succeed at every job interview and a powerful script for salary negotiation which may as much as double the figure your employer offers you.

This is in addition to a resume writing formula that I'm confident will transcend your results, the way it did for my coaching clients over the years.

In this book we will also tackle the plights of job seekers in difficult circumstances: those who have been terminated or long-term unemployed. I am a firm believer that no job-seeker is a lost cause, and that all can obtain jobs and salaries which exceed their expectations and empower them to create the lives they want.

This book is designed to help job seekers all over the world.

Because there are a few small differences between the North American and other job markets, I want to share a few notes for my readers:

- In the United States, Canada and Australia, the document you send potential employers outlining your achievements is called a resume. Elsewhere, that same document is called a CV.
- We have intentionally left our protagonists' salary currency in AED—a currency most readers of this book may not be familiar with. The reason is that we know that appropriate salary and cost of living vary widely around the world, so we do not want the reader to become hung up on specific salary figures. Instead, simply notice that Lisa obtains nearly twice her previous salary using the negotiation tactics I'll be teaching in this book. That is the important thing.

As a job search is arguably one of the most defining moments in someone's career, it is my hope that one day, the step-by-step formula described in this book will be widely taught to students and professionals from all walks of life, and will help professionals find the work they truly deserve, regardless of their current situation.

By choosing to read this book, you have made the decision to generate more and better career choices for yourself and develop an advantage over your competition. Just as importantly, you are about to set yourself apart from the widespread mediocrity that plagues job searches across the world.

I commend you for that. Consider this coaching session to be my gift to you, for your dreams and aspirations to blossom and thrive, and for your true gift in this life to serve others.

Sincerely yours,
Hamza Zaouali.

Table of Contents

Introduction

The Situation at Work

As she drove to work, Lisa dreaded the look of disappointment she was sure she'd see on the face of her manager, Mark, when she stepped through the office door.

What could she say to him? Last week she had exaggerated her potential deal pipeline to buy herself some time. She was certain Mark was becoming impatient at best, or knew she was lying to him at worst. She had already received a written warning last month.

She knew that if she could not get a client to sign a contract within the next two days, she would have to go through another painful performance review. And after that...?

As a sales representative at *Cloudcom*, her role was to call companies, present conference call solutions, and organize online or face-to-face software demos, all in the hope of getting clients onboard for a yearly contract.

For some time, she had been feeling that perhaps sales was not for her. She tried to make it work, but she just couldn't get herself to pick up the phone and do enough cold calls to generate those demos.

'Besides, I'm not really money-driven,' she thought to herself; commissions were never really a motivation.

At 28 years old, she was single and had no children. Having a car loan and student loans to pay off, she had been unable to put aside any savings.

She had been trying to find a role away from the sales sector, but the market was not great. It was as if her life, her job, her career had been at a standstill. Little did she know that after that day, her life would never be the same again.

When she arrived at work that morning, she noticed that Mark was not in his office yet. After bidding, "Good morning," to her colleagues, she sat at her desk, turned on her computer, and immediately picked up the phone so that Mark would see that she was busy when he arrived. In her situation, it couldn't hurt.

It was only half an hour before Mark arrived. As he switched on his computer, Lisa could see him from her desk. She waited, tense, to see what would happen.

As soon as he finished with his computer, he stood up and walked to Lisa's desk.

"Morning, Lisa. Can I see you for a minute?" he asked.

"Morning," replied Lisa, preparing herself for another grueling conversation. "Sure."

Lisa heard the office go suddenly quiet, although she did not dare look at anyone. She was certain that the entire office was watching her follow Mark towards the main meeting room.

"Have a seat," Mark instructed as he held the door.

After the two sat down, Lisa was the first to speak.

"Am I in trouble?" she asked anxiously as Mark sat on the other side of the small, round table.

"You've been in trouble for a few months now, Lisa," replied Mark, "and I think it wouldn't be fair for you or the company to keep this going any longer. We've had several discussions in the past and your results have not improved," he continued. "From what I can see, I don't think you're very happy with this situation either. So I think it's time we both come to the conclusion that this role is not for you."

Lisa was in shock as the words hit her. She knew she was in trouble, but the worst she had imagined was a final warning. Not being fired right then and there.

"So I'm fired?" she asked, her disbelief in her voice.

"I don't like that word," Mark protested, "but I think it's best that your contract is terminated, yes. That is the only way for you to find a company you really enjoy working with and that brings out your full potential."

Lisa sat silently, not knowing whether she should bargain for an extra month or just let it happen. As hard as it seemed, she realized she should not push the matter any further; it wasn't as if she had anything concrete in her pipeline to promise Mark.

But strangely, Lisa did not want the conversation to end. The fear of what would happen once Mark stood up to signal the end of the meeting was terrifying.

Besides, the end of the month was just two days away. Why hadn't he waited?

Mark allowed some time for Lisa to grasp the moment and come to terms with it. But his next words hit Lisa like a shockwave.

"The good news for you is that, as per the company policy, you are not required to serve any notice period. Instead, you will receive all your dues in the next few days, and you'll be free to pursue any other opportunity as soon as you want," he said with a smile.

Although Lisa understood that not having to serve her notice period was better for her—she could dedicate all her time to her job search—she felt like she was being hurled into some unknown abyss.

She saw herself at least staying a few days for the handover. Anything that would give her enough time to process and transition to a life without a job. Lisa couldn't help but feel unwanted.

"Thank you, Mark," she replied stoically. "What can I do in terms of handover today?"

"Nothing for now," Mark replied, already aware of her pipeline and work in progress—or lack thereof. He sounded apologetic. "If you've added everything on the system, we'll take it from there."

It was all moving too quickly, like Lisa wasn't even allowed to catch her breath. But she understood. He needed to do what was best for the business and for the team.

"Sure thing. Please don't hesitate to call if I can help in any way, of course," said Lisa, sensing the end of their conversation nearing. It was nearly time for her to pack her stuff and leave.

"I will," said Mark, and even he seemed uncomfortable with how hurried the meeting had become.

Lisa pushed her chair back to stand up, and as she put her two hands on the table, Mark said something that caught her off guard.

"Listen, I've been in your shoes. I know how you feel right now."

"Really?" she asked, eyebrows rising in disbelief.

"Yes. Years ago, I was let go for poor performance. I was lost and wasn't sure about what I should do next, where I should go, or even what I should think. I hope you won't mind me saying this, but I see a lot of my past self in you today," he confessed.

"Sorry, did you just say that you got terminated?" asked Lisa, just to make sure she heard correctly.

For a moment, Lisa felt better. In a strange way, it was reassuring to hear that Mark, who always seemed successful, had dealt with his own ordeals.

"That's right," he confirmed. "And before that, I was constantly flirting with that prospect anyway; I was very anxious about my career. It's only through coaching and mentoring that I turned the situation around and made it to where I am today," he confessed.

"Coaching and mentoring?" repeated Lisa, attempting to probe further.

"Yes," said Mark. "I used a career coach to help me set my career on the right path and find a job that actually fits with who I truly am. As a result, I started becoming better at what I was doing, and I haven't stopped progressing since then."

"Thank you for sharing this with me, Mark," Lisa replied, puzzled but appreciative all the same. "But I'm not exactly sure how a coach can help me find work."

"Simple." Mark smiled. "By shining a light on your Three Circles and making them work for you."

"My Three Circles?" she repeated, intrigued.

"Yes," Mark confirmed. "But unfortunately I won't have time to go over this today. If you want, I'll send you the email address of the Three Circles Coach; I think he still does free consultations. And you can always give me a call if you need help, I mean it," he assured her.

"Thank you, but I don't think I need a coach," said Lisa, sensing the end of their conversation.

"Suit yourself, of course, but remember this: It's hard to see the big picture when you're in the frame."

Mark stood up and shook Lisa's hand, his expression turning fatherly. "Sorry this role didn't work out for you, Lisa. But you'll be okay, I'm sure of it."

Lisa went back to her desk, grabbed her bag, and left without saying goodbye.

She did not have the energy to go through the "What will you do now?" or "Will you be staying in Dubai?" conversations from her now ex-colleagues. She just wanted to be alone and come to terms with her termination.

Lisa felt every eye in the office on her as she walked towards the exit. As soon as she stepped through the sliding door, the feeling of rejection intensified; it was as if she became a stranger to Mark and the company in one moment.

The reality of her situation caught up with her all at once. She'd seen it many times before: Cloudcom's policy was that when someone was terminated or resigned, there was no notice period to be served. She would receive her salary for the month and the salary she was owed for her notice period.

Under UAE law, she was also to receive the cash equivalent of a single flight ticket back to her home country, and a meager end of service benefit in cash but nothing more. Her employment VISA would be canceled immediately after.

Then she'd have a grace period of just one month before she had to leave Dubai.

Lisa's Career So Far

As she walked towards her car, her heart pounded and shivers raced down her spine. Like every month, her rent, student loans, and car loan payment were due. Her life in Dubai was in jeopardy if she couldn't find work fast.

There was another year of monthly payments towards her car loan before she could settle her debt. She also had five years left on her student loans before she'd completely pay off her college degree. As she sat in her car, she felt like she was in free fall.

Her heart raced with fear and regret.

"How did this happen?" she sighed out loud as she started the engine and began her drive back to her studio apartment in Jumeirah Lakes Towers.

Five years ago, when she graduated with a Bachelor's degree in Commerce with a concentration in Marketing, the only thing she could think about was working in the luxury sector. Coming from a town in Virginia, she always saw herself living in a big city, like New York, Hong Kong, Singapore, or Dubai. This was especially crucial because jobs were disappearing from her hometown.

Besides that, she loved the big cities. She felt more at home where there were many different types of people.

During her first work experience—a six-month internship in New York at Cerrutini, a boutique Italian luxury watch manufacturer—she was so excited that what she thought was her dream at the time had finally materialized.

She quickly became one of the top sales people there. That was also the time she became close friends with Tina, the store's assistant manager.

Tina was older than Lisa and had been working at the shop for about three years by then. Tasked with looking after the new recruits, Tina quickly saw Lisa's determination and ambition. Very approachable, Tina was fun to be around, and she took Lisa under her wing.

At that point in time, ambitious and energized by her early success, Lisa pictured her entire career in New York, growing in that bustling and opportunity-filled city. She would not have imagined for one second that she would soon find herself living in Dubai.

Tina was going there to visit a friend of hers, Sabrina. Since her holidays coincided with the end of Lisa's internship, Tina decided to invite her along.

With no strings attached, Lisa gladly accepted; the commissions she had received allowed her to take a break from the dreary New York winter weather.

When Lisa and Tina arrived, Sabrina had been in Dubai for over four years already. She was working as an executive secretary for the CFO of a large, family-owned company in Dubai. Married to a Tunisian man by the name of Youssef, the couple had an adorable daughter named Hanaa, who was a year old at the time.

Sabrina and Lisa quickly became good friends. After only one week there, Lisa was completely sold on the sunny city. Compared to New York, it was a drastic change, and she started picturing herself living in Dubai.

Convinced by Sabrina to try her luck with the job market and stay a little longer when Tina returned to New York, Lisa gladly accepted. Advised by Sabrina, she walked into several stores at the time and introduced herself to managers in various malls across the city.

After a few job interviews, Lisa was accepted for a permanent sales role at one of the branches of another luxury watch retailer called Watch the Time. Her salary wasn't great, but she enjoyed living in Dubai.

Coming from a small town in Virginia, and having worked in New York afterwards, the fact that she was living in a sunny, metropolitan paradise on the edge of the Arabian sea made up for her low salary for the time being. The city was everything she could have ever wanted.

After a few months at Watch the Time, she began dreading going to work for the first time in her short career. The long hours, an authoritarian manager, and the shop's routine were starting to wear on her. Even smiling at customers was becoming more and more of a chore. For weeks, she had been contemplating leaving the retail sector, when a particularly unhappy and vocal customer tipped her over the edge.

She started sending her profile to other companies away from the retail sales sector. Much to her surprise, she wasn't able to generate many interviews, until she received an interview request for a sales representative role at Cloudcom, a company selling conference call solutions to corporate clients globally.

She hadn't even completed five months at Watch the Time.

When Lisa joined Cloudcom three years ago, she couldn't believe that someone had actually given her a chance to move away from the retail sales sector. Cloudcom was located in Dubai Internet City, one of the two clusters in Dubai dedicated to the IT sector.

"I want something that I can be more in control of," she explained to Mark Higgins during her interview. "With this role," she said, "I will make my own luck. I will be the one approaching potential clients on the phone and following up with them at will, rather than hoping and waiting that one comes into the shop."

At the time, Mark had liked her attitude and wanted to give her a chance.

"What about your dream to work in the luxury sector?" he'd asked.

"I still love the luxury industry, but I'd enjoy it more if I was a customer rather than an employee in that sector. That's why I'm keen on a role where I can earn good commissions," replied Lisa.

Without knowing it, Lisa had pushed the right buttons for the job, and Mark decided to hire her then and there.

As she drove back home that fateful day, Lisa passed by the familiar company names on the buildings.

She remembered how happy she felt at the beginning of her contract with Cloudcom, when she realized she would be working in Dubai Internet City alongside names like Microsoft, IBM, and Oracle. Three years ago, she had felt like she was entering a new and exciting world.

As she drove away from Dubai Internet City, she felt as if that door was closing behind her.

'What am I going to do now?' she wondered, visualizing her resume and thinking about what other job sectors she could apply to.

LISA DUTOIT

Lake Terrace, Flat 1304
Jumeirah Lake Towers
Dubai, UAE.

Single, 28 years old
Mbl: +971 50 000 0000
Email: Lisadutoit@fakemail.com

A motivated and driven Business Development Specialist with 5 years of Corporate and Retail sales experience. Passionate about business development, I use a consultative approach to identify business opportunities. I'm an Expert at understanding customer's needs and areas of challenge to implement relevant solutions. Bilingual in French and English, Bachelor's degree in Marketing - available immediately

CAREER HISTORY

CLOUDCOM INC. Dubai, UAE.   **2016-Present**
Sales Consultant

- Manage client accounts and represent companies in selling web conference solutions
- Proactively identified new business opportunities in line with our service offerings across Telco, Govt, Retail, Manufacturing, Tech, Utilities and FS clients
- Booked demos with new and existing customers to increase sales revenue
- To execute sales strategies in order to explore business opportunity and maximize sales prospect.
- Establish and maintain excellent relationship with potential and existing customers as well as to provide world-class customer service to strengthen customer loyalty and market penetration.
- Visiting client businesses to establish and act on selling opportunities
- Assessing customers' needs and explaining our Conference Call solutions in line with their needs.
- Quoting and negotiating prices, and completing contracts and recording orders arranging delivery of goods, installation of equipment and the provision of services.
- Planned to ensure the successful development and execution of a business development plan.
- Demonstrated in depth knowledge of the competition and their capabilities in order to value position our solutions to the market
- Provided expert training to my clients on our more complex online data products either face to face or by WebEx

Watch the time Inc. Dubai, UAE.   **2015-2016**
Sales Assistant

- Checked supplies, placed orders, created product displays and liaised with retailers to improve product placement
- Delivering excellent customer service to win the sale
- Handling incoming telephone calls from customers or previous customers to assist with their issues
- Attended trade shows and conventions
- Participated in merchandising our products in the most efficient way

Cerrutini & Co. New York, US.   **2014-2015**
Sales Assistant intern.

- Recommended products to customers based on their needs and interests, demonstrated and explained products.
- Delivering excellent customer service to win the sale
- Meeting and exceeding KPI's
- Working within a team to move furniture around

EDUCATION AND TRAINING

Bachelor's Degree in Commerce with Concentration in Marketing,   **2014**
University of Virginia, USA

High School Degree, GPA 3.85   **2011**
Thomas Jefferson for Science and Technology, USA

Retail Sales Foundation Training   **2014**
New York, US

HOBBIES & LEISURE

Leisure Interests: Sport, Travel and Reading

Other: Holder of Full clean driving licence

References available upon request

Although she had been warned multiple times, she just could not get herself to pick up the phone and cold call enough prospects to generate those demos. The worse her situation got, the harder she found it to approach potential clients with any confidence.

"Oh well. It's done now," she muttered with a sigh as she arrived at her apartment's parking lot.

When Lisa arrived to the deafening silence of her studio apartment, it was 9:50 AM. Her night clothes and towels were still on the floor from the morning rush. The daylight streaming through the windows was at all the wrong angles, as if she was intruding in her own apartment.

All her friends were at work still. In fact, the entire city was at work, it seemed. A strange feeling of isolation settled over her like a weight, as if she was being left behind somehow. *'I need to move on,'* she thought to herself, but it wasn't very convincing.

Luckily she had updated her resume two months ago, anticipating the day she would start to receive warnings from Mark. Although she had been sending job applications almost every day for over a month, she'd no luck in securing job interviews for roles outside the sales sector, apart from the odd recruitment agent phone call. The job market was sluggish after hitting a record low during the last global recession and the subsequent property crisis.

She sat at her small desk and turned her laptop on. She opened her personal email to find no new messages worth her time. She then opened another window, went to Google, and wondered what job she would be looking for today.

Lisa knew that sales was the wrong sector for her. She had been trying her luck with other job sectors, like marketing where she majored, administration, retail operations, and even sales training, but nothing came of it.

She knew the market wasn't great. Confusion about what she could do next and irritation with the fact that recruiters and employers didn't bother even replying to her applications mixed like a bitter stew.

The sound of a new email arriving interrupted her thoughts, and she recognized the familiar name: it was Mark. She opened the email immediately.

'Maybe he found a potential deal as he was going through my clients?' she hoped, her heartbeat accelerating.

Hey Lisa,

Someone in HR will contact you soon to confirm the cancellation of your VISA.

I promised to send you the contact details of someone that could be of help.

He goes by the name of the Three Circles Coach. I'm not sure what his real name is; he prefers to remain anonymous. *(Please don't be deterred by that, have at least a free consultation and see for yourself if he can help.)*

You can find his contact details at www.nameyourcareer.com

Whatever you decide to do, your present situation is absolutely not a reflection of your future, I'm sure of it.

Best of luck,
Mark.

Shivers went up her spine as she read Mark's email. Things were moving faster than she could handle. For the first time, the idea of leaving Dubai occurred to her. *'Dubai is an expensive city,'* she thought, *'and if the market is not great, then I'd rather make a quick decision.'*

Lisa contacted a few friends of hers to see if anyone could refer her to their current employer. She received a few answers that promised to pass her resume along, but she wasn't holding her breath.

She spent the entire day sending out job applications. At 6:35 PM, her mobile rang. It was Sabrina, most likely checking in after receiving Lisa's email.

As she picked up Sabrina's call, Lisa could hear the wind of a car in motion on the other end of the phone. Sabrina had just left work for the day.

"Hey sweetie, how's it going?" asked Sabrina.

"Been better..." sighed Lisa.

"Yeah, I read your email. Listen, I'll be by your building in like fifteen minutes. Do you want to come down for a drink?"

"Sure, call me when you've parked," said Lisa.

Although they would call each other during the week, it was rare they would meet on weekdays. Lisa was glad that she wouldn't be alone.

Sabrina and Lisa Meet Up

When Lisa arrived at the cafe, Sabrina was sitting on the terrace, sipping a chamomile tea and looking at her phone.

"Hey!" Lisa greeted.

Sabrina stood up and swept Lisa into a hug.

"How are you feeling?" asked Sabrina.

"Stressed and lost." Lisa forced a smile, trying to keep the conversation light. "I have no idea what I want to do and I've been sending tons of applications but nothing concrete has happened."

"Did you try to change your resume?"

"Of course. I even had it reviewed by a friend of mine in HR. He corrected a few things here and there, but nothing major. I think the market is just not great at the moment."

Sabrina did not respond to that. "How did it end with your boss?" she asked instead.

"Good, I guess." Lisa shrugged. "He said he's confident I'll be able to bounce back and find the right opportunity."

"That's nice of him," Sabrina remarked.

"Mark is really nice. But at the end he suggested I speak to a coach he knows. I'm not sure I will."

"Why not?"

"I mean, when he offered it, it felt like he was saying I couldn't do it by myself. Like I had some sort of condition and needed therapy," she said, only half-joking.

"He didn't ask you to see a doctor, Lisa!" Sabrina laughed.

"I know, but it felt like it!" Lisa laughed in return.

"Well, I don't know if you should see a coach or not, but as an executive secretary, I can tell you that many top executives go through a lot of coaching to get where they are. Like the CFO I'm working with right now said to me once, 'it's hard to see the big picture when you're in the frame.'"

"Wow, that's exactly what Mark said to me this morning. I'm not sure, though. My finances are really tight, and that's another expense I'm not sure I can afford when I can't even juggle rent, student loans, and a car loan."

"Don't worry about that yet. Just start with a free consultation and see if coaching is what you need before you make a decision."

"I guess I have nothing to lose."

"No you don't. As for the money, we'll cross that bridge if and when we get there."

"Fine, fine," Lisa sighed. "I guess I'll get in touch with him."

Both Mark and Sabrina had been so insistent, and they had both spouted the same line about seeing the big picture. It couldn't just be a coincidence. Maybe there really were some career secrets she had never been taught. She doubted that those could help her find a job in only a month— but she was running out of options.

The two friends talked and enjoyed each other's company for another hour or so before they both went home.

The following morning, Lisa sent an email to the Three Circles Coach, asking for a time they could discuss.

The reply came 30 minutes later.

Thank you for reaching out.

My schedule is a little full, but please fill out the attached form and I'll let you know if I can help.

Speak soon,
The Three Circles Coach

PS: Please note that my sessions are conducted via Skype without webcam.

Lisa filled out the form, explaining her situation in full. She also attached a copy of her resume. In the final box, when asked who referred him to her, she mentioned it was Mark.

The Three Circles Coach promptly replied with a time for an initial consultation.

It would be the following day—Wednesday—at 9 AM. Lisa spent the rest of the day sending job applications, and wondered how the first conversation might go.

It seemed so strange that he went by a nickname and not his real name. As she browsed his website again, she found a myriad of client testimonials, both in writing and videos.

Some of the people were job seekers, top executives, and even entrepreneurs located in Asia, Europe, and the US. She couldn't find anyone among his past clients who was actually located in Dubai, and she worried about his amount of experience in her specific job market.

When she went to bed, she was still filled with anxiety. The prospect of returning to Virginia nagged at her again.

Her thoughts raced. She loved her life in Dubai, and the thought of going back home without a job made her feel like a failure. But at the same time, she wanted to be logical, not emotional.

Sleep didn't come easily that night.

The last thing she thought about was the Three Circles Coach saying his schedule was a bit full, and she wondered how their conversation would go.

Nothing could have prepared her for that first discussion.

LISA'S PARADIGM

The Initial Consultation

The following morning, Lisa prepared a notepad in case she wanted to jot down some notes. At 8:54 AM, she sat in front of her computer and checked her inbox for any important emails; there was already one rejection message. Opening it, she read the same type of depressing and impersonal rejection message she received before.

At 9 AM, Lisa opened Skype. When her computer rang, she saw on her screen the username she was expecting: 'The Three Circles Coach.'

"Oh, hi there, is this Lisa?" the coach asked once the call connected. His voice was deep and sounded older.

"Yes, it is," said Lisa. "Good morning".

"Good morning, this is the Three Circles Coach. I believe we have an appointment; are you free to speak?"

"Yes, thank you for calling."

"You're most welcome. So, how can I help?" asked the Three Circles Coach.

Lisa got straight to the point.

"Well, I've been looking for a job for the past two months now, but the job market isn't great at the moment, so I need some help."

"Okay. Roughly how many job applications would you say you've sent in the past two months?" probed the coach.

Lisa hadn't counted or tracked her applications, but after thinking about it for a few seconds, she said, "Probably four or five a day, so around

200 in the past two months." As soon as she mentioned the number 200, she was in shock. "I hadn't realized it was that many..."

Lisa's answer didn't seem to surprise the coach. He carried on.

"So how many companies have you interviewed with?"

"Well, if I don't count calls from recruitment companies, I've had two face-to-face interviews. For sales roles, though. I want to get out of sales."

"We'll get to that, but can I ask you a question first?"

"Sure."

"When you say that you had two interviews after roughly 200 applications, what would you say is your percentage of success?"

"Um—that would be one percent. That's not a lot," she realized with a jolt.

Although Lisa knew something was wrong with her job search, it was the first time she understood of how bad her situation really was.

"That's ok, Lisa; it can only go up from here. Tell me, why do you say the job market isn't great at the moment?"

"Because it isn't," affirmed Lisa, taken aback.

"How do you know?" challenged the coach.

"Trust me, I can feel it. I'm sending job applications almost every day. It was easier for me before. I mean right now, companies are closing down and people are being made redundant, it's all over the news."

"You seem to be describing a crisis," he observed. "So allow me to challenge you a little on this assumption, if that's okay. Are you saying that the job adverts on the web are fake?"

"No. I hope not, although I wonder sometimes..."

The coach replied to her sarcasm with his own. "Well, unless most job adverts are fake and there is some sort of coordinated conspiracy against job seekers in Dubai, you know that for most vacancies, someone is going to get hired, right?"

"I guess so," she admitted.

"So the only question I have for you is, why not you?"

"I'm not sure, honestly. That's why I need some help," Lisa replied sullenly.

"And we're here for that," reassured the coach. "But I won't be able to help if we don't identify the real problem. Would you allow me to ask you a few more questions?"

"Of course," Lisa replied.

"Apart from your perception of the job market, do you see any other reasons for not being successful at your job search?" he asked.

"There's always discrimination," she argued. "My dad was from Jamaica originally, and I think my skin color and the fact that I'm a woman in an Arab country makes finding a job even harder."

The coach didn't reply for what seemed like an eternity. When he did, he didn't sound surprised by Lisa's answer.

"Lisa... would you agree that the vast majority of people with the same background and gender as you in Dubai are at work right now?" asked the coach.

"Some are, of course, but it's harder for people with my skin color and gender to find work," she argued, already defensive. "The stats are here to prove that."

"Stats?" he probed.

"Yes," replied Lisa. "For example, I recently read that ten percent of job seekers with my background are unemployed, compared to two percent for—"

"The stats are probably true," the coach interrupted. "I won't argue with you on that. I can accept the fact that it's harder to find work for people with a specific background or gender. What I disagree with is if you say you don't find work *because* of your background or gender. There's a big difference there."

The coach paused to allow Lisa to process this.

"Besides," he continued, "if ten percent of job seekers with your background remain unemployed, then it means that 90 percent of them are able to find work. If most women with your background are working, why not you?"

Lisa felt cornered, frustrated and penned in. Any reason she might come up with would be swiftly brushed off. Worse than that, he seemed to be implying that if she could not find work, it had to be her fault.

"Well, seems to me that any reason I could come up with wouldn't be what you're looking for," Lisa grumbled.

"If the reasons you offer can be logically challenged, then they can't be the source of our problem," reasoned the coach, like some sort of science teacher.

"Correct me if I'm wrong, but are you trying to tell me that if I can't find work, it's my fault?"

"What made you come to this conclusion?"

"Well, the fact that you keep saying '*Why not you?*' If you're trying to make me feel like it's my fault, I think that's nonsense. The market is challenging, I'm a woman, and I come from a minority background. That's going to make my job search harder!" she snapped. "That's a fact, and there is not much I can do about that, can I?"

Immediately she felt bad. The Three Circles Coach was possibly the only person who could help her, and she was already losing her decorum.

But little did she know, her fears were perfectly in line with what the coach was thinking.

Time for a Choice

The coach said nothing at first. And then, with a deep breath and in a calm voice, he announced, "Right at this moment, I won't be able to work with you, Lisa."

Lisa was shocked. It was the second time in 24 hours that someone told her that! What could she have said that was so wrong for the coach to make this decision? She hesitated, then took a deep breath.

"Okay..." she began slowly. "Is this because your schedule doesn't allow it, or because you feel my situation is unsalvageable?"

The coach said nothing for what seemed to be an eternity. Finally, sounding almost fatherly, he said, "Listen, I'm sorry if I came on a little strong, but right now there's a door between us, and you are at a place where no one can really help you."

"What do you mean?" asked Lisa.

"What I mean is that, even if I find time to coach you, the door between us is locked and you're the only one with a key. If you decide to use that key, then I'll be your guide for whatever is behind that door. But if you don't, I'm afraid that I won't be able to help you. Understand?"

They had already gotten off on the wrong foot, Lisa knew. She tried to keep her confusion and her curiosity in check as she pressed onwards.

"So... what's the key? I'm not sure I follow you."

"The key represents your mindset. I am not going to mince my words, I'm just going to tell you straight away what I think is happening. You can decide to use your energy to challenge me, or to shift your reality. But you won't be able to do both, so choose carefully."

"Okay," she agreed slowly, mentally bracing for impact.

The Three Circles Coach paused for a few seconds, as if to allow Lisa to prepare herself.

"First of all, you suffer from a victim mindset," he stated bluntly.

"A what?" asked Lisa.

"You have a victim mindset," he repeated. "This is a mindset that always blames others, things, circumstances, context... It's a 'there's nothing I can do' mentality. It's the job market's fault, people have more experience than me, it's my background, my nationality, my religion, my skin color, the economy sucks...

"All of those things might be true. But they don't help you. And as long as you are focusing on them, you are not focusing on the things you can do to be better than everybody else on the market.

"Someone afflicted with a victim mindset blames and complains all the time. When challenged, most people with this mindset will tell you that they're already doing everything they can, that their resume, their methods, their attitude are fine.

"Because when you have a mindset like this, you're convinced the problem is outside, not inside. In all my years of experience, I have yet to see someone make it big with a victim mindset. That's why I can't help you. I'm sorry."

Lisa didn't reply. She wanted to argue, but she couldn't.

"You're saying that I can't make it. Why not?" she asked.

"Because we act in accordance with our belief," he stated, before he repeated more firmly, "We act in accordance with our belief. If you believe you can't get a job because of outside circumstances, you're right. If you believe that you can get a job if you improve your skills, you're also right."

He gave it a moment to sink in.

"Listen, Lisa, here's the drill. My clients have a creator mindset. They focus on themselves and take full responsibility. They believe that everything that happens to them is due to their thoughts, their choices, their habits, their methods, and their actions."

"My clients do not spend their time and energy blaming the market, the economy, their employer, their nationality, their background, their gender, or their skin color.

"If there are jobs out there and they can't get interviews or employment offers, they work on themselves. And they keep their egos in check by saying things like 'I am responsible,' 'I need to learn how to...' 'what would I need to change in order to...'" He trailed off, his point made.

The Three Circles Coach paused to allow Lisa to process or argue with the concept.

Although Lisa understood what the coach was saying, she couldn't help but feel like she was being attacked.

"No offense, but I still believe the combination of the job market, my skin color, and my gender have been playing a large part in this outcome. Are you saying these factors have no influence on my job search results?"

"No, that's not what I said," the coach argued. "There are many things that will always influence your results. You only have a problem when you put these things at the center of your world. The truth is that you can keep blaming anything you want for the next twenty years, but it won't change your results.

"You don't have control over these things, and what I am saying is that you might as well never mention them at all because they rob you of precious brain power, creativity, and energy. And you need these resources to focus on the things you can change, not things you can't change. Do you see the difference?"

"I think so," she returned, beginning to grasp the concept.

Even so, she knew she would need to mull it over more later. She wrote in her notebook:

FOCUS ON THINGS I CAN CHANGE,
NOT ON THINGS I CAN'T CHANGE.

"The very problem in this thinking," the coach continued, "is that nothing ever changes when you blame other people or events for what happens to you.

I can show you all the tricks, tools, techniques, and methods to accelerate your job search, but it won't matter if you believe that the market, your skin color, or anything else dictates the results. Do you understand?"

"I think so," she said, though she wasn't sure how *helpful* any of what he said would be. It was still hard for her to believe that she could overcome her challenges simply by focusing on what she could control instead of on what she couldn't.

"The change you're looking for must be inside-out, not outside-in. If you just hope for the market to change, for recruiters to find you, or for luck to strike, you're making a prayer for weakness. Your strength is inside you, and this is where it must start."

The coach fell quiet while Lisa's thoughts raced. The door he spoke of was taking shape in her mind, but she still wanted to dig in her heels. She spent six months blaming things she couldn't change for her lack of results at work and during her job search, which left her powerless. She understood what the coach was saying, but that reaction felt like it was part of her.

"I understand what you're saying. But at the same time, you agreed that the market, someone's background, or gender can influence our results. So how do you reconcile this with having a creator mindset?"

"That's a good question," he conceded. "Imagine you're an athlete getting ready for a race. On both sides of you are the best sprinters in the country; they look strong and they trained hard. We'll call this the market you operate in.

"What I'm saying is that if you think that the market is difficult, that you would need luck to win, I would not bet money on you winning this race. You've empowered the market over your own ability. There is just no way you win with this 'there's nothing I can do mindset,'" he argued.

"There is always something you can do to improve your situation. You can acknowledge external circumstances—but if you believe your results depend on them, it might just be a self-fulfilling prophecy.

"You need to shift your mindset on what you could do to win. You could use your external environment to trigger a different line of thoughts and actions. Someone with a creator mindset will use his environment's pressure and tension to push himself to think outside the box.

"That's when you have a chance to win. In other words, the market has an influence over your results whether you have a creator or a victim mindset. But victims surrender to the market, while creators use it to prepare and adapt. In both cases, it will influence your results, yes, but you can choose how external factors influence them."

The Three Circles Coach paused to give Lisa a moment.

"The market is only here to challenge you to go beyond where you are right now," he continued. "If it was easy, you wouldn't need to market and sell yourself.

"Difficult external circumstances are here to help you grow. Without tension or pressure, there wouldn't be any growth; no world records, no victory worth having, no progress in humanity. Still with me?"

"I get it," she confirmed. "It's about shifting my reality to something that will empower me as opposed to holding myself back."

"Exactly!" the coach crowed. "Most people react to what happens to them. A reaction is instinctive. But when we hit some bumps on the road, we need to grab the steering wheel and respond instead of reacting.

"You have the power to choose how you respond to anything that happens to you. But complaining or blaming is reacting, not responding.

"The truth is that external challenges are here for you to become all you can be. Without this mindset, you are in prison, crying, blaming, and trying to find excuses for your failures."

The coach was silent again, and Lisa took a moment to scribble in her notebook:

I CHOOSE WHETHER A SITUATION HAPPENS TO ME OR FOR ME

"It makes sense, but..." She trailed off, still writing.

"I know how you feel. It's hard to grasp this concept when you've built your reality around the opposite idea. Give yourself some time and think about it logically.

"I strongly believe you can find work. If most people do, why not you?"

"Why not me..." she mumbled. He had said it before, but she didn't feel like he was attacking her anymore. Suddenly, the question was full of possibilities.

"For most vacancies, someone is going to get hired, so why not you?" the coach pushed when she didn't respond.

Lisa was still silent. It felt like she had been rebooted. What had irritated her so much just a few minutes ago was suddenly completely nonthreatening.

The coach was still waiting for a response, and Lisa could practically feel her train of thought switching tracks.

"Why not you, Lisa?" repeated the coach, paternal once again.

"Because of my resume...?" she guessed hesitantly.

"This is partly true, but the real answer is *'Because of something I can change.'* That is the key: taking full responsibility. Do you see what I mean?"

"I do," Lisa replied, taking notes at the same time.

"Taking full responsibility for your results will put you on track for excellence, because you will be focusing on the most critical part of the equation: *you.* Taking responsibility for what happens to you, for the way you think and feel." The coach paused before pressing onwards.

"That isn't going to be easy at first.

"It means you need to surrender to the idea and accept that your current situation is because of your past choices, of your methods, techniques, attitude, or habits. So your job is to grab hold of the steering wheel and change course, to carefully craft a response to your situation instead of simply reacting.

"You will change, learn, adapt, and grow. That's what you'll be doing behind that door if you choose to open it. There is no magic formula, just hard work."

"I think I understand," Lisa mused cautiously.

"I know you do. And don't worry if you don't have all the answers just yet. You'll find them on this new road as you progress. What's important is that you realize how much power you have over any situation in your life when you take full responsibility."

Paradoxically, Lisa felt thrilled and soothed all at once. "Thank you," she said as sincerely as she could.

The coach remained silent, giving her a moment to think.

"Taking full responsibility," she repeated to herself. It was unexpectedly empowering. But fear gripped at her: what if she forgot it as soon as the session ended?

She looked at her notes, which almost served as a mental map to where she was now:

WE ACT IN ACCORDANCE WITH OUR BELIEF.
I WILL FOCUS ON THINGS I CAN CHANGE, NOT ON THINGS I CAN'T CHANGE.
I CHOOSE WHETHER A SITUATION HAPPENS TO ME OR FOR ME.
I WILL RESPOND TO MY SITUATION (CREATOR) RATHER THAN REACT TO IT (VICTIM).
MOST PEOPLE WITH MY PROFILE DO FIND WORK (FACT), WHY NOT ME?
-> PROBABLY BECAUSE OF SOMETHING I CAN CHANGE.

After a good 30 seconds passed, the Three Circles Coach signaled the end of the consultation.

"Before we finish, do you have any questions?"

Lisa looked at the time on her computer and realized the two had been talking for more than 30 minutes.

Already? She hadn't even asked her most pressing question.

"I do, actually," she replied. "How long do you feel it would take before I find a new job?"

"Lisa, the way you ask the question assumes that a job search takes time. Are you expecting me to reply in terms of days, weeks, or months?"

"I guess so..." she replied. "Although I'd prefer if you replied in days."

"Then that's the wrong question. Time has no effect on your job search. You should not ask how much time it takes. Instead, the speed of a job search depends on the number of job interviews. Your question should be: How many job interviews does a job search take?"

It was a simple enough concept. But considering the number of job interviews she already had in the past two months, it wasn't exactly reassuring.

"OK, so how many interviews do you think it will take?"

"I'm unsure at this stage; some people take ten interviews with different companies, and others only need three interviews."

"So what does it depend on?"

"Good question," he replied. "It varies depending on the market and your interviewing skills. Let's shoot for ten interviews!"

"Ten?" Lisa exclaimed, and she felt like she had been doused in cold water.

She tried to gather her composure, but suddenly it seemed almost guaranteed that she would have to go back to her mom's small Virginia hometown, where jobs were few and far between. "So there is no guarantee that I can find work before I run out of money here?"

"No, there isn't." He paused briefly before he carried on thoughtfully.

"Anyone that tells you otherwise is not to be trusted, because of all the factors that are not under your control. For example, the length of a company's recruitment process, your ability to learn and adapt to what we're going to do together, the availability of vacancies at the time of your job search..."

"I'm sorry, but I have to think in terms of time. I don't have long before I run out of money to stay in Dubai," she reminded him insistently.

"I understand that," replied the coach. "Can I ask you a question?"

"I guess," she sighed.

"Are you results-driven or process-driven?"

For Lisa, the answer was so obvious that the question surprised her.

Little did she know, the answer to that question would transform her job search completely...

Are You Process-Driven or Results-Driven?

"Results-driven," replied Lisa confidently.

"Most people would say that," commented the coach. "How about this: do you control results?"

"I guess," she answered cautiously.

"How?" he challenged.

"If you do what you should be doing," she explained.

"But then that isn't the result that you control, is it? Doing what you should be doing is a process. Achieving what you want to achieve is the result. Do you see the difference?"

"Not really," she admitted.

"I'll give you an example: do you know how to bake a cake?"

Surprised, Lisa smiled. "Yes, I do."

"Excellent. Then suppose you're deciding to bake a cake today, do you control the end results?"

"Of course."

"What if you finish baking the cake and realize it isn't as good as usual?"

"It would mean that there was a glitch with the recipe or the preparation."

"Exactly," agreed the coach. "The reason you have a sense of control when it comes to the result is because you master the process. The quality of your cake is a direct result of the quality of your recipe. You control the recipe, not the end result."

"OK," she agreed carefully. "I'm getting it."

"I'm sure you are," he replied. "The challenge that people face when they're results-driven is that their attention is focused directly on the results, and they seldom realize that what they need to focus on is the process: their job search recipe.

"Always waiting, focusing, and hoping for results makes you disappointed when there are none. And that disappointment, everyday, will make you lose motivation for your job search."

Slowly, Lisa was beginning to recognize her own behavior in what he was saying. 'Demotivated' was a bit of an understatement. But something was still unclear.

"But I did get some results so far," she pointed out.

"Exactly the problem," the coach replied. "That's why you never thought of changing your process. As long as you got results, you would pursue that path until you get some more."

"What's wrong with that?" Lisa challenged.

"It's your conversion ratios that directly affect the length of your job search," he explained.

Lisa hmmed, confused.

"Saying that you should follow the same recipe as long as you have some results is exactly like saying that if the cake is edible, you shouldn't change the recipe. Surely you would have higher standards than that, wouldn't you?"

"Of course."

"Then you see the quality of your job search is defined by only two ratios, and these ratios determine whether something needs to change. Do you remember the first ratio I asked you about?"

"Yes," she replied. "The efficiency of my job search was only one percent. We got that by dividing the number of job interviews with the number of job applications I've made."

"Right, good. Which means that you have a 99 percent chance of failure at every job application. Can you see how that would affect the length of your job search?"

"Yeah, there's some work to do on that side..." admitted Lisa.

"Now, let me ask you a question: did you have the same sense of urgency to improve your process before we spoke?"

Lisa contemplated the question for a moment.

"Not really," she confessed. "I thought I just needed to keep applying until it worked."

"There you go. Do you see the problem I have about being results-driven?" asked the coach "That's why when you will find a job is not something you can control: it's an end result."

"So, I shouldn't aim to find a job within a certain time?"

"You can be goal-oriented, of course, but what must drive your job search are your tools, methods, attitude, techniques, and so on. That's how you can influence the speed of your job search. Understand?"

"I think so," answered Lisa, feeling her awareness expand. "What's the other ratio?"

"That would be your interview success ratio. That's the number of interviews you pass divided by the number of interviews you attend. These two ratios are the only indicators of the length of your job search, and they are both a direct result of your job search process," he explained.

Well, the Three Circles Coach's methods certainly seemed thorough. Lisa wrote both ratios in her notebook.

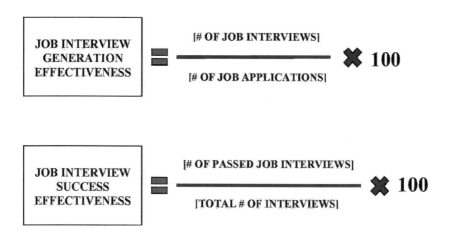

After a brief pause, the coach added, "Taking full responsibility means that the speed of your job search depends on your process. You can measure the speed and the quality of your job search with these two ratios. That's what you should focus on, not time."

"I get it," said Lisa. "Improve my recipe to improve my ratios to improve my results."

"Exactly. Otherwise, with such a low conversion ratio, it'll be as if we're playing lottery with your job search.

"Most people are playing the lottery with their job search, and when they're not getting the results that they want, they blame the market instead of taking responsibility."

"It's so obvious when you say it," she sighed. "I've just been missing it."

The Three Circles Coach remained silent for a moment, letting the concept sink in. Lisa felt like she was waking up after hibernating for years.

"I'm glad you're figuring things out. Taking full responsibility for your results means that you'll be creating these results in the first place, not the market or the economy. You and your recipe.

"When the market is the same for everyone, only people's recipes explain why some get hired for great jobs, and some don't. Do you think your attitude and mindset are part of the process?"

"Probably, yeah."

"Correct. Anything that you think or do can affect your results and is part of your job search process. Anymore questions?"

"How does discrimination fit into this recipe?"

"There are things you can change and things you can't or don't want to change," he admitted. "Imagine if you had a restaurant. You wouldn't be able to adapt to every customer's tastes. People have opinions, stereotypes, perceptions, preconceived ideas...

"Discrimination is a sad but normal occurrence while job hunting. You can't avoid that. Your job is to focus on baking the best dish you can with the ingredients you have. If you do that, you will get plenty of the *right* customers."

"And having a victim or a creator mindset is also part of my recipe?"

"You've got it. The food you cook depends on the ingredients you put in, Lisa," the coach answered.

Lisa took a deep breath and sighed it out. She stared up at her ceiling.

"I feel like I was in prison before. I think I get what you mean about the key.

"Once I take full responsibility for my results, I can open that door. And behind the door lies a creator mindset, tools, techniques, methods that you will teach me and that will make me get more interviews faster and convert those interviews into job offers."

"I couldn't have said it better myself. First, I need you to reflect on all this and see how this can apply to your job search. Do you have any last questions before we end this session?"

"Not for now. Thank you, coach. I really appreciate your time."

"The pleasure was mine, Lisa. Bye for now."

"Bye," replied Lisa.

Lisa felt liberated. She still didn't know what to change in her process, but she felt awake and aware, finally.

The session had knocked her off balance to help her find firmer footing. Still, she felt unsure of where to go now with her newfound energy. How could she improve her resume more than she already had? How could she find open jobs she hadn't already found and applied to?

An email notification interrupted her thoughts. It was Mary, *Cloudcom's* HR Manager. Lisa's VISA had been canceled.

That's when she decided to borrow some money from Sabrina, promising to pay her back as soon as she received her final dues from *Cloudcom*.

A few minutes later, Lisa sent an email to the coach confirming she very much wanted to pursue what they started together and that she would purchase his smallest package via his website.

The coach's reply came two hours later, requesting an appointment for 9 AM the following day.

Shortly after, she received a text message from Sabrina.

> Hey hun, how did it go with the coach? Did you talk to him?

> Intense, but in a good way. I might need to borrow some money from you until I receive my dues from Cloudcom... I should be able to repay you in a couple of days or so. Would that be ok?

Lisa texted back, knowing her friend wouldn't mind.

Career Change or Not?

At 8:55 the next morning, Lisa was all set in front of her laptop, wondering what the day's session would be about. She didn't have to wait long before her laptop rang.

"Good morning, Lisa."

"Good mor—" She cut herself off, unsure what time it was for the Three Circles Coach. "... Hello, coach," she settled on.

"It's 6 AM here," he informed her, likely guessing why she paused. "I'm in London this week."

"I actually wanted to ask about that," said Lisa. "How much do you know about the Dubai market?"

"You think the Dubai job market is particularly unique?" he wondered dryly.

"Isn't it?"

"Yes and no," he replied. "Each job market is different, but the method is the same. Do you really think employers are that different in Dubai?"

"Probably not," she conceded. "But do you have any success stories from around here?"

"Of course. I've coached clients in many countries over the years; that's how I know it's the same method."

"Okay," she agreed slowly. "So what's on today's agenda?"

"I'd like to start with something you mentioned yesterday, about moving away from sales. Is that still the plan?"

"Definitely!" Lisa insisted.

"Then I'm going to challenge you a little here. I need to identify whether your choice is grounded in the right reasons. Alright?"

"Sure," she agreed. "My mind is pretty much made up, though. I don't think sales is for me."

"Okay, can you tell me why your role at *Cloudcom* was terminated?"

"Well, you know I was in sales and I hadn't brought in any new clients for the past three months," Lisa explained. It was her responsibility. "Even before that, hitting my target was a bit hit and miss. The economy is challenging for a lot of companies, so finding new clients is hard."

The coach was quiet for a moment before he asked, "Since the economy is challenging, have there been many layoffs?"

Sensing that the situation could get difficult, Lisa tried to correct her course.

"Well, it's not just the economy. I just don't want to be in sales. That's why I've applied to other types of roles, but nothing's come of it."

"Correct me if I'm wrong, but do I hear the cries of a victim mindset again?"

Lisa blushed, and she was glad there was no video link.

"Maybe," she sighed. "But to be honest with you, if Mark didn't see any potential in me, I trust his judgment."

"Did he say that?"

"Not in those words, but he still fired me."

"That he did, unfortunately, but was it because he didn't feel sales was for you?"

"Well no, not exactly. It was purely based on my poor results, I guess. But without sounding like a victim, the market really isn't great."

"So have many of your colleagues been terminated, too?" repeated the coach.

Lisa knew what he was getting at. Reluctantly, she confessed, "No. Some of them are doing pretty well, actually."

"Thank you for being honest. So let's suppose you're right and sales is not for you. What made you come to that conclusion? But this time, try answering with a creator mindset."

"Because I tried and I don't enjoy it."

It was the truth, at least. She had suffered during the past months and wasn't ready to contemplate the idea of getting into the same situation.

"The thing you have to remember is that your chances of finding a role in a sector you haven't been exposed to are always going to be much slimmer than your chances of finding a role in a field where you already have some experience."

"I have friends that did that, though," said Lisa.

"Of course, there are plenty of people who have. But it's a much bigger risk for employers. If you don't have a previous track record in the role you're applying to, you are competing with candidates who do. So why would an employer or a recruiter give *you* a call, Lisa?"

"I feel capable of doing other things, though."

"We all can," he agreed, "but that doesn't add any credibility to your profile in the eyes of an employer."

Lisa thought for a second before trying to finally settle the matter.

"I don't think someone can be good at something he doesn't enjoy. Do you?"

The Three Circles Coach chuckled briefly. "Fair point. But at the same time, **it's hard to like something you haven't been very good at.** Wouldn't you agree?"

Lisa knew what he was implying, but she couldn't decide if she should defend herself or not.

As if the coach was reading her mind, he added, "Which one came first? Disliking sales or the poor results?"

"I loved my job at *Cloudcom* the first six months," she insisted firmly. "I was excited to go to work every morning. I was learning new things, I believed in the product I was selling, and Mark was great to work with.

"I even broke the company's records very early. I made the fastest first deal in the company's history. I was ahead of my target during the first six months."

"Wow," he mused quietly. "Why didn't you mention this on your resume?"

"I never thought about it, I guess. Thanks for the suggestion."

"Of course. But what happened after your first six months?"

"I think I relied too much on my early clients, and I stopped generating new ones. So when some of my existing clients ended their contracts with *Cloudcom* to cut costs, I had to start all over again. With the market being more challenging, I guess I was never able to get back to my original level."

"I see. Thank you for sharing this with me so openly," said the coach. "Based on your experience, what's the best advice you could give someone beginning a sales career?"

"That you should stick to a rigorous routine of generating new clients; the moment you stop, it becomes harder to get back on track. Habits are what make people successful, and once you get used to not calling clients, it just seems harder to break that habit again. I guess my advice would be to never get comfy in sales."

"Wow. That's the kind of advice that a great sales manager would give. And great sales managers can do this thanks to experiences like the ones you've had at *Cloudcom*."

At that point, Lisa remembered her last conversation with Mark. '*He mentioned a point in his career where he wasn't performing, either.*'

"The choice you have in front of you is to use this experience to learn and pursue your growth in the sales field, or to start all over again in a new field. It all depends on one question: do you believe your unhappiness with your previous role came from the role itself, or from your lack of results?" the coach pressed.

"If you started disliking sales after your results went south, that's a natural reaction. But it doesn't mean you should avoid sales roles in the future. You might just need some training, a different attitude, or a different environment to improve your results."

Lisa was silent, thoughts still circling around her conversation with Mark. The coach carried on.

"I've seen this situation a lot. Job seekers that convince themselves they should try different sectors without even knowing which one.

"They apply for roles outside of their core experience for weeks or months until they're demotivated and end up accepting anything that would end the agony of their job search. That's not how you build a career you can be proud of."

Both of them were quiet as Lisa digested everything that had been said.

For months, she convinced herself that sales was not the right career path for her. But she realized now that it was her lack of results that led to her disdain, not the sector itself, and certainly not the market or the economy.

"I guess my lack of results made me come to this conclusion," she mused slowly.

"I'm glad you've had the courage to face this truth head on," the coach encouraged her. "You mentioned that you've been applying to different kinds of roles. Do you think this has played a role in your lack of interviews?"

"Definitely," she agreed. "The only two vacancies I got calls for were for business development specialist and sales consultant roles."

"And if your level of energy was low in relation to pursuing your sales career, your interviewers probably picked it up during the interview," said the coach.

He paused again to let Lisa absorb the concepts, and she scribbled in her notepad:

SOMEONE WHO WANTS TO ENTER A NEW FIELD IS ALWAYS GOING TO HIT APPREHENSIVE EMPLOYERS AND FIERCE COMPETITION FROM PEOPLE IN THAT SAME FIELD

(—> MUCH HARDER TO GET JOB INTERVIEWS)

RESULTS IN A JOB (OR LACK OF) AFFECT MY RELATIONSHIP WITH THIS JOB.

IT'S NOT BECAUSE I DO NOT LIKE A JOB THAT I SHOULD CHANGE MY CAREER PATH. MY RESULTS CAN ALSO AFFECT MY PERCEPTION.

IF I BELIEVE I'M IN THE WRONG JOB SECTOR, THIS WILL HAVE CONSEQUENCES ON MY ENERGY LEVEL AND INTERVIEWERS WILL NOTICE IT.

"I think I understand," said Lisa. "But I probably need some time to reflect on all this. Honestly, I really don't enjoy cold calls, for example, and having a sales job often means a lot of them."

"I know, and we're going to get to those ungratifying tasks soon," replied the coach. "But before we end this session, I would like to talk to you about the meaning of job fulfillment."

"I'm listening," she replied, intrigued. Her pen was poised over her notepad.

What is Career Fulfilment?

"Tell me, what is career fulfillment?"

"When you have a career that makes you happy?"

"Right. So what makes you happy, Lisa?"

"I guess it's doing a job that I enjoy."

"What kind of job is that?" asked the coach.

"A job that would stimulate me, where I would enjoy each task day in, day out."

"You sound like you're certain of that. What about the boring tasks?"

"I don't think a truly fulfilling job would have boring tasks," Lisa reasoned.

"Really? And what job is that?"

"That's my problem: I don't know."

"Does such a job even exist?

"So, what?" she demanded. "There's no such thing as a fulfilling job?"

"That's not it. What I'm saying is that there is no such job that only includes tasks that you enjoy. Every job has its boring tasks, bad days, and failures."

"So how do you reconcile that with being fulfilled?"

"Great question. Fulfillment at a job is defined by what it means for the people you serve at the job, not a lack of boring tasks."

"I'm not sure I follow," Lisa admitted.

"That's okay. Fulfillment in life is serving others, not doing things that you enjoy. This is the most fundamental difference between pleasure—tasks you enjoy doing—and meaning—tasks that impact others positively." He paused for a second.

"If you're looking for a job that only includes tasks you'll enjoy, you'll be looking for a long time. Most importantly, that perspective could make you miss out on a truly fulfilling job."

"How so?"

"If your standard for happiness is doing tasks that only please *you*, then you might miss the true impact you're having on other people's lives when you serve them successfully." The Three Circles Coach paused before elaborating.

"Have you ever wondered why people feel fulfilled despite doing the most difficult jobs?

"Think about a bricklayer who works outdoors in the cold or extreme heat, or think about a police officer or a taxi driver who spends his days patrolling in a car. A teacher can feel fulfilled despite teaching almost the same material year after year, and a salesperson can feel fulfilled despite having to do cold calls all day. Do you know why?"

It took Lisa a moment to think it over before she suggested, "Because they're not doing it for themselves?"

"Exactly! And doing it for others brings meaning to your work. It makes the task or the job matter to others. The moment your equation for happiness only includes *your* satisfaction, you will never find a truly fulfilling job, regardless of what you're doing.

"Fulfillment at a job is about a combination of passion and the impact it creates in other people's lives, despite the tasks that you find unpleasant."

"I think I understand."

"I don't doubt it. Remember, we've established that you enjoyed sales when you were successful. Most people enjoy what they are successful at. But if you fail to see how it helps others improve their own lives, you will soon miss the fuel to go through these tasks.

"I'm willing to bet that this is what happened at *Cloudcom*. Success cannot happen without struggle and failure. That's the price of learning a skill that can transcend your work and impact the people that truly need your work. **Fulfillment in life is service to others, not pleasure for oneself."**

Lisa was silent for a moment, her eyebrows rising. Finally, all of the pieces were lining up.

"Thank you, coach. This means a lot to me."

"I'm glad; this is critical to know. You need to climb that mountain before you can get to the top and enjoy the view. When you expect life to be happy without the struggle to master a skill that could truly impact others, you're doomed to fail at anything you try."

"I wish I'd known this before I started working at *Cloudcom*," Lisa admitted, the realization hitting her like a softball to the chest.

"I wish they taught this in schools," the coach sighed, briefly melancholic. "Can you imagine if people's main focus in life was to serve others, instead of only thinking of their own benefits?

"Can you imagine a world where everyone's yardstick for happiness is the impact they leave on others? Successful companies have this in their DNA. Successful managers serve their employees, not the other way around. Successful employees serve their colleagues, their bosses, their clients. It's what makes everything meaningful."

"No wonder all the statistics say most people aren't satisfied at work. It always seemed so discouraging."

"It doesn't have to be like that. You don't have to become a statistic."

"I agree," said Lisa, certain of it in that moment.

"When you're not working in a way that impacts others," the coach continued, "you're depriving the world of your input, energy, and results. You haven't been enjoying sales by chance: you've enjoyed it because it clicked with your inner talent and because you can make a difference there."

The coach paused to let Lisa wrap her mind around everything.

His next question would trigger the most important paradigm shift in Lisa's career.

Thinking Like an Entrepreneur

"Tell me, who do you work for right now?"

"No one, obviously."

"And who were you working for before you lost your job?" the coach asked.

"*Cloudcom*?"

"No, try again," he returned playfully.

"My manager?" tried Lisa.

"Nope."

Confusion was setting in again. "I'm not sure what you're expecting," she confessed.

"Let's try something different," he tried. "How would you define the term 'client'?"

"Someone who pays you in exchange for a product or service?"

"Correct. So how is that different from an employer?"

"I see what you mean. But you're acting like I'm a company selling my services to employers," Lisa replied.

"The term 'freelancer' would be more appropriate."

"But I'm not looking for a freelance opportunity," she pointed out, bewildered. "I'm looking for a permanent job."

"What's the difference between the two?" he challenged.

"A freelancer needs to find his own clients, and is hired on a temporary basis for specific tasks, projects, or expertise. What I'm looking for is a permanent job."

"Did you have a permanent job at *Cloudcom*?"

"Yes."

"So why aren't you employed there anymore?"

It was as if a lightbulb had suddenly clicked on. "Because there's no such thing as a permanent job," she answered.

"Bravo!" he cheered. "Looking for a job is about finding clients who will pay you for your services. We're all freelancers serving client after client throughout our career. Does it make sense?"

"It does," said Lisa.

"So I want you to become an entrepreneur when you look at your career, not an employee, and certainly not a job seeker."

Lisa was silent. As much as she wanted the session to continue, her thoughts were racing.

"I think that we should stop for today," the coach suggested, as if reading her mind. "We'll reconvene tomorrow at 9 AM, if you're free."

"Sure. But before we end the call, can I ask you why they call you the Three Circles Coach?"

"I knew you would ask eventually," he mused wryly. "We'll talk about this during our next session. Trust me, it will have everything to do with your job search. But for now, just remember this: the first and most important of all three circles is 'service to others.'

"It's on this circle that your career and of course your job search should be based on. You're no longer looking for work, you're looking to help others with your sales expertise. Regardless of the state of the market, there are plenty of companies that need your work. When you succeed at selling, you help a client solve a problem.

"There is an enormous number of companies that need your help, and there are plenty of clients that need your specific services or products. And the best part is, when you master the other two circles, you'll find that you can pick and choose the best job for you.

"The true purpose of the three circles job search is to generate choices for your career. We'll talk about it more tomorrow."

Intrigued and energized, Lisa's heart raced at the prospect of choosing the *right* job for her.

Thoughts still buzzing, she thanked the coach before they hung up.

The 3 Circles of an Effective Job Search

The following morning, Lisa was in her kitchenette preparing her coffee when she heard the familiar sound of her laptop ringing. She answered it quickly.

"Hello, Lisa."

"Hey, coach."

"Before we begin, I'd like to make sure we're on the same page. What kind of job have you decided to look for?"

"Our session yesterday was a bit of a breakthrough. For the first time in a long time, I'm confident that I should pursue my career in sales.

"I've always enjoyed it, and my results at *Cloudcom* just made me lose sight of that. Beyond all, I think that my ability to serve others is by selling something that I feel can help them."

"What about the cold calls?"

"I think they're a necessary evil if I'm truly committed to adding value in other people's lives.

"Yesterday's session made me realize that serving others was what I loved the most in sales, whether it's contributing to the team's effort in hitting our objective or solving customers' problems. I even love it when my work makes my managers happy. I don't think what happened at *Cloudcom* will happen again."

"I'm glad we're on the same page." He sounded pleased. "Now, this session is going to be about your job search strategy."

Lisa readied her pen and notepad.

"Job seekers often feel rejected, ignored, unwanted, or not good enough, and their self-esteem takes a hit. They become afraid and needy. These emotions will turn off employers and recruiters. Have you noticed this?"

"Yeah," she sighed.

"Unfortunately, those feelings become the norm among job seekers, especially when they're unemployed. But it's the most ridiculous feeling to have."

"How so?" asked Lisa.

"It's illogical," explained the coach. "You can't reject someone you don't know."

"So why do recruiters and employers reject so many people?"

"They don't," he answered simply. "They simply ignore resumes that don't offer a solution to their challenges. It can't be personal: they don't know you. It's critical that you become a company when you're looking for work.

"A company's service getting rejected is okay. You still take responsibility as the CEO, but you don't take it personally. Instead, you do what every great CEO does: you change and adapt your offering to what the market demands," he elaborated. "Do you know why companies fail?"

"A lot of reasons," Lisa replied. "Lack of funds, fierce competition, the economy..."

"Not if you're a CEO who takes responsibility for your company," he challenged.

Lisa chuckled nervously. "Sorry. Old habits die hard."

"That's okay. Old reflexes just need to be replaced with new ones. Companies fail when they're not efficient at **marketing** their products or services, **selling** their products or services, or **serving** their customers correctly. Do you know why most job seekers fail?"

"If I think like a company, then job seekers fail for the same reasons," she answered.

"Absolutely correct. Imagine your marketing, sales, and customer service are like these three circles." The Three Circles Coach shared his screen to reveal a PowerPoint slide. Three overlapping circles appeared, one by one.

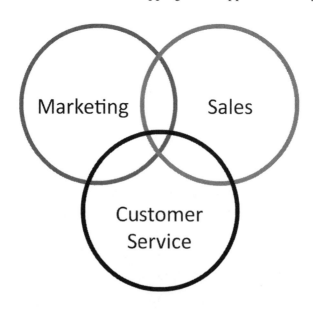

"It's at the junction of these circles that magic happens and our work together will end. But let's not get ahead of ourselves here."

Lisa smiled as she listened attentively.

"Your resume said you majored in Commerce with a concentration in Marketing. Let's hear your simplest definition of the term 'marketing.'"

Lisa felt like she was back in college again. She paused for a moment and then said, "Any activity that promotes your brand or product."

"Not bad, but that's still too complicated. Can you think of just one verb that defines marketing?"

"One verb? Other than 'marketing' itself?"

"Right."

She paused, racking her brain before she conceded, "I can't think of one."

"That's okay. The simplest definition of marketing is 'attracting.'"

The Three Circles Coach paused to let Lisa ponder the idea.

"I'm not sure 'attracting' could be used in every marketing category," she mused after a moment.

"Can you think of an example?" challenged the coach.

"What about branding? Isn't that part of marketing?"

"Of course. But what's the purpose of branding?"

"To improve the perception of a product, a person, or a company," Lisa answered easily.

"That's the definition, but what's the purpose? Why are companies spending millions on branding?"

"Because the better a person, product, or company is perceived, the more customers will trust it, and the more they'll do business with that brand," she explained.

"Right. So are you saying that someone or something that is perceived favorably becomes more *attractive*?"

Even after thinking it over, Lisa couldn't come up with an objection. "I haven't heard this definition for marketing before," she mused, "but I like it. It would have been helpful to have it when I was a student. But what does it have to do with my job search?"

"That's your first circle. The reason job seekers fail is because one or more of their circles aren't working properly," the coach reminded her.

Lisa nodded, before remembering to answer out loud. "Right."

"So becoming attractive to employers is the first thing we're going to focus on. If your phone doesn't ring, it means your presentation isn't attractive enough."

It was empowering, starting to feel like her own CEO. The stakes were high, but it was exciting.

"Your marketing circle is anything you do that entices employers to call you. Can you think of one thing that does that?" asked the coach.

"My resume should be doing that, right?"

"Right. Your resume is your marketing brochure. It should make employers feel like you have solutions for their challenges. The way you write your job application email should play a big part, too, but we'll cross that bridge when we get there. For now, let's agree that your resume is the pillar of your marketing strategy."

"So what about the sales circle?" asked Lisa.

"What do you think? Let's suppose that an employer found your resume interesting enough to give you a call. What's the next step?"

"A job interview?"

"Exactly. This is where you have an opportunity to sell your skills against the job you're interviewing for. Can you think of a one-verb definition of selling?"

"I'm not sure," she confessed reluctantly. She was a salesperson, after all.

"Selling is about convincing others," he answered, his words simple but powerful. "You do that by addressing their challenges and providing sufficient proof that you can help them. **Selling is the promise that there's a better tomorrow for your clients if they hire you.**"

Lisa remained silent, save for her pen scratching over paper.

THE GOAL OF MY MARKETING IS TO GENERATE JOB INTERVIEWS

THE GOAL OF A JOB INTERVIEW IS TO CONVINCE EMPLOYERS I CAN HELP THEM

"What about the third circle?" she asked. "Serving others makes a career fulfilling, but how do you apply that to my job search?"

"Serving your customers during a job search means that you should adapt to their way of thinking, searching, and selecting. Make it easy for them to decide if your services are what they need. You do that across your job search process.

"Your resume should be easy to read, your interview should be adapted to what they're looking for, your attitude, your tone of voice, and absolutely everything you do should be serving others, not you.

"Your customer service circle crosses the other two circles because your entire process should be designed for employers and recruiters. That means you need to know their way, their tools, their methods. Does it make sense?"

"It does, but it sounds really complicated. How can I know all this?"

"Maybe because you're not thinking like an employer?"

"But how can I put myself in their shoes?"

"How do you suppose successful companies do it? They're not their customers, are they?"

Lisa mulled it over before she guessed, "They ask themselves what the customer would want?"

"That's correct, but incomplete. It is not only *what would customers want?* How your clients feel is more important."

"You lost me again," she sighed.

The coach did not answer immediately, and he sounded thoughtful when he did.

"The issue with most job seekers is that they don't care about what employers really want, but instead go with what they *think* an employer wants.

"For example, by following some urban legends, like *'your resume must be of a certain length,' 'you need—or don't need—a picture on your resume'* and other superficial issues.

"But employers don't really care about that, as long as you're operating within the legal framework of your country. Just wildly guessing what employers want is exactly why people are wrong. What I'd like you to do instead is to make an effort to be in their shoes for a moment.

"See the world with their eyes. Empathize with them, and you *will* think like them. That's the essence of what true customer service is."

"Okay, but *how*?" Lisa asked plaintively.

"Just imagine you're an employer. Have you ever wondered how painful it is to hire the wrong person?"

"Pretty bad, I guess."

"That's it?" He sounded incredulous. "I'm not sure you realize what's really at stake here. We're trying to establish the fundamental difference between you and the rest of the job seekers out there.

"If you get this right, you will transcend your job search in a way you could not have imagined before. Would you like to try again? How does it feel to be an employer who is trying to hire someone onto his team?"

"Okay, here's the thing," Lisa began. "I may be wrong here, but to me employers are the ones who have the money and the choice over which candidate to hire. They're the ones that can fire someone or refuse to get back to applicants after they spend hours writing a resume or filling out an application.

"That's not what you're looking for, but I don't think they're in such a bad place."

The coach was quiet at first, and then he sighed, slow and world-weary.

"There's the root of your problem," he declared.

Lisa stayed quiet, waiting for him to continue.

"You think that employers are already in a good position and don't need our help."

Lisa tried to interject, but the coach pushed onwards.

"I can tell you this from experience; when you make the decision to hire someone, you're making a risky financial commitment. If you fail, you will never get a refund on your investment.

"You go through dozens of resumes that are mostly mediocre and vague. You start interviewing a few profiles and you come across people who have exaggerated their skills, that showcase the wrong attitudes, or that lie outright.

"You skim through people who are just there to get a job or money, with little consideration of what the employer is truly looking for." Clearly, he was on a roll.

"And even if you pass through this anxious process and you end up hiring the best of a bunch of mediocre candidates with the hope that it can work out with a bit of training and support, you start investing and hoping things will be okay.

"But then their attitude and results are nowhere near what's expected, the new hire gets demotivated easily, and the more you try to make things better, the less it works. The more demotivated an employee becomes, the more negativity spreads through the team, and it becomes a drain on morale. How fair does this sound to you?"

Lisa remained silent, picturing herself in that situation.

After a brief pause, the Three Circles Coach asked, "Have you ever thought about what Mark went through before deciding to let you go? How do you think he felt watching you stagnate week in and week out? Like every good manager, I can only imagine that he tried to re-motivate you, to speak to you, to listen to you.

"How did he feel when nothing he did was working? Have you ever considered what he must have said to his boss when he had to explain that the money spent on you was lost forever? And how he had to explain to the rest of the team that instead of being in a growing company of happy people, he had created an environment where people are afraid of losing their jobs, too, and might start looking for another one?

"That's only a snapshot of what employers out there are *feeling*, but this is happening to every company and manager out there, and once an employee is terminated or resigns, they have to start all over from scratch with a new recruit. Have you ever really tried to be in their shoes?"

Lisa was speechless. She wanted to defend herself, but how could she?

"No, I haven't," she answered.

The past few months must have been agonizing for Mark, coming to the conclusion that he should let her go and count his losses. She was so focused on herself and what it meant for her that she never even considered how employers might suffer, too.

"I feel selfish now," she grumbled.

"That means you're starting to see things from their eyes. Employers have lost great people to the competition. They've spent money and invested in them. They even have employees right now who are underperforming and doing their head in.

"It's with this frame of mind that they're looking at what you're offering. These are the people who will read your resume and potentially interview you."

"You make it sound like it's a nightmare to have employees."

"It's not. A manager's biggest joy is when employees become happily successful. This is when he feels he's impacted someone's life. But we're focusing on the pain points of your target audience for now.

"Despite the most advanced recruitment techniques and tools, employers continue to hire employees that complain about everything. This is the national sport in most companies.

"So, how cautious do you think an employer should be with their next hire?"

"Very," Lisa answered. "But that freaks me out. How can I address them now that I know that?"

"That's the best part, Lisa. Your competition is mediocre; they think about themselves first. If you start feeling like an employer, not just thinking like one, your job search will show it.

"You'll start doing and saying things differently because of this vantage point, and that is the essence of true customer service. It's not about understanding what employers want; it's feeling as if you were them. That's the difference between sympathy and empathy.

"If you're hoping to truly serve them during your job search, I want you to sync up with their fears and worries. That's when your third circle will take all its meaning and cross with all your marketing and sales activities."

Lisa was still shaken, unmoored like a ship at sea. She couldn't get herself to say anything relevant.

"I think I understand," she settled on.

"Good. Do you have any questions about the three circles?"

Lisa refocused on the purpose of the session.

"Why do the circles overlap?"

"In order to reach the sweet spot, everything you do should include the three circles. Take your resume, for example.

"We agree that this is your marketing brochure, but it should also be written in a way that convinces an employer to call you; it should sell you.

"It should be easy to read and answer their one fundamental question: 'Why should I meet Lisa Dutoit?' Do you see how just a resume can include your three circles?"

"I do," she replied.

"Great! Now, would you say that your job application emails, your job interviews, or any activity during your job search include all three circles?"

"Not quite," she admitted. "This is still new."

"I'm glad you're starting to realize how much improvement can be done. The three circles should be present in everything you do or they won't meet in the middle."

The Three Circles Coach added what two circles crossing meant:

For the crossing of the Sales and Marketing circles, Lisa heard a mouse click that revealed what the coach wanted to show her, just as he said, "**Attracting employers and convincing them to take the next step leads to great career opportunities and choices.**"

"It makes sense," Lisa commented.

The coach moved on to the junction between the Sales and the Customer Service circles. "**Convincing employers and serving them with five-star customer service, both during your job interview and during your employment, impacts the company and its stakeholders in a meaningful way.**"

"Like we talked about earlier," Lisa added.

"Right. And finally..." The coach clicked his mouse again, revealing what the Customer Service and Marketing circles created when they crossed.

"When you serve your employer in the best way possible throughout your job search and you help him achieve results through your services, your personal brand will get a big boost.

"That's how you get recommended for further interviews, and how you become attractive to even more employers and career opportunities," continued the coach. "The idea of a job search is *not* to find a job, it's to generate *choices*. You should look for several jobs, not one."

Lisa was quiet as she took notes.

THE PURPOSE OF A JOB SEARCH IS NOT TO FIND A JOB, IT'S TO GENERATE MANY CAREER OPPORTUNITIES FOR ME TO CHOOSE FROM!

It was so logical once she was really thinking about it. She added:

SERVING OTHERS AND HELPING THEM ACHIEVE RESULTS BOOSTS MY REPUTATION AND THUS MY PERSONAL BRAND, WHICH REINFORCES MY ATTRACTIVENESS (MARKETING)!

"Whether you're on the job or during the recruitment process, the three circles work," the coach stated.

"I get it. I've never seen this before..." said Lisa. "They're like an engine, aren't they?"

"Can you elaborate?" asked the coach, sounding intrigued.

"I mean the more results I get, the more attractive I become, and the more opportunities I attract."

"Amazing. That's exactly what I was about to say."

The coach clicked his mouse to show the final part of the theory.

"I'm completely on board with this model," Lisa declared. "I love it! Where do we start?"

"First, you need to understand where you are right now with these circles. If you ask me, your current circles look like this." The coach's screen changed as he showed a different slide, this time with the three circles separated:

"That's kind of scary, but I get it. As long as these circles aren't big enough to cross with each other, I won't get career opportunities, I won't create an impact in the lives of others, and I won't improve my personal brand," Lisa observed. "So how do we get them to cross?"

"We're going to start with your marketing circle," the coach obliged easily. "Do you have any other questions about this model?"

"Why circles?"

The coach chuckled. "It's the size of each circle that makes them overlap. It's the quantity and quality of each circle that dictates its size. When done properly, each circle will be big enough to cross with the other two."

It was a simple concept, and Lisa grasped it better than she could have hoped. It was obvious that her circles weren't overlapping just yet, although she wasn't sure why.

They decided that it was enough for one day, and the next session would begin tackling Lisa's marketing brochure. Although Friday was the first day of the weekend in Dubai, the same couldn't be said for London, so the Three Circles Coach was working that day.

The truth was that Lisa's mind was racing with excitement, and was drained at the same time. She would have appreciated a couple of days to process everything before her next session.

But she knew that her days in Dubai without a job were numbered, so she had to push on. The two agreed to have their session at 5 PM the next day.

As Lisa pondered over her notes, she couldn't believe how much her career perspective had changed. Just the previous day, she was convinced that the only way to be fulfilled was to run away from sales and try a new job sector. That's when she had a strange epiphany.

Grabbing her pen, she wrote an analogy that she thought only she could ever understand:

A JOB SECTOR IS LIKE ICE CREAM, AND EACH JOB COMES IN A DIFFERENT FLAVOR, DEPENDING ON THE COMPANY'S ENVIRONMENT, THE MANAGEMENT, THE INDUSTRY IT OPERATES IN, ETC.

IF I NO LONGER LIKE A FLAVOR, IT DOESN'T MEAN THAT I SHOULD STOP EATING ICE CREAM!

SECTION 1:
THE MARKETING CIRCLE

The #1 Purpose of a Resume

"Good afternoon, Lisa!"

"Hello, coach."

"Ready for today?" asked the Three Circles Coach. He sounded excited, and his enthusiasm was infectious.

"Ready!" replied Lisa eagerly.

"Great! Becoming attractive to employers is the first thing we are going to focus on. If your phone doesn't ring, that means that the way you present yourself isn't attractive enough.

"So tell me," the coach continued, "if companies have marketing brochures to explain how their services or products can help their customers, do you remember what your marketing brochure is?

"My resume," said Lisa easily.

"That's correct. And who wrote your resume?"

"Myself," she answered, proud but anxious. "I've had it reviewed by a friend of mine who's in HR. Other than a couple points, he said it was great, so I don't think it will require a lot of work.

"Besides, I've received a few phone calls from recruiters and I've already been to two interviews. So I don't think it's a bad resume. What do you think?"

"Well," the coach began carefully, "it depends. According to you, what's the number one purpose of a resume?"

"To find a job?" Lisa guessed cautiously.

"Not quite," replied the Three Circles Coach.

"To sell myself, then?"

"That's close, but still not what I'm looking for," returned the coach.

"So what is it, then?" asked Lisa.

"The number one purpose of a resume is to get you contacted by recruiters and employers. If you want to measure the effectiveness of your resume, you measure it by the ratio between job applications you send and the phone calls you receive."

"You told me that was one percent, correct?"

"If I don't include the recruitment agency phone calls," Lisa confirmed, sullen. "That's shocking," she admitted, "but I'm not sure I agree with that ratio."

"Why not?"

"We've established that there are many aspects of my job search that could affect my marketing circle, didn't we?"

"Yes, please continue," the coach encouraged.

"Isn't my one percent a reflection of my overall marketing circle? Not just my resume, but also my overall approach to a job application?"

"That's right," agreed the coach. "And we're going to look at all these aspects one by one. But for now, trust me when I say that in 99 percent of the cases when people can't generate enough job interviews, their resume is the number one suspect."

"Why is the resume so important?"

"It plays the biggest part in an employer's decision to interview you. Your resume can be found on many online and company databases, it's on LinkedIn as your profile, it's sent to job openings, and it can be passed along by your network.

"Your resume is truly the basis of your job search. Does that make sense?"

"So far," she answered as she took notes in her notepad.

IF I'M NOT ABLE TO GENERATE ENOUGH JOB INTERVIEWS,
MY RESUME IS THE #1 SUSPECT.

THE #1 PURPOSE OF A RESUME IS TO GET CONTACTED BY RECRUITERS AND
EMPLOYERS. THAT'S THE ONLY TRUE MEASURE OF THE EFFECTIVENESS OF A RESUME.

"Now, suppose you receive an employer's phone call today. What do you assume happened to trigger that call?"

"An employer found my resume interesting?" replied Lisa.

"And before that?" further probed the coach.

"He received it?"

"That's one way. Or he could have found your profile online. In a more general way, providing your resume is well-written, there are three steps before you receive a phone call from an employer. First, your resume must be found. Next, your resume must be opened by the recruiter. Finally, your resume must tell them '*Why should I call this person?*' So if you want to receive more calls from recruiters, you must work on increasing the effectiveness of these three stages."

The coach shared his screen again:

Be Found → Be Read → Be Contacted

The concept was clear, but how to put it into practice still seemed hazy.

"I understand the process, but I'm not sure how I can use it to receive more phone calls," Lisa stated.

"Here's an example: let's suppose that right now, for every 100 jobs you apply to, your resume is only read five times. Do you agree that this means it's ignored 95 percent of the time?"

"Sure," agreed Lisa.

"So what if you could get your resume read not five times, but 30 times? Wouldn't your resume be read six times more?"

"So if I increase my result at each of these three stages, the result at the end could be phenomenal."

"That's correct! And as soon as you understand how these marketing stages work and apply specific methods for them, you will mathematically receive more phone calls. Making sense?"

"Yeah," she replied.

"Your target customers are recruitment agents, in-house recruiters, or line managers in sales departments. They're the ones who have to find you, and the message you want them to read is on your resume. You want your resume to be read as often as possible.

"In fact, **the more recruiters read it, the more chances you will have to be contacted.** And since your resume is the message you're trying to get through, it needs to include triggers for recruiters to call you and find out more about you."

He gave her a moment to absorb the message before he said, "If you don't mind, I'll be sending you a document that outlines my resume writing formula.

"I want you to take a good look at your resume, because you'll soon replace it with a more powerful and attractive one. We start there, Lisa. Do you have any questions before we end this session?"

"Not right now. I look forward to receiving your resume writing formula, coach."

"Sure thing. Please try to revamp your resume over the weekend, and let's reconvene on Monday. Okay?"

"Deal!" Lisa agreed, eager to get started.

What Lisa didn't know was that the task would prove to be the most difficult and yet rewarding step of her entire job search.

Closed Door

After the two hung up, silence seemed to creep into the apartment again, looming like a specter. She looked at her phone to check her messages, and noticed the familiar notification from her bank.

Like every month for the past two years, transfers were made from her bank towards her car and student loans. Without her salary for the month, it left her with just AED 347: not enough to pay for her utility bill, or her phone bill. She worried silently over the delay in receiving her final months' salary.

This was the first time she'd been in danger of going broke in Dubai. As she pondered different scenarios, she thought that perhaps it was time to tell her mom what had happened and possibly borrow money until she could stand on her own two feet again. It was morning time in Virginia due to the time difference.

She tried to keep her message as neutral as possible.

> Hey mom, would you be free for a quick call on Skype? I need to speak to you.

Her mom replied promptly.

> Hey sweetie, sure. Give me 5 min as I'm arriving at work, will call you from the office.

The call came a few minutes later on her phone.

"Hey, Mom," Lisa greeted.

"Hey, sweetheart. Is everything okay?" her mom asked. She already sounded worried.

"I'm okay," Lisa sighed. "What about you?"

"I'm good. I wanted to speak to you, too, actually, but you go first. What's going on?" said her mom.

"Not a lot, I just wanted to keep you in the loop. I resigned from my job three days ago. It wasn't what I was looking for," said Lisa, immediately feeling a knot of guilt for the lie. She always wanted to make her mom proud, and she didn't want her to worry.

Her mom was silent for what seemed to be an eternity, until all she said was a very careful, "Okay..."

"Don't worry! I've already had other interviews and I'm hoping to find work soon."

"Oh, good," said her mom, still sounding cautious. "I thought you liked your job at *Cloudcom*. What happened?"

"The market isn't great in my industry and my results weren't at a level where I was comfortable. I thought maybe a different industry would be a strategic move before I find myself in a difficult situation with my manager."

"Well, I'm sure you know what you're doing. Is that what you wanted to tell me?"

"Yeah," said Lisa, trying to find the words to ask for financial support. Her mom spoke before Lisa had a chance to ask her.

"I'm sorry it didn't work out, Lisa," her mom crooned gently, "but I actually wanted to speak to you, too."

"What's up?"

"You know I've always wanted to travel the world once the mortgage on the house was paid."

"Yeah," replied Lisa, her heart beating faster.

"Well, I made the last settlement last month and my employer agreed to a twelve month sabbatical!"

"Really?" Lisa gasped. "How will you pay for your trips?"

"I've put the house up for rent, and I found a lovely couple that agreed to a one-year contract! Isn't that exciting?"

"Wow, that's amazing!" Lisa gushed, hoping she sounded convincing despite the anxiety sitting heavy on her shoulders.

It felt like the entire world was leaving her behind. But this trip was her mom's dream. After Lisa's dad passed away when she was fourteen, her mom had worked hard to provide for her daughter. Now that her dream was coming true, all Lisa felt was guilt for not being excited.

"I know what you're thinking, young lady," her mom said when Lisa didn't say anything else.

"You do?" asked Lisa, surprised.

"You're worried about your mom, aren't you?" she said. "Listen, you don't have to worry about me. I've been saving for this trip, and I finally have the money to make it possible. You don't need to worry."

Lisa felt tears filling her eyes. Voice shaking, she said, "I'm not worried. I know you'll be okay."

"Oh, sweetheart, you're crying..."

"No, I'm not," Lisa protested, making it even harder to hide. "... okay, I am. I'm just happy for you," she said, feeling genuinely so for the first time in the conversation.

"Thank you, sweetheart. And don't worry, we'll be on Skype and I'll keep you updated with my every move, I promise."

"I'm counting on that, Mom. You deserve this."

"Thank you," said her mom, also trying to hold back tears.

"You're crying, too," laughed Lisa, her eyes still damp.

"No I'm not," said her mom, still clearly crying. The two laughed.

"Will you send me pictures?" asked Lisa.

"Of course!" said her mom. "Even better: I've created a small travel blog to share my daily activities."

"That's so cool! But I still expect to speak to you on Skype."

"Of course, you silly girl, I wouldn't have it any other way."

Lisa asked her mom what countries she would visit first, where she would sleep, and how she would travel. Her mom was truly excited, and Lisa felt truly happy for her, forgetting her own situation for a while.

"Listen, Lisa, I gotta go, I'm late for my first meeting," her mom said. "I'm glad you're having interviews already. I'm sure you'll find a much better job for you."

"Thanks, Mom. Let's speak soon," replied Lisa.

"We will, sweetheart. Look after yourself, okay?"

"I will. Have a good day."

"You too, sweetheart. Bye now." Lisa's mom hung up in a rush.

Lisa burst into tears, hands covering her face. She hadn't cried that way in years, and she wasn't even sure why she was crying. She was so happy for her mom, but it was like she was being left in the dust.

She couldn't go back home. She tried to gather her composure as she digested that realization.

"I'm going to do this," she said resolutely. "Even if I have to go back to New York." It wouldn't be her first choice, but Lisa was in survival mode, her safety net gone.

It was only 7:10 PM, and she thought that she could use a little exercise. After changing her clothes, she went to the last floor of her building. The building's gym was free to use, and as she chose her favorite music playlist, she jumped on the treadmill and started running.

After twenty minutes, she felt exhausted but better, like her mind had rebooted. As she was catching her breath, she started thinking about her progress with the Three Circles Coach.

She had been so oblivious about the job market, her attitude, her mindset, and even her career.

The three circles certainly shifted her perception of her job search. It was no longer a slow, boring experience, despite her current financial situation. It was fascinating in a way she hadn't expected. As if looking for work was its own branch of science.

After returning to her apartment, she quickly showered and prepared to work on her resume. She passed by the fridge and grabbed a cold slice of pizza for a late dinner, getting ready to get to work.

The Resume Writing Formula

Lisa's notepad was still open on her desk, and she glanced over her notes briefly.

I'M NOT A JOB SEEKER, I'M THE CEO OF MY COMPANY
SELLING MY SERVICES TO OTHER COMPANIES.

MY MARKETING IS MY ABILITY TO ATTRACT EMPLOYERS
AND GENERATE JOB INTERVIEWS.

JOB INTERVIEWS ARE MY SALES PROCESS, MY PROMISE TO EMPLOYERS FOR A BETTER
TOMORROW.

SERVING OTHERS STARTS BY FEELING MY CLIENTS' PAIN POINTS AND
ALIGNING EVERYTHING I DO THE WAY THEY WOULD WANT IT.

IF I'M NOT ABLE TO GENERATE ENOUGH JOB INTERVIEWS,
MY RESUME IS THE #1 SUSPECT.

THE #1 PURPOSE OF A RESUME IS TO GET CONTACTED BY RECRUITERS AND
EMPLOYERS, THAT'S THE ONLY TRUE MEASURE OF A RESUME.

She was energized, at least. It was better than nothing.

She read her resume with a fresh set of eyes as she waited for the email from the Three Circles Coach. It felt flat suddenly, even if she couldn't put her finger on why. It listed dull tasks she had done, but offered nothing enticing.

The terms were mostly vague: words like "responsible for," "in charge of," "coordinating," and other widely used expressions that could mean anything.

'How can my resume truly make employers see that I can help them?' she wondered. 'If I were an employer, I would look for clues that tell me that the person's profile could help me grow my market.'

Granted, being terminated for lackluster performance wasn't exactly going to give her a competitive edge.

She turned to the internet for help, asking Google how to describe a position she had been terminated from, but she found nothing tangible. Most articles were general, offering no clear method that she could apply. Just general tips scattered across articles.

She kept searching until a notification finally popped out on her screen, showing an email from the Three Circles Coach.

Hey Lisa,

I hope you enjoyed our session as much as I did!

Once you have processed all of the information we covered today, I'd like you to start thinking about how you could write a resume that actually serves employers and recruiters.

Please find attached a document that outlines my resume writing formula. It's an easy formula, but you will need to adapt it to your specific situation.

To help you start on the right track, I have also attached a resume template that you should follow. Aesthetics can be changed to your liking once we're done.

Finally, I have attached a short document to help you get started. Please follow it first, and you will find yourself on the right track in no time!

It would be great if you were able to prepare a first draft of your experience at *Cloudcom* for us to review on Monday.

I'll answer any questions you might have during our next session.

Speak soon,
The Three Circles Coach.

PS: Please focus on your most recent experience for now. Once we review this together, you'll have a good feel for how the rest of your experiences should look. Good luck, Lisa!

Just as the coach described, there were three documents attached:

1. "The Resume Writing Formula"
2. "Resume Template"
3. "The 5 Steps to Begin Writing Your Resume."

She opened the first document called "The Resume Writing Formula", and started reading:

THE RESUME WRITING FORMULA

1. Keywords
2. Action Verbs
3. Quantities
4. Results

1. Keywords:

Spoiler: Your resume will rarely be read by a human being at first.

The most important thing to keep in mind is that most of your job search will begin in databases. Whether it's LinkedIn, internal resume databases, or job portals, your resume will be part of a database that is searchable by recruiters. We call this an ATS (Applicant Tracking System).

If your resume is one of 500 job applicants, it would be naive to think that a recruiter would open all 500 resumes and read each one of them. That would be too time consuming, and that's why databases exist.

The recruiter will type in keywords that match what he has in mind. He will then only read the resumes that come up in his search results.

The higher you rank in employer searches for your desired job description, the more often your resume will appear and be read.

The idea is to have a resume that is enriched with relevant keywords that a recruiter is likely to search for.

To make sure you understand the importance of having the right keywords on your resume, here's a quick example:

Suppose that right now your resume comes up in recruiters' search results one out of ten times. After you add a few industry specific keywords, let's say your resume comes up in three out of ten times. ***That is already three times more often!***

Q: What if I send my resume directly to generic email addresses like hr@companyurl.com or apply@companyurl.com?

Most generic emails are used as an entry gate to a database. The ATS simply parses them into the recruiter's database. Parsing is the process of adding each detail of the resume into pre-defined _(and thus searchable)_ fields on a database. In 95% of cases, there is no human behind generic inboxes.

Q: So how do you know which keywords recruiters are searching for?

The answer is in the job description, or the job ad. This is the place where recruiters are unveiling the words they're searching for on a resume. Read them with a recruiter's eye and you'll realize which keywords must be put on your resume.

Keywords density:

The more often a relevant keyword appears on your resume, the higher you will rank in the search results for that specific keyword.

Of course, you shouldn't "stuff" your resume with keywords in a way that spoils the reading experience. Remember that the experience that a recruiter has when reading your resume is part of your customer service circle. One way to repeat a specific keyword is to add it in the summary, the title of your resume, or in the description of the education/degree section.

For technical profiles:

If your job involves technical jargon _(like tools, methods, techniques, software...etc.),_ consider adding them into a table at the end or at the beginning of your resume.

IMPORTANT:

Some ATS's still struggle with parsing information from tables, graphs, text boxes and illustrations.

Instead of using the "table function" of your text editor, feel free to use tabs instead. And then save your document in PDF to ensure it will give the same visual effect regardless of who opens your resume. _(For graphs, text boxes and illustrations, however, please avoid relying on them for keywords, some old ATS's will struggle to extract the content inside.)_

2. Action Verbs

Action verbs describe what the subject of the sentence does. Any verb that is vague will not create the necessary impact in the recruiter's mind. Try to stay away from verbs or sentences that could mean different things. For example:

Responsible for / in charge of: you can be responsible without actually doing anything.

There's a fundamental difference between what you are and what you do. Employers are looking for doers. Instead of saying "responsible for training interns," say "trained interns" for example.

Managed: This is a job seeker's favorite, yet this is one of the vaguest verbs you could use on a resume. What does "managing" include? Does it mean that you are coaching or mentoring people? Are you monitoring their progress? Are you training them?

TRY TO BE SPECIFIC WITH ACTION VERBS SO THAT YOUR RESUME STANDS OUT.

Coordinated: Another vague term.
'To coordinate' could mean forwarding emails between two teams or departments, which doesn't showcase any skill set. **Again, please use specific action verbs.**

Solving the writer's block with action verbs:

Apart from making your resume much more specific, action verbs also happen to solve an issue that is often referred to as the *'writer's block.'* This is when you feel that you don't know what to write on your resume and you agonize trying to write something relevant.

The easiest way out of this is to stop thinking about what to write, and instead focus on how to start each bullet point. If you start a sentence with the right action verb, you will trigger the right thoughts for the rest of the sentence to emerge.

The best way to do that is to go on Google and search for *"action verbs on resume"*. Read them carefully, and the moment you find a verb that triggers a thought, use it.

<u>Controlling the recruiter's perception</u>:

A final, huge advantage of action verbs is that they trigger the reader's imagination.

For example, if I were to write that I *"trained fifteen people twice a month,"* chances are that the recruiter will ***immediately imagine*** me in a classroom standing up in front of 15 people, even if that thought was happening for just a second.

When you repeatedly use action verbs throughout your resume, the employer will imagine you in so many working situations that he will *feel* that you are a competent "doer," even if he can't prove it yet. That's what your resume should focus on: **creating a feeling of trust.**

<u>Use the past tense:</u>

When choosing the past tense or with the suffix "ing", I usually recommend the past tense. Why? Because when a verb ends with the suffix "-ing," the impression it gives is that the action is still ongoing *(e.g.: "monitoring three projects at the same time")*.

In other words, you haven't necessarily finished *"monitoring three projects at the same time."* For me *(just my personal opinion)*, this form conflicts with recruiters' desire to hire someone that can get the job done *(not just start it)*.

Instead, say *"monitored 3 projects simultaneously."* The past tense implies that this task is over, which creates more impact in the mind of the employer.

3. Quantities / Numbers

Since you intend to write a resume for employers, I highly recommend that you write it in a language that they understand: numbers. Company managers live and die by the numbers they report every month.

Everything in an organization, whether private or governmental, is about numbers: profit, loss, productivity, salaries, working hours, efficiency, turnover, investments, time, size, Key Performance Indicators (KPIs), etc. **That's the employer's language.**

Lack of numbers is by far the most damaging thing for your resume. Why? Because it becomes vague and it won't stand out. The moment someone can say something like *"Recruited an excess of 145 candidates per year"* instead of *"In charge of recruiting the best candidates for various roles,"* which sentence do you think carries the most power in the mind of a recruiter?

Quantifying the skill you're highlighting *(i.e.: recruiting)* communicates a certain level of seniority and uniqueness to your profile *(you will never find someone that has the same numbers than you.)*

Same thing for results: *"generated substantial revenue."* Try to *always* quantify your sentence towards something like this: *"Generated $65,000 per month in the last 6 months."*

Do you see how the proper use of action verbs *(and the past tense)* combined with specific numbers creates a more powerful impact?

For every sentence you add to describe your experience, ask yourself:
- *Supervised a team → How many?*
- *Implemented projects → How many projects, what size were they (budget/length/people involved)?*
- *Organized client meetings → How many, how often?*
- *etc.*

And remember, **WRITE EVERY NUMBER AS A FIGURE, NOT AS A WORD.** Figures contrast in a sea of words and attract attention. And finally, every sentence should allude to a relevant skill set. As you're reading your tasks again, ask yourself:

WHAT IS THE SPECIFIC SKILL HIGHLIGHTED HERE?

Ask yourself this at every sentence and make sure it does allude to a specific skillset or result.

4. Results/Achievements

Last but not least, your achievements.

Employers hire people based on their results. For an employer, your salary is an investment. And like every investment, they will be screening your resume for signs of potential return on investment. **You need to show that you can bring more than what you cost to an employer.**

The best indication of future results is past results.

For example, top athletes get paid a fortune. Why? Not because they're good, but because their past results reassure their employers about the prospect of a return on investment.

There are plenty of athletes who are good but don't perform well during competitions. Their past performances usually keep them where they are, unable to close a high ticket deal with a club or get paid millions to play at a tournament.

If a new player comes to play for your favorite team, the first thing you will look at is where he comes from and his track record *(hey wait, did I just define what recruiters are doing when looking at your resume?)* while he was playing for other teams.

As with athletes, your past performances will dictate whether employers will want to give you a trial, an audition, or a job interview for an opportunity to join their team.

While athlete's past performances are often recorded and easily accessible publicly, that's not the case for you. You will have to highlight it on your resume. Remember, it's not whether you have experience in your job that matters; it's about what you have achieved for your past employers. So here again, numbers are essential.

There are three types of results that are more important than anything else: *money, time, and variations (%).*

Money:

This is the biggest consideration for employers. It is the lifeblood of any business, and the more disconnected your resume is from money, the less likely an employer is to see a potential return on investing in you. **Try to always allude to financial results for the company.**

For example, if you are in customer service and you have been awarded *"customer service agent of the year twice in a row,"* what do you think employers will think? They will think that with someone like you on their team, the quality of their customer service will improve and more clients might renew their contracts for example.

Do you see what I mean when I say that your job is connected with the financial performance of a company?

Time:

We have all heard the adage that says *"time is money."* Well, that's because, among other costs, employees are being paid every second they spend at work, whether they're being productive or just standing at the coffee machine.

If you can show that you have saved time *by putting in place a system that saved 2 days of work every month* or *by finishing a project 2 months/2 weeks before the deadline*, the employer will also translate this in terms of money. Being more productive means employees can now do other things with that time.

Variations _(Percentages)_:

Percentages matter when you want to highlight variations like growth or reductions. Suppose you are currently heading a team. How big was the team before you took charge?

If it was smaller before you took charge, you can say:
→ _**"Grew the team by 50% in the space of 12 months"**_

Or if it was bigger when you joined and the company had to let go of a few people, you can say:
→ _**"Reduced the team operational cost by 50% in the space of 12 months."**_

Same thing for revenue, productivity, market size, client base, delivery, etc.

Other types of results could include:

Promotions: _**"Promoted twice within 24 months."**_
→ This indicates to a prospective employer that you must be doing something good to deserve a promotion.

Top employee of the month/Top performer on your team:
→ _**"Consistently in the top 5 performers on my team (250 people)"**_

Employee appraisal:
→ _**"Scored XX during the last employee appraisals."**_

If you trained people, what have they become?
→ _**"Trained 2 team members who became top performers within 3 months."**_

Without saying that you're good, you're allowing the employer to assume that you _must_ be good.

Other questions that could help you extract more achievements:
- *What has changed since you've joined an employer?*
- *How has the company/your team/department evolved since you joined?*
- *Suppose you were to leave today, what would be your legacy? How would you be remembered?*
- *Imagine someone calling your manager for a reference – what would he say about your achievements?*
- *Remember your last performance appraisal? How did it go?*
- *etc...*

WORD OF CAUTION:

1. If you can't find achievements to list easily, that's normal. Communication between employers and employees is not always the best, and some managers worry that if they praise an employee too often, the employee will ask for a raise.

Please don't hesitate to ask colleagues or managers *(current or otherwise)* to help you extract these achievements. You'll be amazed at how others will highlight things you weren't even aware off. Remember, **it's hard to see the big picture when you're in the frame.**

2. **"Fake" achievements:**

I am not talking about lies *(which you should avoid at all costs)*. I am alluding to things that you think are achievements, but they aren't for the employer.

Example:

"*Learned to master SAP quickly*" → Good for you, but that doesn't mean that the employer benefits here. You're expected to master companies' systems as fast as possible.

"*Quickly adapted to the new environment.*" → Again, good for you. But why would an employer care? You're supposed to adapt, that is the minimum expected.

"*Consistently arrived on time.*" Same as above. If you think this is a special achievement, I would be concerned about what your daily performance is like.

The only achievements that should be on your resume are results that the team, the company, or others have achieved <u>through your work, or recognition of past performance (promotion, award...etc.)</u>.

It's not about you. It's about your customers. Remember, an employer is the one paying you, so mention anything and everything that increases the value that your past employers got for the money they paid you. That's what employers will find attractive on your profile.

Remember, you're an investment. You either show the return on investment through the results you have produced in the past, or the employer will look for someone else to invest in.

(This is for an IT Specialist, but you can adapt it to your own technical sector)

You must prove your expertise with the number of years.

Equipment / Protocols	Skills	Expertise	Details
Cisco Switches & Routers *(2900, 3600 3X50x, 6500)* **Nexus 2K, 5K & 7K** **Load balancers, Checkpoint** *(Nortel,Alteon , F5)* **Firewalls** *(Nokia and SPLAT)*	Configuration	★★★★★	- **7 years of experience** *(BNP, Orange, Dimension Data)* - Multiple trainings from Cisco and F5
	Migration	★★★★★	- **3 years of intensive experience** *(BNP)* *(Over 130 network infrastructures)*
	Implementation	★★★★★	- **4 years of experience** *(Orange & BNP)*
	Administration	★★★★★	- **7 years of experience** *(multi-manufacturer environment)* BNP – Orange – Dimension Data
	Troubleshooting	★★★★☆	- Support level 1, 2 and 3 - 18 months of on-calls 24/7 at BNP
	Project Mgt / Coordination	★★★★☆	- **2 years of intensive experience** (BNP) *(over 5 big programs)* - Supervising, Training & Monitoring Staff members - Risk Assessment – Project Follow Up
Network Protocols *VLAN, 802.1Q, Spanning Tree (MST, PVST), EtherChannel, VPC, HSRP/VRRP, static and dynamic routing, OSPF, VRF, ACL, NAT*	Analysis Implementation network design	★★★★★	- **7 years of experience** *(BNP, Orange, Dimension Data)*

(Here's another example for a Trading Document Specialist...)

Skills	Terms	Expertise	Details
Payments	Cash Against Documents(CAD), Bank Collections Letters of Credit Avalized Drafts	★★★★★	- **14 years of experience** *(Saint Louis Sucre, Bauche SA, ED&F MAN Sugar Limited)*
Shipping documents	Bill of Lading Certificate of Origin with legalisation Invoice with legalisation Certificates with inspection companies	★★★★☆	- **14 years of experience** *(Saint Louis Sucre, Bauche SA, ED&F MAN Sugar Limited)*
Incoterms	Mainly FOB, CFR, CIF, FCA, FAS, EXW (from overseas warehouses)	★★★★☆	- **14 years of experience** *(Saint Louis Sucre, Bauche SA, ED&F MAN Sugar Limited)*
I.T. Proficiency	**ITAS**: 6 years (ED&F MAN London and Dubai) **SAP** Sales and Distribution (SD) module: 3 years and 6 months (KUEHNE+NAGEL, Saint Louis Sucre) **BV Laytime**: 2 years (Bauche SA)		

Not all resumes will require a table, but it is great if you do not want to overcharge your resume with technical jargon. The idea is to keep the description short and simple *(each bullet point should have one topic and fit in one line ideally)*. Just as importantly, it increases the density of your technical keywords!

A table is great for a reader (*recruiter/employer*), but not all ATS's are great with tables... So to optimize it for ATS's, you can convert it into tabs.

(In MS Word, select the table, go to table's layout menu, click on "Convert to Text", and select "Tabs".)

IMPORTANT: THE STRUCTURE OF YOUR RESUME.

This is what I highly recommend:

Put a 3-line title on your resume that goes as follows:
>   1st line: The role you feel your profile fits the most
>   2nd line: number of years of total experience and specific experience
>   3rd line: You can say that you are, for example, *"Bilingual English/Spanish"* and/or you can state your education level: *"Master's degree in Education leadership"*

If you have more than 3 years of solid experience, **start with the "Professional Experience" section after the summary.**

For work experience older than 10 years ago, I would recommend keeping only the achievements part, with one or two lines of description of the purpose of your role.

Try to build each bullet point with:
→ [Action verb + Quantities] or [Action verb + Result]

To increase the readability of your resume, each bullet point should fit in 1 line *(as much as possible)* and present only 1 skill or result.

Don't forget to showcase your achievements in the "Education & Training" section. If you've been accepted in one of the top five universities in your country, say so. If you have made it on the dean's list, mention it.

Don't worry too much about the size/length of your resume for now. The first phase is a brainstorm. The final phase will clean things up and optimize your resume.

Write your summary at the end, when the rest of your resume is done. **The summary should be four to six lines on your resume.** The important thing is that it gets read, so keep it short!

IMPORTANT: *Each work experience should be separated into two sub-categories:* **Responsibilities & Achievements.**

The purpose is to "force you" to separate tasks (which highlight your skill set) and results (which showcase the results you created for your employers)

Lisa reached the end of the article and couldn't decide if she was thrilled or terrified. It seemed logical enough, but there were so many parts!

She grabbed her pen and notepad and summarized it as simply as she could.

RESUME WRITING FORMULA

1. KEYWORDS

2. ACTION VERBS

3. QUANTITIES (NUMBERS)

4. RESULTS

She could always go back to the article for a more in-depth refresher.

If there were any lingering doubts about the coach's ability to help her, those doubts had vanished. After reading the *'Resume Writing Formula,'* it was amazing how little she had known about the topic. The entire situation was still terrifying, but her determination easily rivaled her nerves.

She opened the second document, entitled *'Resume Template.'*

The Resume Template

First Name Surname

Target City - Country

Citizenship

☎ +XX X XXX XXXX

✉ XXXX.XXXXX@XXXX.COM

🔗 ae.linkedin.com/in/FIRST-LAST/

YOUR TARGET / LATEST JOB TITLE
XX Years of Experience in XXXXX, XXXXX
Degree, Certification and / or languages spoken

SUMMARY

XXXXXXXXXXXXXXXXXXXXXXXXXXXXXXXXXXXXXXXXXXXXXXXXXXXXXXXXXXXXXXXXXXXXXXXX
XXXXXXXXXXXXXXXXXXXXXXXXXXXXXXXXXXXXXXXXXXXXXXXXXXXXXXXXXXXXXXXXXXXXXXXX
XXXXXXXXXXXXXXXXXXXXXXXXXXXXXXXXXXXXXXXXXXXXXXXXXXXXXXXXXXXXXXXXXXXXXXXX
XXXXXXXXXXXXXXXXXXXXXXXXXXXXXXXXXXXXXXXXXXXXXXXXXXXXXXXXXX

PROFESSIONAL EXPERIENCE

Job Title   **Mar XX – Jan XX**
Company   *City – Country*

(If the company is not known well, add a brief explainer about what it does and the purpose of your role)
XXXXXXXXXXXXXXXXXXXXXXXXXXXXXXXXXXXXXXXXXXXXXXXXXXXXXXXXXXXXXXXXXXXXXXXXXX
XXXXXXXXXXXXXXXXXXXXXXXXXXXXXXXXXXXXXXXXX

Responsibilities
- Action verb + quantities if possible
- Action verb + quantities if possible
- Action verb + quantities if possible
- Action verb + quantities if possible
- Action verb + quantities if possible

Achievements
- ✓ Action verb + quantified results / achievements
- ✓ Action verb + quantified results / achievements
- ✓ Action verb + quantified results / achievements
- ✓ Action verb + quantified results / achievements

Job Title   **Mar XX – Jan XX**
Company   *City – Country*

(If the company is not known well, add a brief explainer about what it does and the purpose of your role)
XXXXXXXXXXXXXXXXXXXXXXXXXXXXXXXXXXXXXXXXXXXXXXXXXXXXXXXXXXXXXXXXXXXXXXXXXX
XXXXXXXXXXXXXXXXXXXXXXXXXXXXXXXXXXXXXXXXX

Responsibilities
- Action verb + quantities if possible
- Action verb + quantities if possible
- Action verb + quantities if possible
- Action verb + quantities if possible
- Action verb + quantities if possible

Achievements
- ✓ Action verb + quantified results / achievements
- ✓ Action verb + quantified results / achievements
- ✓ Action verb + quantified results / achievements
- ✓ Action verb + quantified results / achievements

To download this template for free, please go to:
www.nameyourcareer.com/jobsearchtemplates

EDUCATION & TRAINING

→ *Education:*

Master's Degree in....   **Mar XX – Jan XX**
School (Top 10 School in XXX)   *City – Country*

Bachelor's Degree in....   **Mar XX – Jan XX**
School (Top 10 School in XXX)   *City – Country*

→ *Certifications:*

PMP (Project Management Practitioner) Certified   **Mar XX – Jan XX**
Institute name / Employer's Name   *City – Country*

Other Certification   **Mar XX – Jan XX**
Institute name   *City – Country*

→ *Trainings:*

Training topic   **Mar XX – Jan XX**
Institute name / Employer's Name   *City – Country*

Training topic   **Mar XX – Jan XX**
Institute name / Employer's Name   *City – Country*

Training topic   **Mar XX – Jan XX**
Institute name / Employer's Name   *City – Country*

How to Showcase Key Skills:

Equipment / Protocols	Skills	Expertise	Details
Cisco Switches & Routers *(29XX, 26XX 3X50x, 65XX)* **Nexus 2K, 5K & 7K** **Load balancers, Checkpoint** *(Nortel, Alteon , F5)* **Firewalls** *(Nokia and SPLAT)*	Configuration	★★★★★	- 7 years of experience *(BNP, Orange, Dimension Data)* - Multiple trainings from Cisco and F5
	Migration	★★★★★	- 3 years of intensive experience *(BNP)* *(Over 130 network infrastructures)*
	Implementation	★★★★★	- 4 years of experience *(Orange & BNP)*
	Administration	★★★★★	- 7 years of experience *(multi-manufacturer environment)* BNP – Orange – Dimension Data
	Troubleshooting	★★★★☆	- Support level 1, 2 and 3 - 18 months of on-calls 24/7 at BNP
	Project Mgt / Coordination	★★★★☆	- 2 years of intensive experience (BNP) *(over 5 big programs)* - Supervising, Training Staff members - Risk Assessment – Project Follow Up
Network Protocols VLAN, 802.1Q, Spanning Tree (MST, PVST), EtherChannel, VPC, HSRP/VRRP, static and dynamic routing, OSPF, VRF, ACL, NAT	Analysis Implementation network design	★★★★★	- 7 years of experience *(BNP, Orange, Dimension Data)*

LANGUAGES & INTEREST

Languages:
- English – Native
- French – Fluent
  - *Studied in France for 2 years, worked in French for 18 months.*

Hobbies:
- Boxing 3 times per week: Ex Regional Champion (2006)
- Swimming: Once a week

Must be a local ph. number in relation to your target market

Include your email ID and your LinkedIn Profile (hyperlink)

Type the city you're targeting, not the city you're living in.

4 to 6 lines as a summary or career objective

Include months and years

Job title comes first, not the company

Add 1 line to explain what the company does (*unless it's a known company*)

Purpose of your role for the company: ***Why did they hire you?***

Divide each section into 2 sub-categories:

- Responsibilities (*each task should reflect a specific skillset*)
- Achievements (*each point should highlight a specific result for the employer or a recognition of your performance, like a promotion, award…etc.*)

Ensure your job title supports your target job. If your official title sounds too <u>vague</u> or not up to <u>date</u> with what you're really doing, do not allow it on your resume.

i.e.: *If your designation is 'project coordinator' but your role is to manage projects from A to Z, do not be afraid to put:*

- **Project Manager (called "Project Coordinator" internally)**
or
- **Project Coordinator (Acting as Project Manager since XXXX)**

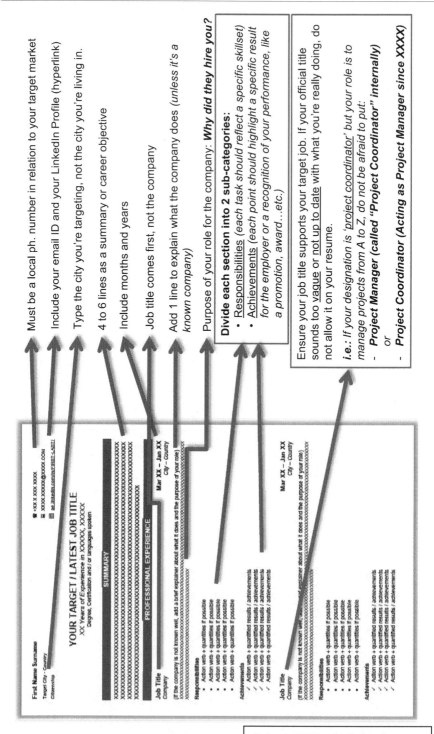

To download this template for free, please go to:
www.nameyourcareer.com/jobsearchtemplates

If relevant, include the ranking of the school, your own ranking in terms of results, or that you've made the dean's list.

Include official training and "on the job" or self-taught training. Make sure you separate training and certification into 2 distinct sub-sections.

If you come from a technical field, use a table to mention any technical jargon. And to make sure the content is ATS friendly, pls convert it into "tabs". (In MS Word, select the table, go to table's layout menu, click on "Convert to Text", and then select "Tabs")

Although using rating stars to illustrate your level of expertise is good, it is crucial that you "prove" the level of expertise you say you have, by mentioning where and how long you have been exposed to it.

For languages, please don't just say "fluent" or "advanced". Prove it by quantifying how long you've spoken that language and in what context.

Please remember:
- Once you wrote your responsibilities & achievements, sort them by order of value. Put the most important skill / achievement first and then the second one and so on.
- Even "on the job" trainings are worth mentioning. A trained professional will always be more attractive than someone with no relevant training in the field. And you'll be able to increase the keyword density.
- Ideally, your resume should go to the end of its last page. Otherwise try to optimize it so that it fits with the previous page.

To download this template for free, please go to:
www.nameyourcareer.com/jobsearchtemplates

The resume template was surprisingly helpful and already included most of what the coach described in the previous article. It also looked fairly nice and well-structured without getting complicated.

Her next step would be to migrate her current resume into the new format, and then follow the model.

She was finally ready to open the last document the coach attached: 'The 5 Steps to Begin Writing Your Resume.'

The 5 Steps to Begin Writing Your Resume:

Lisa printed the coach's *'Resume Writing Formula'* document and the *'Resume Template.'* As the printer buzzed and whirred, Lisa opened the last document, *'The 5 Steps to Begin Writing Your Resume,'* which read as follows:

BEGINNING TO WRITE YOUR RESUME:

The 5 Steps for an effective start

Step 1: Migrate your old resume into the new template

Step 2: Separate each experience into 2 subsections: *"Responsibilities"* and *"Achievements"*.

Step 3: Go on Google and type:
"List of Action verbs + resume" Read each action verb and pick the ones that apply to your experience.

Step 4: Once you have done step 1, 2 and 3, follow this model:

<u>For the **"Responsibilities"** section:</u>
Action Verb + Quantified <u>skill based</u> task
➔ Rewrite it if it does not allude to a relevant skillset
➔ *Try to keep every bullet point in 1 line and with only 1 topic*

<u>For the **"Achievements"** section:</u>
Action Verb + Quantified result
➔ *Try to keep every bullet point in 1 line and with only 1 topic*

Step 5: Ask yourself "How many, how often, how much, how big or small, how far". In other words, try to quantify every sentence. Remember: it's the numbers that make you unique. Nobody has the same numbers as you.

It was amazing how structured and powerful writing a resume could be. '*If I do this right,*' she thought, '*I can destroy the competition.*'

Lisa worked on the Cloudcom role for three hours straight. Although the last document made it easier to build up momentum, she struggled to revamp her experience at Cloudcom in a way that was powerful enough for her. She added a few quantities, but she didn't know how to quantify her experience like the document described.

But each time she returned to her resume over the weekend, she was more creative and specific, like she was stretching a new muscle.

The achievement part, however, was a different story. Considering a lack of results had gotten her fired, thinking about results at all was challenging. She managed to create two bullet points, but she wasn't sure of their relevance.

On Sunday, she stopped at her experience at Cloudcom and sent the coach the first draft of her resume, along with the previous version.

Lisa had several questions, and she couldn't wait for her next session... It would be at 4:30 PM the following day.

Lisa's previous description of her role at Cloudcom:

CLOUDCOM INC. Dubai, UAE.   **2016-Present**
Sales Consultant

- Manage client accounts and represent companies in selling web conference solutions
- Proactively identified new business opportunities in line with our service offerings across Telco, Govt, Retail, Manufacturing, Tech, Utilities and FS clients
- Booked demos with new and existing customers to increase sales revenue
- To execute sales strategies in order to explore business opportunity and maximize sales prospect.
- Establish and maintain excellent relationship with potential and existing customers as well as to provide world-class customer service to strengthen customer loyalty and market penetration.
- Visiting client businesses to establish and act on selling opportunities
- Assessing customers' needs and explaining our Conference Call solutions in line with their needs.
- Quoting and negotiating prices, and completing contracts and recording orders arranging delivery of goods, installation of equipment and the provision of services.
- Planned to ensure the successful development and execution of a business development plan.
- Demonstrated in depth knowledge of the competition and their capabilities in order to value position our solutions to the market
- Provided expert training to my clients on our more complex online data products either face to face or by WebEx

Lisa's new description of her role at Cloudcom.

PROFESSIONAL EXPERIENCE

Sales Consultant   **Mar 16 – Present**
CloudCom Inc.   *Dubai – UAE*

Cloud Communications is a leading Web Conference reseller and partner located in Dubai and London.

→ *My role was to develop the GCC Market and offer leading Web Conference solutions to clients across various industries.*

Responsibilities
- Managed around 35 client accounts and represent companies in selling web conference solutions
- Proactively identified new business opportunities in line with our service offerings across Telco, Govt, Retail, Manufacturing, Tech, Utilities and FS clients
- Booked demos with new and existing customers to increase sales revenue
- Executed sales strategies in order to explore business opportunity and maximize sales prospect.
- Established and maintained excellent relationship with potential and existing customers as well as to provide world-class customer service to strengthen customer loyalty and market penetration.
- Visited client businesses to establish and act on selling opportunities
- Assessed customers' needs and explaining our Conference Call solutions in line with their needs.
- Quoted and negotiated prices, and completing contracts and recording orders arranging delivery of goods, installation of equipment and the provision of services.
- Planned to ensure the successful development and execution of a business development plan.

Achievements
- Provided expert training to my clients on our more complex online data products either face to face or by WebEx
- Demonstrated in depth knowledge of the competition and their capabilities in order to value position our solutions to the market

The Resume Writing Session

"Hi, Lisa."

"Hi, coach."

"Well done on your resume. How did it go?"

"It wasn't as easy as I expected. I think my responsibilities are fine, but I'm struggling with the achievement part."

"That's pretty normal," commented the coach. "But before we begin, I would like to make sure you understand my resume writing formula. Can you explain it to me in your own words?"

"Sure," replied Lisa. "First, it's the keywords and their density on my resume that make it come up more often in search results," she explained. "Then, once they open my resume, the second ingredient is a list of job tasks that we try to quantify. Each task should represent a relevant skill set, or it shouldn't be there. And my seniority and my expertise in whatever skill is best represented by numbers, right?"

"Yes, that's the 'responsibilities' part of your resume," replied the Three Circles Coach, clearly pleased. "What else?"

"The third ingredient is my results at a job. They should outline the benefits my previous employers got beyond just doing the job itself. Speaking the employer language, I will quantify my results in time, money, or percentages. The fourth and final ingredient is 'action verbs.' They trigger the employer's imagination to see me in action while reading my resume. That's why they need to be specific and carefully chosen," said Lisa confidently.

"Excellent! Now, let's get started."

The coach shared his screen; Lisa's resume was open on it.

"Now, I'd love to challenge you on your responsibilities first."

"Sure," agreed Lisa.

The coach zoomed in on Lisa's resume so just her experience at *Cloudcom* appeared.

PROFESSIONAL EXPERIENCE

Sales Consultant
CloudCom Inc.

Mar 16 – Present
Dubai – UAE

Cloud Communications is a leading Web Conference reseller and partner located in Dubai and London.

➔ *My role was to develop the GCC Market and offer leading Web Conference solutions to clients across various industries.*

Responsibilities

- Managed around 35 client accounts and represent companies in selling web conference solutions
- Proactively identified new business opportunities in line with our service offerings across Telco, Govt, Retail, Manufacturing, Tech, Utilities and FS clients
- Booked demos with new and existing customers to increase sales revenue
- Executed sales strategies in order to explore business opportunity and maximize sales prospect.
- Established and maintained excellent relationship with potential and existing customers as well as to provide world-class customer service to strengthen customer loyalty and market penetration.
- Visited client businesses to establish and act on selling opportunities
- Assessed customers' needs and explaining our Conference Call solutions in line with their needs.
- Quoted and negotiated prices, and completing contracts and recording orders arranging delivery of goods, installation of equipment and the provision of services.
- Planned to ensure the successful development and execution of a business development plan.

Achievements

- Provided expert training to my clients on our more complex online data products either face to face or by WebEx
- Demonstrated in depth knowledge of the competition and their capabilities in order to value position our solutions to the market

"First of all, well done adding some numbers and keeping your action verbs in the past tense. However, can you explain the first sentence of your responsibilities to me?"

Lisa read the sentence to herself.

'Managed around 35 client accounts and represented companies in selling web conference solutions.'

She paused before answering. It already seemed clear to her.

"I managed around 35 clients while representing our partners' web conference solutions."

"Okay, that's already clearer. I guess if you say that it was your partners' web conference solutions, it's because *Cloudcom* is a reseller. But when you say *'represent companies,'* that's really vague. Can you see why?"

"I see what you mean, but I already said that *Cloudcom* was a reseller."

"You want to make it easy for recruiters. Remember who you're serving with this resume. If you make me feel like I have to put the pieces of the puzzle together to understand, it won't necessarily stick."

"That makes sense," Lisa sighed.

"Now, what do you mean by *'managed?'*"

"These clients were under my supervision," she explained.

"So were they given to you?" asked the Three Circles Coach.

"Not at all," said Lisa, indignant. "I had to acquire them all myself."

"You see, that's the problem with words like *'manage'* or *'in charge of'* or *'responsible for.'* They blur your skill set and what you really did. In this case, they even diminish your skills."

"So what would you put instead?" asked Lisa.

"Based on what you told me, I would say: **'Acquired, secured, and developed a portfolio of 35 new clients from scratch in less than six months.'**"

"Wow." The sentence was already more powerful than what she had written.

"And do you suppose this would go to the *responsibilities* or the *achievements* section?"

"That's a result."

"That's correct, well done."

They reviewed each sentence, and the coach rewrote them as they went.

Lisa's old resume	The coach's comments	Lisa's new resume
Proactively identified new business opportunities in line with our service offerings across Telco, Govt, Retail, Manufacturing, Tech, Utilities and FS clients.	*No real skill promoted here... What actions have you done here? And how many/how much?*	Promoted our web conference solutions to around 20 new companies per day *(mainly via cold calls)*. *(Under Responsibilities)*
Booked demos with new and existing customers to increase sales revenue.	*How many demos per week did you book on average?*	Booked up to5 product demos per week with new and existing customers. *(Under Responsibilities)*
Executed sales strategies in order to explore business opportunities and maximize sales prospects.	*What does it mean? What did you do?*	Unclear and vague, No specific skills come out of that sentence. → *Removed.*
Established and maintained excellent relationships with potential and existing customers, and provided world class customer service to strengthen customer loyalty and market penetration.	*That sentence is too long, try to make it fit in one line for maximum impact. Do not hesitate to add extra bullet points if needed.*	Built strong relationships with around 95 clients thanks to world class customer service. *(Under Responsibilities)*
Visited client businesses to establish and act on selling opportunities.	*What value does this add? It does not show any skill. Be more specific, don't make them guess.*	Met with an average of 3 prospects every week to demonstrate our web conference solutions at their premises. *(Under Responsibilities)*

Lisa's old resume	The coach's comments	Lisa's new resume
Assessed customers' needs and explained our CRM solution in line with their needs.	*That's not bad. Keep it, but with a twist.*	Collected and analyzed customers' needs and presented our solution in line with their requirements. *(Under Responsibilities)*
Quoted and negotiated prices, completed contracts, and recorded orders.	*Be more specific. How many proposals did you do? Rephrase it.*	Issued 2 to 3 proposals daily and handled contract negotiations, payments, and activations from A to Z. *(Under Responsibilities)*
Planned to ensure the successful development and execution of a business development plan.	*??? It does not mean much. No visible skill set showcased here, either.*	Unclear and vague → *removed.*
Demonstrated in-depth knowledge of the competition and their capabilities in order to value position our solutions to the market.	*"Demonstrating" is not a skill, and this sentence can't be backed by data or numbers.*	Unclear and vague → *removed.*
Provided expert training to my clients on our more complex online data products either face-to-face or by WebEx.	*That's not bad but there are no numbers. Here's what I would write instead:*	Personally trained around 10 new client users per month, which fast tracked the adoption rate of our software. *(Under Responsibilities)*

As soon as they finalized the rewrites, it was obvious each sentence carried more weight and was more to the point. However, there was still only one achievement.

"I'm not sure what other achievements I can add," Lisa admitted.

"That's okay. The results are always the biggest challenge."

"Really?"

"Yes," replied the coach. "Professionals don't always keep track of their various achievements, and months or years later, they forget. On top of this, achievements are from the company's perspective, so if someone has been in environments where his or her results are not recognized, then it's often the part on the resume that proves the most challenging," the coach explained.

"If your results are neatly presented on your resume, you'll be the exception, and that's a huge competitive advantage, regardless of the market you're in. Remember, most resumes are vague and average. When you show results on your resume, employers are immediately thinking *'That's what I want for my company: results.'*"

"That makes sense, but I was terminated for poor results, remember?" Lisa pointed out.

"I do," replied the coach. "But it doesn't mean you haven't had good results before that. Let's see what we can string together," suggested the coach. "Didn't you mention that you broke the company's record during your first six months?" he asked.

"Oh, that's right!" she remembered.

"So we could write *'Made the fastest 1st deal in the company's history,'*" he suggested.

"It definitely sounds impressive."

"And you were ahead of your target in the first six months, weren't you?"

"Of course," she replied with a sense of pride.

"How do you reckon we could phrase that?"

"What about *'Was ahead of my targets within the first 6 months'*?"

"That's not bad," commented the coach. "But I'd suggest *'Exceeded my target within my first 6 months on the job.'*"

"That's more powerful," Lisa agreed.

"That's because I used a power verb. You said *'Was ahead of'* and I changed that to *'Exceeded,'*" he explained. "I'm thinking as a marketer, not a job seeker. I try to charge my messages with positive emotions."

"I get it," said Lisa. "I don't think I can do the same thing on my own, but I get it."

"Of course you can! Let's see if we can extract more achievements."

"Sure," said Lisa.

"Did Mark ever appreciate anything you did during your tenure at *Cloudcom*?"

Lisa was silent for a while. Thinking past her recent firing wasn't easy.

"Oh, I know," she murmured. "Mark praised me once because I trained a new team member and she was able to hit her targets very quickly."

"And how would you bring this to life on your resume?" asked the coach.

"I could say *'Trained a new staff member who quickly achieved her target.'*"

"Not bad, but you made a small mistake," commented the coach. "You've put the achievement part at the end of the sentence. How do you think a marketer would turn this sentence around to highlight the achievement first? Remember, start with an action verb."

Lisa was quiet for a moment.

"I could say *'Empowered a new team member to achieve her targets within her first quarter, by coaching and mentoring her.'*"

"That's much better," said the Three Circles Coach, clearly pleased. "Any second thoughts?" he asked, challenging her further.

"Maybe," she mused. "How about: ***'Turned a new team member into a top performer in less than 3 months by mentoring and training her?'***"

"Now *that's* impressive!" the coach crowed. "I couldn't have said it better!"

Finally, it was starting to get fun. Lisa felt a bubble of pride beginning to expand as she read the sentence again.

'Turned a new team member into a top performer in less than 3 months by mentoring and training her.'

"Now, why do you think this sentence would be appreciated by a potential employer?" probed the coach.

"Because if I was an employer, that would help my business grow," she answered confidently.

"Great! Do you think you could give your resume another go?" he asked.

Encouraged by her results, Lisa was quick to reply, "Of course!"

The Three Circles Coach spent a minute reading what they had done and formatting it so most bullet points would fit within the same line. Lisa couldn't believe the final result.

Sales Consultant
CloudCom Inc.

Mar 16 – Present
Dubai – UAE

CloudCom is a leading Web Conference reseller and partner located in Dubai and London.

→ *My role was to develop the GCC Market and offer leading Web Conference solutions to clients across various industries.*

Responsibilities

- Promoted our Web Conference solutions to around 20 new companies per day *(via cold calls)*
- Booked as much as to 5 product demos per week with new and existing customers.
- Built strong relationships with my clients thanks to a world-class customer service.
- Met with around 3 prospects every week to demonstrate our Web Conference Solution.
- Collected & understood customers' needs and presented our solution in line with their requirements.
- Issued 2 to 3 proposals daily, handled contract negotiations, payments & activations from A to Z.
- Personally trained around 10 new Web Conference users every month which fast-tracked my clients' adoption of our software.

Achievements

- ✓ Acquired, Secured and Developed 35 new clients from scratch *(generating almost AED 1 Million)*
- ✓ Exceeded my target within less than 6 months on the job.
- ✓ Made the fastest 1st deal in the company's history.
- ✓ Turned a new team member into a top performer in less than 3 months by mentoring & training her.

"What do you think?" the coach asked.

"I can't believe it!" Lisa gushed. "It's like day and night. I see how the figures we added come out. It's easy to read, the bullet points fit, and the separation between *'responsibilities'* and *'achievements'* is great. I see how enticing it could be. It's no longer than the old one, but it's so much more impactful!"

"I'm glad you see all that." The coach paused as if he was trying to structure his next comment. "At first, your resume will be read in around seven seconds. If it passes that first test, recruiters will have a second, more thorough read.

"Everyone is different, but the way recruiters read resumes is more or less the title first, your current location, each job title, a line or two of the description, the dates of each experience, and your last degree," he explained. "You've got to optimize each step to increase your chances for a second read."

"How?" asked Lisa.

Another chart showed up on screen.

The title of your resume		Make sure it's in line with the job adverts you're applying to.
Your current location		Avoid putting your exact address; the city and country are enough. If you put your exact address, an employer looking for someone to recruit at the other end of town could assume that this would be too much of a commute.
The job titles of each experience		Companies give different titles. Make sure the one you put on your resume is in line with the most common designation for your type of work. If you don't want to do that, add the most common job title in brackets. Remember, even in job titles, keywords are critical.
The first 1 or 2 lines within the description of your experiences (responsibilities and achievements)		Separating responsibilities and achievements will entice the recruiter to read the first 1 or 2 lines of each of these subcategories. **IMPORTANT: Make sure the most impactful bullet point is at the top of this subsection and the rest of the bullet points are ranked by order of importance.**
The dates and duration of each of your experiences		Make it easy for recruiters to understand the duration of each experience. **IMPORTANT: If you had experiences that lasted less than 12 months, please add an explanation: e.g.: 'Internship,' 'Temporary contract,' 'part time while studying,' etc.** Otherwise the recruiter might think that you're jumping from one job to another and that you're not very stable/loyal.
Your latest degree		If you have been studying in a great school, say so with something like: 'ranked as one of the top 5 logistics schools in Virginia.'

When Lisa finished reading, she could see the importance of each point, and she understood the details.

"Any questions?" the coach asked after a moment.

"On your resume template, there's no space for a picture. Is that on purpose?"

"It sure is. A picture attracts the wrong attention from employers and—"

Lisa interrupted before he could finish. "You said that a resume should attract attention."

"Yes, just not based on looks," replied the coach. "People are fickle, and they could see the picture in a way that wouldn't serve you. They could discriminate based on your looks, your religion, your race..." He trailed off. "You will find that in many countries, a picture isn't allowed on your resume to avoid discrimination."

"Don't you think that's being overcautious?"

"No. I think that's being meticulous about your personal brand. Discrimination already happens without pictures. You don't need to make things harder on yourself."

"Okay, it makes sense. But can't they just find my picture on LinkedIn anyway?"

"They can, but their first impression will be based on your skills, rather than looks. Your first impression is key. Besides, if they look you up online, they're already interested. Just make sure that on LinkedIn, you have some strong recommendations from previous employers to keep scoring extra points in the screening process."

"You really have thought of everything."

"Thank you. The important thing is to think like a recruiter, while you keep your marketing hat on," replied the coach. "Do you have any more questions?"

Quantifying Responsibilities and Achievements

"Actually, yeah. It's about quantifying my experiences. Are all jobs really quantifiable?"

"You bet!" exclaimed the coach. "I was conducting a lecture for final year students at a university once and when I explained that every job can be quantified, I found a few people arguing that *'not every job'* could be quantified. **Don't fall into this trap.** Here are the examples that I gave to the class to settle the point."

The Three Circles Coach took a deep breath as he began explaining what happened that day while he was giving the lecture.

"First, they looked at their marketing teacher who was present in the classroom and took her as an example to back their claim that not all jobs can be quantified.

"So I asked them a question: *'If I'm a university dean and I have to find a teacher for an 85-student class, do you think that if your teacher adds on her resume that she has been handling classes of up to 120 students, this would make the dean more confident about her ability to handle a class of 85?'"* he explained.

"Students agreed, of course, but I wanted to make sure that everyone was on board with the concept, so I asked another question:

*"And do you not believe that if the dean had the choice between 10 resumes and only one mentioned the right numbers, wouldn't that teacher receive a phone call anyway **even** if she doesn't have as much experience as the others?"'* said the coach.

"I'm with you so far," Lisa started, "but how would a teacher quantify results?"

"They asked the same question," he commented. "What about the percentage of successful students? Imagine two teachers' profiles: One of them shows that 73 percent of her students have passed and the other shows that

93 percent of her students have passed. Which one would you call first for an interview?"

"Okay, you win," Lisa huffed playfully. "What about a nurse, then? That type of work is all about people."

The coach obliged. "Well, let's say a nurse is overseeing around fifteen patients in a ward versus eight patients for another nurse. Even if the recruiting hospital has a ratio of ten patients per nurse, which resume do you think the recruiter will contact first?"

The coach paused for a second to allow Lisa to grasp the concept once and for all.

"Every job can be quantified if you look at it from the employer's point of view. How could you justify being a good investment for your employers if you can't quantify the return on that investment?

"The answer can *only* be in numbers, and certainly not in meaningless adjectives like '*passionate,*' '*diligent,*' '*results-driven,*' '*detail-oriented,*' or any other unprovable fluff.

"No one is naive enough to believe that when a recruiter reads something like '*results-driven*' he thinks '*Wow, he's results-driven, I better call him.*'

"Those words carry no weight and should only be tolerated in the summary or the objective section of your resume. Remember, you are a company selling your services, so always try to speak like your target customers: in numbers."

"Got it," Lisa assured him. "I just think people don't want to be reduced to numbers."

"That's because they see their resume as themselves, not as what it should be. Their resume is only a marketing brochure of their services."

Lisa was comfortable with the concept by then, but still not 100 percent convinced. She remembered a friend of hers, back in Virginia.

"Okay, one last example. A friend of mine is a social worker, and I can't imagine she could ever accept putting numbers on her resume. She would feel like she was dehumanizing her work."

"Dehumanizing," the coach repeated. "I heard this before, actually, but that can't be further from the truth.

"A social worker has families or people to help. Their files are on their desk and they're eager to be contacted. If you had to hire a social worker, numbers are all they have to represent the measure of what they do.

"Things like: *'Successfully closed 58 cases in the last six months,' 'held the lowest rate of reopened cases in my department with 98 percent of my files closed with sustainable solutions,'* or *'won the 'best customer service award' twice based on surveys filled out by the people I was in charge of helping.'*

"Doesn't that sound like a very *human* social worker?" asked the Three Circles Coach.

"Yeah, fair point."

"Being efficient or productive is always at the service of others, and that's what employers are looking for. There is no job that can't be quantified. It's about asking yourself the right questions.

"You are always measured because you're an investment for an employer. So the key is to ask yourself what you're being measured against and bring that to life on your resume. **Never make the mistake of believing that someone's job can't be measured.**"

She was convinced, even if it took a little while. Still, that left the matter of applying for jobs in other countries. Going back to Virginia wasn't an option anymore.

Applying to Jobs Abroad

"Suppose that I want to submit job applications abroad," Lisa began. "New York, for example. If recruiters look at someone's location and only call job applicants that live close enough, won't it be hard for me to find a job abroad?"

"Not necessarily. I've coached many clients that found jobs abroad. You just need to imply that you're already there."

"How so?" asked Lisa, intrigued.

"Instead of putting your *current* location, you replace it with your *target* location. You wouldn't mention whether this is your current or your target address; what you mean is entirely up to you. So if you were to apply to a role in New York, I would suggest you have a resume that implies that you're there already."

"Isn't that lying?" asked Lisa.

"Only if you say that it's your current location. Otherwise, it's up to you what you mean by the location you put in. After all, it's your resume, Lisa."

"Okay," she agreed. "But wouldn't my phone number give me away?"

"That's the second thing you should be careful about when applying abroad. Can you buy yourself an American SIM Card?" asked the coach.

"I can get a friend to purchase one for me and send it over," Lisa mused out loud.

"There you go. Otherwise you could just type the phrase: *'how to get a virtual SIM card number'* on Google and you'll find services like https://www.worldsim.com where you could also have a US sim card sent to you, along with a local mobile number.

"It works for many countries and depending on which country you're in, incoming calls might even be free. Check it out."

Lisa scribbled down the website URL. She hadn't known that a service like that actually existed!

"Thank you, but what if an employer calls that number and finds out that I'm in Dubai?"

"At the time of the call, you could be traveling anywhere in the world. That's your right. You can just say that you're *out of the country at the moment* and ask if it would be possible for him to call you on your other number to avoid roaming charges.

"Your aim would be to tell them that you can shorten your 'trip' and take the next flight anytime, but ask if you could first have a preliminary interview via phone or Skype.

"If things work out well, then you might consider traveling for a face--to-face interview, but only after you've established that there is a clear opportunity and a fit between yourself and an employer. A difficult situation to handle, but the right script helps it work more often than not."

"That makes a surprising amount of sense," Lisa acknowledged.

"Remember, the true purpose of your resume is to generate phone calls and interviews. You don't want recruiters disqualifying your profile based on your location, and a phone call will give you a chance to reassure them."

"OK..." agreed Lisa. On one hand, she was pleased with the possibilities that this technique offered, but on the other, she wasn't completely comfortable.

"It still sounds like I'm tricking them into believing I'm at a certain location when I'm not," she confessed.

"I can see why you'd think that," replied the Three Circles Coach. "You're thinking like an employee and not like a company."

"What do you mean?"

"Have you ever tried to call a company's customer support department on their local number, only to realize it's being answered in a completely different country?"

"Yes, it happens a lot," Lisa acknowledged as she cottoned on to the coach's point. "I get it. I need to think like the CEO of my company. Serving my customers internationally and putting a local number they could call me on is a good customer service practice."

"Exactly," said the coach, sounding pleased. "Of course, you don't want to lie and mention on your resume that it's your current location, but apart from that, why wouldn't you put a local number and a location you can easily serve your customers?"

"I guess you're right," she agreed.

"Lisa, my biggest problem with job seekers is that they consistently do what they're told without questioning whether it's good for them or not. Entrepreneurs and companies do what they should to market themselves and compete effectively.

"As long as you're not doing anything illegal, make sure everything you put on your resume actually serves you."

"I understand."

"You know, there's so much hypocrisy out there. Companies are happy saying they serve customers in so many countries they're not located in, and add local numbers to strengthen that impression, and yet HR personnel wouldn't accept that job seekers market their services in the same way. Why not?"

"It does sound pretty hypocritical," Lisa acknowledged. "If companies are doing it, why *not* job seekers?"

"Exactly. It's *your* company, *your* career, *your* resume, and *your* future. Stay legal and don't lie, but at the same time, don't follow pre-established rules that don't serve you."

Lisa was really starting to like that mindset. She was her own company, after all. She was just doing what every other company was already doing.

Tackling Short Experiences and Terminations On a Resume

Lisa knew she would be speaking to recruiters in no time. But so far, nothing she had learned would help her explain what happened at *Cloudcom* in a way that didn't make her look awful. The Three Circles Coach was her best card, but he was also the last card in her hand. She cleared her throat.

"How should I present my experience at *Cloudcom*? The ending of that experience, mostly."

"You don't have to mention that it ended," replied the coach.

"So, I should keep the word *'present'* even after my contract ends?" It felt a little like lying all over again.

"Yes. For up to three months after the end of your notice period, allow yourself to not have a perfectly updated resume. Your job is not to allude to any negative customer experience.

"The sole purpose of your marketing brochure is to attract customers so you can have a conversation with them.

"The job of your customers is to ask you any questions they want and decide whether you are the right fit or not. So don't shoot yourself in the foot. Let employers form an opinion by speaking to you. By not mentioning an end date, you might avoid the question all together."

"It makes so much sense, but what if he asks me and finds out that I'm no longer employed at *Cloudcom*? Wouldn't he think that I lied to him?"

"Not quite. Sending a resume that is not 100 percent up-to-date happens all the time, and recruiters know that. Besides, you'll be honest during the interview, but you'll also help the employer see your side of the story before he assumes something based on an end date.

"The decision will be his after that. Even if he asks you why it says *'present'* on your resume after you explain everything, you could just say that he doesn't have the most updated version of your resume and you can send him one right away. Can you see my *'customer service'* circle constantly at play here?"

Lisa understood the coach's point, but that didn't help with the worst case scenario.

"Okay, but how would you explain to a recruiter that you were terminated if he was to ask?"

"You do what great CEOs do, Lisa; you bite the bullet and show that this is a great learning experience for you. You will find that most people are understanding when you do not try to hide the truth.

"It's the first time it happened, so it's not like you have a track record of being let go. You can say that you have both agreed that this was not the right role for you. I would also explain how this experience made you more mature in your career, which will surely serve the next employer, don't you think?"

"I guess you're right," she replied, already thinking of a proper scripted answer for that question. It didn't seem like the sort of thing she should improvise.

"For argument's sake, what if I'm out of work for longer than two or three months?"

"For two or three months, you can say that he doesn't have an updated resume, but if you have a gap longer than that, it could signal to other employers that you're unwanted, unless you have a logical reason," explained the coach.

"Like a maternity leave, traveling, joining a charity, writing a blog, helping someone in his business, freelancing... it puts the recruiter at ease if you've added that on your resume, and it stops him from thinking that you were unwanted by other employers. Always show that you're still kicking!"

Lisa hummed in agreement before she wondered, "But wouldn't activities away from my career path make it trickier to find work?"

"Not if you do it right. Let's suppose that you haven't found work in three months," said the coach, and Lisa had to stomp down her anxiety to focus on his words, "and you decide to write a blog, for example.

"You could write a blog about sales techniques, all the scripts you could think of, all the rebuttals to common objections. You could have articles that talk about the sales industries that pay the highest amount of commissions, and so on. You could share these articles on LinkedIn, and who do you suppose would read them?"

"Sales professionals?"

"Including sales managers, who happen to be employers."

"So... I really could keep marketing myself."

"Exactly. Don't let unemployment derail your career; do something in line with your career.

"If you decide to write articles on LinkedIn, your LinkedIn profile would be visited more frequently, on top of showcasing your sales industry knowledge and helping others with your articles. Can you see how your *'marketing'* and your *'customer service'* circles cross?"

"But what about the 'sales' circle in this case?"

"Sales is about convincing people to take the next step with you, re-member?"

"So then they would contact me."

"Right! So what would you add at the end of the articles?"

"I could add my email address, but wouldn't that look a little desperate?"

"It could, unless you make sure that your *'sales'* circle crosses with your *'service to others'* circle," replied the coach. "How could you present your email address in a way that is helping others?"

Lisa paused to think it over. "I could say that they could contact me if they have any questions. And now my three circles cross!" She snatched up her pen to take a few notes.

IF MY JOB SEARCH LASTS FOR MORE THAN 3 MONTHS, I SHOULD START AN EXTRA ACTIVITY TO AVOID GAPS ON MY RESUME.

THE ONLY GAPS THAT ARE TOLERATED ARE THOSE THAT WON'T PORTRAY MY PROFILE AS BEING UNWANTED BY EMPLOYERS.

(I.E.: MATERNITY BREAK, TRAVELING, LOOKING AFTER A FAMILY MEMBER, ETC.)

IDEALLY WHATEVER I DO DURING THESE PERIODS OF UNEMPLOYMENT, IT NEEDS TO BE RELEVANT TO MY CAREER DIRECTION, OTHERWISE IT WILL LOOK LIKE I'M INTERRUPTING MY CAREER.

(GOOD EXAMPLES ARE FREELANCING, ARTICLE WRITING, DOING VIDEOS, ETC.)

As she set her notepad down, Lisa mused, "I actually know someone who has been unemployed for nine years," as her thoughts turned towards her mom's cousin Leonard in Virginia. "Do you think that it's because the gap on his resume made him look unwanted?"

"It could be for many reasons," the coach acknowledged. "But if he's unconsciously promoting himself as being unwanted, he needs to get out of that cycle."

"Honestly, he gave up trying to find work. It seems kinda hopeless by now," said Lisa.

"No case is hopeless! I've had my share of supposedly hopeless clients, and as long as he's ready to change the way he markets himself, his phone will ring again."

"If you say so," Lisa laughed, skeptical but willing to play along.

The coach went quiet. Not hearing any reply for almost 20 seconds, she probed, "Coach?"

She had been a bit flippant, but she hadn't been that bad, had she? The line disconnected a moment later and she flinched. She tried to call him again, but after a moment he wasn't even online anymore.

After a few minutes, a notification popped up, indicating an email from the Three Circles Coach, and Lisa felt a flood of relief.

Hey Lisa,

Sorry we got disconnected. I actually had to go, so it was good timing.

It's time for you to apply what we discussed and let me know when you've finished your resume.

I look forward to seeing the final version. Use what we did together with your experience at *Cloudcom* as a template for your other roles and you'll be fine.

On another note, I found your comment a little upsetting. No one is a lost cause.

And it hurts seeing people get dismissed because at one point in their career they had a setback and might have not been able to stand back up.

As time passes, they fall even deeper into hopelessness. It could have been anyone of us and you know it.

Speak to you soon,
The Three Circles Coach.

Lisa's heart was racing. She had been a little insensitive, but she hadn't anticipated the coach's reaction. Maybe he had gone through a long period of unemployment himself, but she didn't know enough about him to guess.

Perhaps she could rewrite Leonard's resume using the Three Circles Coach's method. She wasn't even sure if Leonard had a proper resume, but she could *try*.

At 42 years old and with no degree, Leonard was living in a small town that had lost many jobs in the last decade, far away from cities and recruiters. The task looked daunting and would raise some eyebrows in her family.

To make sure she wouldn't back down, she sent a text to her mom:

> Hey mom, I need a small favor. Please don't ask any questions, but can you please send me cousin Leonard's resume ASAP? (I'll explain why next time we speak)

If anyone had Leonard's resume, her mom would know how to get it. The answer came back a few minutes later:

> Hey hun, sure... but???

Lisa was feeling better already. There was nothing to lose.

But for now, she needed to tackle her own resume, while she was energized. She drew three columns in her notepad.

In the left column, she wrote the lines of her current resume. In the middle, she started revamping each sentence. On the right, she finalized each one, trying to make sure that each line would actually reflect a skill or a relevant result.

She made sure that by the end of the process, each line would have three of the four resume ingredients: *Action Verb + Quantity + Keywords* for each subsection—responsibilities and achievements.

Watch the Time, Inc. and Cerrutini

There were very few tasks that actually showcased her sales skills, and no figures, either. More shocking still, there was almost no mention of any achievements. *'How did Mark decide to interview me when he saw that?'* she wondered. *'No wonder no one else did.'*

Watch the time Inc. Dubai, UAE.   **2015-2016**
Sales Assistant

- Checked supplies, placed orders, created product displays and liaised with retailers to improve product placement
- Delivering excellent customer service to win the sale
- Handling incoming telephone calls from customers or previous customers to assist with their issues.
- Attended trade shows and conventions
- Participated in merchandising our products in the most efficient way

Responsibilities	1st draft	Final Draft
Checked supplies, placed orders, created product displays, and liaised with retailers to improve product placement	*Irrelevant, I do not want to go back to retail.* → *removed.*	
Missing sales tasks	*Greeted each customer and directed him to specific products based on his needs.*	**Greeted up to 50 customers a day and promoted our products in line with their needs.**
Delivering excellent customer service to win the sale	*Delivered some of the highest customer service on the entire team based on daily surveys.*	**Consistently awarded one of the highest customer service scores based on daily surveys.**
Handling incoming telephone calls from customers or previous customers to assist with their issues.	*Handled each phone call to the shop and convinced them to come and visit us.*	**Handled around 10 customer phone calls each day and convinced them to come and visit us.**
New additions	*Contacted key customers on the phone to let them know of new product arrivals.*	**Contacted up to 30 customers per week on the phone to promote our new product arrivals.**
Attended trade shows and conventions	*Networked and promoted our products during trade shows.*	**Networked and promoted our products to visitors during trade shows.**
Participated in merchandising our products in the most efficient way	*Played an active role in optimizing our merchandising in line with clients' behavior during their visit.*	**No extra change**
New idea	*Trained new staff*	**Trained and coached new team members to quickly excel at their jobs.**

As some of her responsibilities made her think of a few achievements, Lisa drew a new table:

Achievements	1st draft	Final Draft
	Was awarded employee of the month in my second month.	Won the "best employee of the month" award 4 times in less than 9 months.
	Sold around AED 350,000 of product.	Sold around AED 350,000 of product in less than 9 months.
	Exceeded my sales target after only 6 months on the job.	No change

Putting it all together on her resume, it was in stark contrast with her previous one:

Sales Assistant   Nov 15 – Feb 16
Watch the time Inc.   *Dubai – UAE*

Watch the time Inc. is a watch retailer with 8 outlets across the Middle Eastern region.

→ *My role was to promote our products according to customers' needs and deliver on my sales target.*

Responsibilities
- Greeted up to 50 customers a day and promoted our products in line with their needs.
- Consistently awarded 1 of the highest customer service score based on daily surveys.
- Handled around 10 customer phone calls every day and convinced them to visit us.
- Contacted up to 30 customers per week on the phone to promote our new product arrivals.
- Networked and promoted our products to 100s of visitors during trade shows.
- Trained and coached 2 new team members to quickly excel their job.

Achievements
- ✓ Won the "best employee of the month" award 4 times in less than 9 months
- ✓ Sold around AED 350,000 of products in less than 9 months.
- ✓ Exceeded my sales target after only 6 months in the job

Reason for leaving: Was contacted by the regional Head of CloudCom for a role with them.

Bolstered by how much marketing and sales treasure her resume was actually hiding, she continued with her experience at *Cerrutini*.

Although it was a similar experience as the one at *Watch the Time, Inc.,* she tried to focus on the fact that *Cerrutini* was a luxury watchmaker instead of copying what she had already done. Using three columns again, the result was nothing short of motivating.

Sales Assistant
Cerrutini & Co.

Apr 14 – Oct 15
New York, US

Cerrutini & Co. is a luxury Italian watch maker with over 50 outlets and 280 employees worldwide.

➔ *My role was to promote our watches according to customers' needs during a 6-month internship.*

Responsibilities
- Served and consulted with around 20 customers a day on average to identify their needs
- Cold-called around 25 5-star hotels and concierges to establish a referral partnership.
- Tailored each customer experience in line with our Maison's brand guideline
- Delivered a 5-star client experience before, during and after their visits.
- Ensured a World Class After-Sale Service by personally following up with clients after every purchase

Achievements
- ✓ Quickly exceeded my KPIs and delivered my internship at 24% above my sales target.
- ✓ Achieved the highest customer return ratio across a team of 8 sales assistants.
- ✓ Selected for a full time position as a sales assistant at the end of my internship.

Reason for leaving: End of my internship + wanted to pursue a career in Dubai.

Certain that recruiters would find it attractive, Lisa felt great. It showcased her sales skills in a variety of different contexts, and the strong results she had extracted would surely help employers zoom in on those results.

She still needed help with her summary, but she was looking forward to having her last resume writing session with the coach before she could start applying to jobs again.

Leonard's Email

Finally satisfied, she sent her latest draft to the Three Circles Coach. Just as she thought she was done with her day, an email came in. It was Leonard.

Hey Lisa,

How have you been and how is Dubai?

Your mum called me at lunch and asked if I could send you my resume. You'll find it attached.

I'm not sure how you could help but whatever you do, thank you.

Please don't hesitate to call if you need any info.

Speak to you soon,
Leonard.

When Lisa opened his resume, she was in shock.

Leonard was divorced with no children. He had no specific career path. Dropping out of high school at 17 years old, he started doing temporary work.

After a couple of years, he got a training certificate as a warehouse worker. A few temporary contracts later, he was finally offered a permanent role at a medium-sized logistics company. That was when Leonard met Emma from the accounting department and ended up marrying her.

After a company restructuring and ultimately a takeover from a larger competitor, his job became redundant. On the forefront of strikes which were covered by the local media, Leonard did what he felt was the right thing at the time, organizing protests and speaking to the regional and national press.

He had been on a mission, not just for himself but also for the 52 employees who lost their jobs as a consequence of the takeover.

Criticized by his wife and his own family members for exposing himself and the family name in public, he continued his fight against what he called the 'capitalist machine' and was even invited on a few TV shows.

When the media moved on to other topics, Leonard found his message ignored and decided to look for work. He was 33 years old then, and two years of unemployment later, Emma asked for a divorce.

Unsurprisingly, employers were wary of Leonard's profile, seeing him more as a danger to the company's stability and ignoring his experience as a warehouseman.

"I told you," was what he kept hearing from his wife during his unemployment until the divorce. After his divorce, Leonard was seen more with pity and viewed as a classic case of personal failure.

He was invited to most family reunions, for the Fourth of July and some birthdays. That was how Lisa knew Leonard.

His story was well known across the family, and after nine years of unemployment he was the example that children were to avoid at all costs. "Study and get good grades or you'll end up like Leonard," was a sentence that Lisa had been familiar with as she was growing up.

The adults in the family looked down on him, labeling him lazy. "If I was him, I would take any job to get back on track," pretended some. "He will never amount to anything in life," replied others.

As Lisa read his resume, she felt at a loss. The Three Circles Coach was right: it could have happened to anyone. Even so, she didn't know how to deal with a nine year gap on Leonard's resume.

"Of course, she could speak to him and revamp his past experiences according to the Three Circles Coach's method. *'But what about the gap? No employer will ever give him a call with a nine year gap,'* she thought. *'We must fill this gap.'*

She put the matter to rest for the time being. She could ask the Three Circles Coach later. She closed her laptop and checked her mobile for the first time in hours. She saw a text from Sabrina:

> Hey hun, how is it going?
> Would you like to come for
> lunch tomorrow? Let me know.

Lunch at Sabrina's

The following day, Lisa prepared some cupcakes and took them with her to Sabrina's. She arrived at Sabrina's just after noon, and immediately Hanaa, Sabrina's 5-year-old daughter, ran towards the door and jumped into Lisa's arms.

Sabrina's husband, Youssef, was in the kitchen baking couscous. Fish couscous, based on the smell. Youssef was originally from Tunisia, and he cooked the most fabulous couscous in town.

Lisa was playing with Hanaa in a corner of the living room when Youssef and Sabrina emerged from the kitchen with the couscous dish.

That was when Lisa realized that she hadn't eaten a healthy meal in days. They sat around the table and Lisa complimented Youssef on the delicious dish. After the usual small talk, the conversation quickly shifted to Lisa and her job search.

"So how are your sessions with the Three Circles Coach going?" asked Sabrina.

"Great, I think," Lisa replied, and she launched into an explanation of how simple and sharp the coach's resume writing method was, how she was seeing her experience in a new light, and how it boosted her self-esteem. She was excited for whatever was coming next.

After lunch and tea, Sabrina was fixing one of the toys her daughter had on her mat. She seemed to be lost in her thoughts.

"Sabrina's lost in space," Youssef observed, grinning.

"What?" Sabrina snapped out of it. "Sorry. I was thinking about my last job search."

"I bet you found work much faster than me," Lisa mused, trying to probe further.

Sabrina looked at Youssef, still sipping his tea. He raised his eyebrows expectantly.

"Trust me, it wasn't easy," Sabrina replied.

"What happened?" asked Lisa.

"When Hanaa was born, I stayed at home for a year to look after her. With Youssef working freelance, we didn't have a stable income on a monthly basis, and you know how expensive Dubai is."

"At the time, I figured I could find work easily. I had experience and great references, or so I thought..." Sabrina sighed. "The truth is, after reactivating my network, I didn't have much coming my way.

"Maybe I wasn't doing it right, I don't know, but I quickly realized I'd better start applying to jobs the old fashion way, through online portals. After two months of nothing, I felt pretty low. Youssef was supportive, but I was angry, and we'd already eaten up all of our savings. We were stressed.

"I dreaded Youssef asking how things went with my job search. We started arguing a lot. Youssef was feeling down for not being able to support his family." She squeezed Youssef's forearm. "I was feeling awful for not being appreciated or recognized the way I thought I should be.

"It built up, and eventually we would go days without talking to each other. It's hard when you have a family counting on you, and every week brought its load of false hope. It wasn't easy."

Youssef held Sabrina's hand as she started getting emotional.

"I'm glad everything worked out," said Lisa, already feeling bad for pushing.

But Sabrina seemed determined to finish what she started.

"We wanted to help each other, but we were awful at it," she continued.

"What do you mean?"

"Like giving advice to someone who doesn't need it. 'Have you tried to follow up on that application?' 'Are you ready for your interview tomorrow?' 'How was your job hunt today?' Too many questions, and I was asking them, too.

"'Are you working on a new project?' 'How did your meeting go with the client?' 'Are they going to extend your contract?' We were scared, we had no answers, and we felt terrible. Throw in the sleep deprivation from Hanaa, and we were ready to blow. We almost went back to New York."

"Did things get better once you found work?"

"No. We thought they would, but things only got better when we got better."

"Got better at what?" asked Lisa.

"We were hoping our relationship would go back to normal once I found work or once Youssef secured a big contract. But we were the problem, not the work. We were needy, and no one wants to hire needy people.

"I guess we were frustrated, angry and scared, so with so much negative energy, I think we were unconsciously pushing away any opportunity. So one night we agreed to support each other, no matter how scared we got.

"No more questions. We just had to trust each other. We talked about other things, we lived simply, we learned to appreciate each other again, and leave our worries at the door. Pretty soon, we were back on track as a couple.

"The strange part is that my phone started to ring more after that, and I don't know why. I can't explain it. It's like we had to cure ourselves before we hoped for anything else to work out."

"God changes not the condition of a people until they change what is in themselves," Youssef said out of the blue. Seeing the confusion on Lisa's face, he explained, "It's a verse from the Qur'an."

"Oh, don't start," Sabrina laughed, elbowing her husband in the arm as she smiled.

"What did I say?" asked Youssef, amused.

"Sorry, Lisa," said Sabrina chuckling.

"It's fine, don't worry," Lisa replied, glad the mood had lifted.

At 5 PM, Lisa decided it was time to go home and prepare for her coaching session the following day. She added another note to her notepad once she was home:

No one wants to hire needy people!

She connected with her mom via Skype, and they talked for over an hour. The topic of Leonard was inevitable.

"So, did Leonard send you his resume?" asked her mom eventually.

"He did," Lisa confirmed, unsure how to explain what she was trying to do. She wasn't sure herself.

"And...?" prompted her mom.

"See, I've actually hired a coach for my job search, and I've learned so much! He's got this resume writing formula that I'm using now for my own resume, and it's incredible. I'm surprised I ever found work before."

"I always thought your resume was fine, with your experience and the degree," her mom replied thoughtfully.

"Well, now it's ten times better."

"Sounds exciting."

"It is! And it's changed how I'll conduct myself during interviews, too. I have way more to show."

"I'm glad to hear that, but your profile is really different from Leonard's, isn't it?"

"Oh, definitely. But I have nothing to lose by redoing his profile with everything I've learned."

"I agree, but..." Her mom trailed off.

"What's wrong?"

Her mom sighed. "I just don't want Leonard to get his hopes up just to be disappointed again. It's all been hard enough on him already."

"I know, and I'll be careful when I manage his expectations. I don't want anything bad to happen to him."

"Just don't make him expect a miracle."

"No, I won't, I promise. I haven't even tested *my* new resume, so I won't know if this method even works until then."

"Alright, sweetie," her mom agreed. "Thank you for trying when everyone else gave up. He needs someone like you."

"Thanks, Mom. I'll keep you posted, okay?"

"I'll look forward to it," replied her mom.

"Sure thing," assured Lisa. "Now, tell me more about this trip of a lifetime of yours," prompted Lisa playfully.

After their conversation ended, Lisa checked her email, and she was glad to see the Three Circles Coach's name.

He suggested a session at noon the following day, and Lisa accepted immediately.

Final Touches on Lisa's Resume

The following day, Lisa woke up early, eager to speak to the coach. She went to the gym, wrote in her notepad what she wanted to discuss, and waited. At 11:55 AM, she received the call she was waiting for.

"Hello?"

"Hello, Lisa!" said the coach, clearly in a good mood.

"Hey, coach!" replied Lisa, relieved that the coach didn't seem upset with her.

"Listen, before we begin, I'm sorry our conversation ended like that last time."

"No problem. Sorry if I seemed a little harsh."

"That's okay. Now, let's talk about your resume!"

"Did you read it?" asked Lisa anxiously.

"I did," replied the coach. "Color me impressed."

"Thank you," sighed Lisa, anxiety beginning to ease.

"I mean it. I don't have much to say, honestly, so let's focus on the last part of your resume: writing a summary."

"I have a small question first. I've seen resumes sometimes with a summary, and sometimes with an objective. What's the difference?" asked Lisa.

"Good question. In most cases, you should write a summary. An objective is for when you need to explain the new direction your career is taking.

"Use an objective when you're starting your career and you have little to no experience, you're trying to change your career, or you've had a career gap of more than a year. Otherwise, you should write a summary," he explained.

"Got it," she commented.

"The easiest way to do this is for me to write the summary. But first, understand this: the purpose of a summary is to make the employer want to read your resume in detail."

"That makes sense," Lisa acknowledged.

The Three Circles Coach shared his screen to reveal her resume. After he went through her resume again, he began writing:

With 5 years of experience in sales and a Bachelor's degree, I have a solid track record of exceeding my sales target for every employer I have served. My ability to build strong relationships and my passion for delivering world class customer service with my clients has helped me generate a substantial amount of extra revenue thanks to client loyalty. I thrive in multicultural environments, which served me well in helping my employers grow in both size and reputation internationally.

"Et voilà! What do you think?"

"Wow. I mean, that's me, but how did you write that in one shot?" she asked, stunned.

"Because you wrote an amazing resume," he replied earnestly. "I just used the info you shared with me."

Lisa read her summary again. It had everything an employer could want.

"Is there a specific method that you used?" asked Lisa, eager to know how he did it.

"There are a few rules that I try to stick to. I try to keep it between four to six lines, or the recruiter might skip it. I start with an overall experience and degree and connect it to the main result expected for a given role.

"So for you it's *'With five years of experience in sales and a Bachelor's degree, I have a solid track record of exceeding my sales target for every employer I have served,'*" he explained.

"Then I explain how I do that. *'My ability to build strong relationships and my passion for delivering world class customer service with my clients has helped me generate a substantial amount of extra revenue thanks to client loyalty.'*

"Finally, I speak about a personal trait that employers could find attractive. *'I thrive in multicultural environments, which served me well in helping my employers grow in both size and reputation internationally.'*"

"Interesting," Lisa mused quietly.

"Just make sure you incorporate all three circles. You serve them with a concise format and by putting the information that would help them first.

"You market yourself when you say how your previous employers have benefited. You're being extremely convincing when you outline results and key actions that they know you can produce for them."

As Lisa read the summary again, she finally felt proud of her career.

LISA DUTOIT

Dubai - United Arab Emirates
Single, Driving License

☎ +971 52 000 0000
✉ Lisadutoit@boogymail.com
🔗 www.linkedin.com/in/lisa-dutoit

Business Development Specialist

5 years of Experience in both B2B and B2C sales
Bachelor Degree in Commerce with a concentration in Marketing

SUMMARY

With 5 years of experience in sales and a Bachelor degree, I have a solid track record of exceeding my sales target for every employer I have served. My ability to build strong relationships and my passion for delivering a world class customer service with my clients has helped me generate a substantial amount of extra revenue thanks to client loyalty. I thrive in multicultural environments, which served me well in helping my employers grow internationally in both size and reputation.

PROFESSIONAL EXPERIENCE

Sales Consultant
CloudCom Inc.

Mar 16 – Present
Dubai – UAE

"It's so obvious now! Everything I have on my resume includes the three circles. I get it, coach."

"I'm glad you can see that," said the coach. "Tell me, have you ever had any sales technique training?"

"Of course. In New York I had retail sales foundation training on the basics of sales, and I had great training at *Cloudcom* about cold calling and SPIN selling for consultative sales."

The coach was typing this part on his screen.

"Any reason why you didn't put that on your resume?"

"I guess I hadn't thought about it. I see how it would add value for an employer," said Lisa, reading what the coach just typed.

EDUCATION & TRAINING	
Education:	
Bachelor's Degree in Commerce with Concentration in Marketing, University of Virginia, USA *(Ranked in the top 30 universities in the US)*	2014
High School Degree, GPA 3.85 Thomas Jefferson for Science and Technology, USA	2011
Training:	
Cold Calling and SPIN Selling *(Several Trainings)* *Cloud Communication (internal trainings)*	2016 – 2017 *Dubai, UAE*
Retail Sales Foundation Training *Cerrutini & Co (internal training)*	2014 *New York, US*

"Most professionals play down the training they've had while employed, but knowing that you are a trained professional is important for an employer," he explained.

"Besides, this is a great opportunity for you to add relevant keywords on your resume. And now," the Three Circles Coach zoomed out to allow her entire resume to fit on the screen, "let's put ourselves in the shoes of an anxious recruiter looking for potential risks."

"Okay," Lisa agreed slowly. She had been so sure her resume was finished.

"After your resume comes up more often in the search results thanks to the keywords we've added, do you remember how we said that it will be read in six or seven seconds at first?"

"Of course."

"The plan now is to look at anything that could prevent you from getting that second read through. Here are the points I told you will be looked at during the first screening." He opened another document on his screen.

The title of your Resume
→ *Make sure it is in line with what you're applying to.*

Your current location
→ *Be sure to show that you're near your clients; replace your current address with a target location and make sure you have a local number if you're applying to jobs abroad.*

The job titles of each experience
→ *Make sure the job titles that you've had are in line with how the majority of the companies refer to that job. Otherwise, add an explanatory job title in brackets. For example, if one of your job titles was 'Client Relationship Specialist', you could add between brackets (Business Development & Account Management). Also helpful for keywords.*

IMPORTANT: Remove any word that does not serve you from your job titles: i.e.: 'intern,' 'volunteer,' 'freelance,' 'founder,' etc. None of these words communicate any expertise/skill set/specialism.

Rank each bullet point by order of importance:
→ During the first read, your resume will be read in around 7 sec. Make sure the first two lines of your 'responsibilities' and your 'achievements' are the most impactful. You should sort your bullet points in order of impact and importance to an employer.

Dates and duration of each of your experiences
→ *Watch out for any job duration that has lasted less than 1 year. An employer will frown at this and will worry you might leave shortly after being hired. Make sure you put a reason why a role has ended. The reason should be logical and reassuring to an employer.*

Your latest degree.
→ *Here, feel free to add anything related to the quality of the school you have studied in, or your highest marks/GPA, etc."*

Lisa took a few screenshots of the document so she could look at it later. Already, she recognized a few things she could do herself. Her resume didn't *need* the word *'intern'* attached to her job title at *Cerrutini*, and it could stand to be rearranged a bit. But she had left *Watch the Time, Inc.* of her own free will.

"I mostly get it, but," Lisa began, "I resigned from *Watch the Time* after just four months. I'm not sure how to make that sound reassuring."

"Just remember this rule: **if you stayed less than one year, put a reason.** Don't let the employer assume anything."

"But I resigned," she reminded him.

"Then say that," he replied. "Just say it in a way that makes you look good. Something like *'Was contacted by the Regional Head at Cloudcom for a role with them.'* Don't give an employer room to assume the worst. You could even add: *'Left to pursue a career that was more in line with my aspirations.'*"

"I get it," said Lisa. "Now that I'm in the right career track, it would reassure the recruiter about my attitude towards the job."

"Exactly. And you're also stating between the lines that you don't wish to get back to retail."

"Alright. For the record, though, *Cloudcom* didn't approach me. I applied."

"I know. You probably applied online. But who gave the first phone call?"

"Mark."

"And who asked you to come for an interview"

"Still Mark," replied Lisa.

"So did Mark contact you, or did you contact Mark?"

Lisa paused for a moment before she replied, "I applied online and he contacted me."

"There you go. In my example, you didn't say that *'Cloudcom'* approached you, but that 'Mark' contacted you, which is true. It was prompted by your job application, but that's irrelevant.

"It's all in the wording; you're not lying by saying that the Regional Head at *Cloudcom* called you," said the coach. "Whatever you put, the most important thing is to put a reason on your resume that will reassure the recruiter and serve you as well," he added.

"OK, I see what you mean," she agreed. "But for argument's sake, what if I was terminated before I completed a year?"

"Same thing. Just say that you were contacted by Mark for your next role."

"Okay," said Lisa. "But it sounds so..." She trailed off, searching for the right words.

"Like marketing?" suggested the coach.

"No. I know it's not lying, but it still feels like hiding the truth. I'm really not comfortable with this," confessed Lisa. "I mean, how can we serve others by manipulating the truth to our own benefit? Do you see what I mean?"

"I do," said the coach.

"You do?" she parroted back at him.

"Yes," he replied. "It's called being naive about how the world works."

"Naive?" she repeated, bewildered. "Too honest, maybe, but naive?"

"Listen, I'm going to tell you something that I will only say once. Remember this, even if you forget everything else."

"Okay..." she agreed warily.

"The vast majority of people suck at attracting success," he began. "It's not that they don't have the resources to do so. They have the time, they're smart, they're talented. But they suck at attracting success. Marketing is about attracting success.

"You see, most people dress up for work, and they speak with words that make them sound smart. They do that unconsciously because that's what everyone does. But when it comes to their resume, that's another story.

"You have people that clearly lie on their resume; we know that's dishonest. And you have people that just say the truth regardless of how it looks to recruiters. Both are wrong, Lisa. Creating a resume that truly works for you is like dressing up.

"You're not lying by controlling how others perceive you. You're just allowing them to focus on who you really are. Your marketing brochure is just that: a nice suit that flatters you and lets them focus on what you can do for them.

"No career is perfect, but if you're hoping that people will ignore any imperfection on your resume, you're being naive. Dressing up your marketing brochure, as long as you don't lie, is true marketing.

"Only then will recruiters have a chance to see how awesome you can be. Your resume is part of your personal brand. It is a reflection of how you want recruiters to perceive you. Be attractive on your resume, as you would when you dress up for a job interview."

Well, he was certainly passionate. And Lisa couldn't think of an argument.

"Most people's resumes look good at first glance," he continued. "But recruiters are trained to look deeper than that. And if they get worried, that's how you fail.

"You're an honest person and you won't resort to lying, but don't be naive. Nothing is perfect, but dressing up that resume will truly allow people to focus on the good things that you have in store for them.

"So never lie, but don't be naive. You're competing and always will be," he stated firmly. "My job over the years has always been to help my clients shine.

"The first time I saw your resume, I looked at it as a rough diamond. We're polishing it until it shines. As a creator, not a victim, you can only focus on what you can do, so don't fool yourself into thinking that leaving a rough part on your resume is being honest. It's being negligent. And you're certainly not giving the best customer experience by doing that."

For a long moment, Lisa didn't do a thing. Finally, she picked up her pen and notepad and wrote:

MARKETING IS ABOUT CUTTING AND POLISHING A ROUGH DIAMOND SO THAT IT SHINES. DOING THIS ALLOWS THE RECRUITER TO TRULY ENJOY READING MY RESUME AND FEEL REASSURED.

"Okay, I'm with you now. Everything I do needs to be attractive, otherwise people will fail to see what I can truly do. I'm already doing this with other areas of my life, so I need to expand this to my resume as well. Thanks."

"You're welcome. Do you have any questions?"

Lisa felt pretty much done with her own resume. However, there was still the matter of Leonard.

"Coach, imagine if you were helping someone who was unemployed for... let's say nine years. How would you fill this gap on his resume?"

"Simple," he replied, already guessing why she was asking. "Ask him to list all the activities he's done in the past nine years. Chances are that he's been helping neighbors or friends in a variety of tasks.

"Try to give these tasks a hypothetical job title. Fill the gap with a hypothetical role using the resume writing formula."

"Got it. Thank you. I'll try my best, I just hope he'll cooperate. He's so demotivated."

"Motivation comes from progress. Once his phone rings for the first time in years, see if he still thinks there's no hope. If his three circles are out of sync, we just have to fix them, that's all."

"Okay," said Lisa. "I guess he doesn't have much to lose anyway..."

"And neither do you. You'll figure something out. After all, just look at your resume now. Isn't this a reflection of who you truly are?" He zoomed out to show Lisa's new resume.

LISA DUTOIT

Dubai - United Arab Emirates
Single, Driving License

☎ +971 52 000 0000
✉ Lisadutoit@boogymail.com
in www.linkedin.com/in/lisa-dutoit

Business Development Specialist

5 years of Experience in both B2B and B2C sales
Bachelor Degree in Commerce with a concentration in Marketing

SUMMARY

With 5 years of experience in sales and a Bachelor degree, I have a solid track record of exceeding my sales target for every employer I have served. My ability to build strong relationships and my passion for delivering a world class customer service with my clients has helped me generate a substantial amount of extra revenue thanks to client loyalty. I thrive in multicultural environments, which served me well in helping my employers grow internationally in both size and reputation.

PROFESSIONAL EXPERIENCE

Sales Consultant   **Mar 16 – Present**
CloudCom Inc.   *Dubai – UAE*

CloudCom is a leading Web Conference reseller and partner located in Dubai and London.

→ *My role was to develop the GCC Market and offer leading Web Conference solutions to clients across various industries.*

Responsibilities
- Promoted our Web Conference solutions to around 20 new companies per day *(via cold calls)*
- Booked as much as to 5 product demos per week with new and existing customers.
- Built strong relationships with my clients thanks to a world-class customer service.
- Met with around 3 prospects every week to demonstrate our Web Conference Solution.
- Collected & understood customers' needs and presented our solution in line with their requirements.
- Issued 2 to 3 proposals daily, handled contract negotiations, payments & activations from A to Z.
- Personally trained around 10 new Web Conference users every month which fast-tracked my clients' adoption of our software.

Achievements
- ✓ Acquired, Secured and Developed 35 new clients from scratch *(generating almost AED 1 Million)*
- ✓ Exceeded my target within less than 6 months on the job.
- ✓ Made the fastest 1st deal in the company's history.
- ✓ Turned a new team member into a top performer in less than 3 months by mentoring & training her.

Sales Assistant   **Nov 15 – Feb 16**
Watch the time Inc.   *Dubai – UAE*

Watch the time Inc. is a watch retailer with 8 outlets across the Middle Eastern region.

→ *My role was to promote our products according to customers' needs and deliver on my sales target.*

Responsibilities
- Greeted up to 50 customers a day and promoted our products in line with their needs.
- Consistently awarded 1 of the highest customer service score based on daily surveys.
- Handled around 10 customer phone calls every day and convinced them to visit us.
- Contacted up to 30 customers per week on the phone to promote our new product arrivals.
- Networked and promoted our products to 100s of visitors during trade shows.
- Trained and coached 2 new team members to quickly excel their job.

Achievements
- ✓ Won the "best employee of the month" award 4 times in less than 9 months
- ✓ Sold around AED 350,000 of products in less than 9 months.
- ✓ Exceeded my sales target after only 6 months in the job

Reason for leaving: Was contacted by the regional Head of CloudCom for a role with them.

Sales Assistant   **Apr 14 – Oct 15**
Cerrutini & Co.   *New York, US*

Cerrutini & Co. is a luxury Italian watch maker with over 50 outlets and 280 employees worldwide.

➔ *My role was to promote our watches according to customers' needs during a 6-month internship.*

Responsibilities
- Served and consulted with around 20 customers a day on average to identify their needs
- Cold-called around 25 5-star hotels and concierges to establish a referral partnership.
- Tailored each customer experience in line with our Maison's brand guideline
- Delivered a 5-star client experience before, during and after their visits
- Ensured a World Class After-Sale Service by personally following up with clients after every purchase

Achievements
- ✓ Quickly exceeded my KPIs and delivered my internship at 24% above my sales target.
- ✓ Achieved the highest customer return ratio across a team of 8 sales assistants.
- ✓ Selected for a full time position as a sales assistant at the end of my internship.

Reason for leaving: End of my internship + wanted to pursue a career in Dubai.

EDUCATION & TRAINING

Education:

Bachelor Degree in Commerce with a concentration in Marketing University of Virginia *(Ranked in the top 30 universities in the US)*	2014
High School Degree, GPA 3.85 Thomas Jefferson for Science and Technology, USA	2011

Training:

Cold Calling and SPIN Selling *(Several Trainings)* *Cloud Communication (internal trainings)*	2016 – 2017 *Dubai, UAE*
Retail Sales Foundation Training *Cerrutini & Co (internal training)*	2014 *New York, US*

LANGUAGES & INTEREST

Languages:
- English - Native
- Spanish - Advanced
  Learned at School for 12 years and practiced sporadically with friends and while traveling.

Hobbies:
- Running 5Kms or 10Kms twice a week
- Traveled to many Middle Eastern and African Countries *(for both leisure & business)*

"Wow," Lisa breathed, emotion building.

"Are you okay?" the coach asked when her voice trembled.

"I am," she hurried to assure him. "Before this, everything just felt... so hopeless. Now, just doing my resume..." Abruptly, she stopped talking as she began to cry in earnest.

"A resume is a reflection of you," the coach pointed out. "The more care you take in creating it, the more it will make you feel amazing about yourself.

"Looking for work when you're unemployed challenges your self-confidence and your self-esteem. Unemployment is rough for anyone. But focusing on the positive things about you and putting it on paper can work miracles for some people.

"It's not *just* a resume: it's the choice you made about how you see yourself before you allow others to form their own impressions. It's the reflection of your entire career, taking a stance that any negative situation you encountered has strengthened your career.

"It's not *just* a resume, Lisa, it's who you really are and how much good you brought to others across your entire career. You should feel proud of that."

"... Thank you, coach."

"The only one to thank here is you. I'm just the diamond cutter. You're the diamond. And now it's time to reveal your shine to the world."

Suddenly, it felt as if he was saying goodbye. "We have another session, right?" she asked, gripped with anxiety.

The Three Circles Coach was silent at first, and then he took a deep breath. "Actually, your package ended an hour ago."

"What?" But how was she supposed to make it all work without him?

"You'll be fine. You're ready," he assured her.

"You *know* I'm not."

"Listen, Lisa, with your resume, you're going to be able to generate job interviews. Fifty percent of your job interview preparation was made while writing your resume. Fifty percent of the recruiters' questions are already answered."

"What about the other 50 percent?" asked Lisa.

"If you feel you need my help in the future, just send me an email and I'll send you a link for you to take another package," said the coach.

She didn't even have money for her bills.

"But I do not think it's necessary now," added the coach. "Just remember, you're the CEO of your company selling your services, so think like a marketer. Think outside the box."

"But what does that even *mean*?"

"Is there a way to find hidden jobs online with less competition? Can you contact decision-makers directly instead of waiting for someone in HR to call you? There is so much information out there, so many techniques you can use to accelerate your job search. Remember, to find the right answers, you must ask yourself the right questions."

"Right."

Lisa wrote what was probably the last notes from her sessions with the Three Circles Coach:

THE BEST WAY TO FIND ANY ANSWER IS TO ASK MYSELF THE RIGHT QUESTIONS:

→ HOW CAN I FIND HIDDEN/INVISIBLE JOBS WITH MUCH LESS COMPETITION?

→ CAN I FIND THE CONTACT DETAILS OF DECISION-MAKERS INSTEAD OF WAITING FOR HR TO FIND ME?

The prospect of tackling the job market on her own was daunting, but she wanted her last session to end well nevertheless.

"I understand."

"You'll be fine, Lisa," repeated the coach.

"I'll do my best. And your help was priceless. I can't thank you enough."

"I'm genuinely excited for you, you know," he replied. "You're about to embark on one of the most exciting parts of your career.

"Right now, your job is to find an amazing employer that you will serve with everything you have, and that will take your career to the next level. They're out there, hoping that someone like you exists. It's time to be excited, not frightened."

She was pretty sure she was going to miss the reassuring speeches.

"Thank you again, coach."

"It has been a pleasure, Lisa. I'll send you a final draft of your resume and a couple of documents in a few minutes. Please keep me in the loop with your progress, okay?"

"I promise," said Lisa.

"Great. Good luck."

"Bye. Have a great day."

And just like that, the call and her sessions were over, and she wasn't sure what to do. If she was a diamond, she was pretty sure she was still in the rough.

But she couldn't afford a pity party. "You have the most amazing resume in the world, Lisa," she told herself. "A real employer magnet."

She just needed a plan of action before she started sending job applications.

'*Uploading my resume on the main databases will work for me while I send my applications to the relevant job adverts,*' she thought, writing the first step in her notebook:

1. REGISTER /UPDATE MY PROFILE ON EVERY JOB PORTAL AND LINKEDIN.

Plus, recruitment companies also had large databases of candidates that recruiters checked on a daily basis for their clients' vacancies.

2. REGISTER WITH NEW RECRUITMENT AGENCIES ON A DAILY BASIS.

With that, she knew that she could start applying to jobs individually, as her resume would be available for recruiters on various databases in the meantime. She could take care of that for the rest of the day, and the next day she could handle applications.

Lisa's Final Resume and the Job Application Email

After a brief coffee break, Lisa checked her inbox and saw an email from the Three Circles Coach entitled *'Your final Resume + a job application template + cover letter + LinkedIn tweaks.'*

Lisa,

Please find attached the final version of your resume. I'm certain that it will open more doors than your previous one.

I'm also attaching **a job application email template** that I suggest all my private clients use.

If you choose to use the email template, just customize it to your profile and you'll be ready to go. Same thing for the cover letter, although job application emails have mostly replaced the need to write a cover letter nowadays.

Beyond all that, remember: you are the CEO of your company. The three vital organs of your company are your marketing, sales, and customer service circles. They must cross at all times. (You will also find them crossing in the job application email template attached.)

As you continue on your marketing journey, please do not stop at what other job seekers do. There are many other things you can do, Lisa. For now, I have attached a fourth document entitled: *'Optimizing Your LinkedIn Profile.'*

I hope this will help you, and I'll be looking forward to hearing from you!

Good luck, Lisa,
The Three Circles Coach.

The first thing Lisa opened, of course, was her resume.

She read her resume in full, as if she was reading it for the first time.

"So perfect," she breathed out loud.

Before redoing her resume with the Three Circles Coach, Lisa recalled how shaky she was in her career, but her resume offered the opposite image. It was simple, easy to read, and full of quantified benefit statements.

Before, she wasn't sure why a recruiter would even consider giving her a call. But now, her resume reflected how confident Lisa was in her abilities and track record. For the first time in her career, Lisa felt proud. Not an egoistic type of pride, but a serene pride.

She loved how her resume even prevented questions she would have dreaded answering during a job interview, like why she had a short experience at *Watch the Time.*

At that moment, she thought about her three circles and wondered if it would apply to just her resume. She grabbed her pen and started drawing.

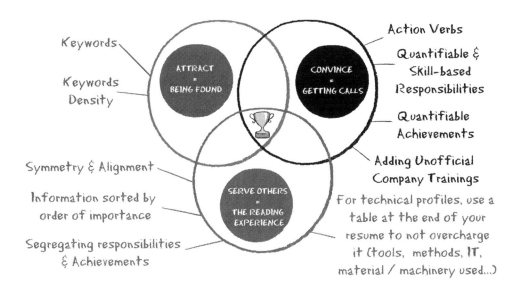

Her resume fit the three circles like a glove.

The second document she opened was 'The job application email template.'

Dear *First Name,*

Mv name is *[First Name – Last Name]* and I have come across your job advert for the XXXXXX role at *[ABC Company].*

I was wondering if you'd be interested in meeting with a young and ambitious *[Your Job Title]* Professional that considers the following as the most important keys to my success:

1. Adjective + [What employers have achieved by hiring you for a similar role]
   Think about the overarching goal of your job for an employer?
2. Adjective + [Specific key performance indicators that explain point 1]
3. Adjective + [An extra skill that you have that explains point 1.]

I have attached my resume where you will find my achievements in these areas throughout my X years of experience in the XXXXXX Sector.

If you feel these achievements are in line with your expectations, I would be eager to meet you to discuss how I could add value to *[ABC Company].*

In the meantime, please feel free to call me should you have any question of course. *(My mobile number is XXXXXXXXX)*

Thanking you in advance for the time you will dedicate to my application.

Best Regards,

First name **Last name**
Your mobile number
Your LinkedIn profile URL

To download this template for free, please go to:
www.nameyourcareer.com/jobsearchtemplates

The first thing that Lisa noticed was that the template was in stark contrast to the emails she was sending. It was easier to read and navigate, easy to tailor, and the three points in the middle allowed anyone reading it in a rush to go straight to those points.

Everything in the email was inviting the reader to go to the next step, which was opening her resume.

The three points in the middle would be clear benefit statements of why an employer should pay attention to her application. The mobile number was mentioned twice and there was even a curiosity trigger that would make employers want to open her resume if they wanted to see more results.

Not wanting to delay her job search any further, she decided she would customize the template to her specific profile before she even opened the last document.

How could she write three compelling points about her profile to attract employers? She took her notebook and drew a table, much like the one she created when she was writing her resume. Just above the table she copied the sentence from the Three Circles Coach's template:

'I was wondering if you'd be interested in meeting with a young and ambitious [Business Development or anything relevant] Professional who considers the following as the most important keys to my success:'

Instructions	1st draft	Final draft with an adjective
1. What employers have achieved by hiring you for a similar role	*Made money for them and exceeded my targets*	**Relentless at exceeding my targets in every role I've had.**
2. Specific key performance indicators that explain point 1	*Did cold calls nonstop and met clients (online and face-to-face)*	**Nonstop cold calling attitude and weekly client meetings.**
3. An extra skill that you have which explains point 1	*Built strong client relationships that allowed me to do repeat business*	**Effective at increasing repeat business from my customers.**

Putting it all together, she was pleased with her new job application email

Dear XXXXXXX,

My name is Lisa Dutoit and I have come across your job advert for the Sales Consultant role at *[ABC Company]*.

I was wondering if you'd be interested in meeting with a young and ambitious Business Development Professional that considers the following as the most important keys to my success:

- Relentless at exceeding my targets in every role I've had
- Non-stop cold calling attitude and weekly client meetings
- Effective at increasing repeat business from my customers.

I have attached my resume where you will find my achievements in these areas throughout my 5 years of experience in the Sales Sector.

If you feel these achievements are in line with your expectations, I would be eager to meet you to discuss how I could add value to *[ABC Company]*.

In the meantime, please feel free to call me should you have any question of course.
(My mobile number is XXXXXXXXX)

Thanking you in advance for the time you will dedicate to my application

Best Regards,
First name Last name
Your mobile number
Your Linked In profile URL

To download this template for free, please go to: www.nameyourcareer.com/jobsearchtemplates

Immediately after, Lisa opened the cover letter template the coach attached in the email. Unsurprisingly, it was also very straight to the point and easily customizable.

Dear XXXXXXXX

I was thrilled to read your ad for a *[job title]* at your *[City branch / center / offices]*. Having a strong track record in the same field for the past *XX years,* the role completely matches with my profile, especially on the points you mentioned in the job description:

- Proven track record in *[take a point from job description]*: XX years *[comp. name & comp. name]*
- Hands-on experience in *[take a point from job description]*: XX years *[comp. name & comp. name]*
- Practical knowledge of *[take a point from job description]*: XX years *[comp. name & comp. name]*
- Exposure to *[take a point from job description]*: XX years *[comp. name & comp. name]*
- Comfortable at using *[take a point from job description]*: XX years *[comp. name & comp. name]*
- Training in *[take a point from job description]*: XX years *[comp. name & comp. name]*

I have included specific figures on my resume in relation to my daily tasks and my achievements in similar roles. Should you find them in line with your requirements, I will look forward to meeting you and discuss how I could help you *[the real purpose(s) of the role for an employer, i.e.: expand, grow, improve, reduce, revamp, XXXXX... etc.].*

Thanking you in advance for the time you will spend reading my application.

Yours sincerely,

[Use a mobile app to create your signature + insert it here—just type "signature" in Google Play or App Store]

[first name last name]

All in all, she was glad the coach didn't ask her to come up with some sort of compelling or emotional plea as to why a company's vision, mission, or values matched with her own. She remembered finding a lot of articles online in relation to that, and the task of doing this for each company would have been daunting and time consuming for Lisa.

Instead, the coach's template was simple, factual, and most of all, easily customizable.

Here again, she recognized the three circles: the template *served* the recruiter by allowing him to quickly skim through it and find the relevant information, the bullet points *attracted* the reader's attention, and they aimed at *convincing* them of the relevancy of her profile in relation with the role at hand.

Almost out of nowhere, Lisa noticed that she could also use parts of her resume summary in her cover letter, too.

How to Put Your LinkedIn Profile On Steroids!

After tailoring the cover letter to her specific profile, Lisa had built up momentum, and she went straight back to the Three Circles Coach's email to open the last document: *'Optimizing Your LinkedIn Profile.'*

OPTIMIZING YOUR LINKEDIN PROFILE:
The 9 points that will boost your profile!

LinkedIn is by far the most visited database for recruiters. The following points will allow you to make sure your profile is treated as a priority by LinkedIn algorithm.

1. ADD AN INDUSTRY AND A LOCATION

Make sure the location is the same as the city you're targeting. i.e.: If you're looking for work in New York, make sure your location on LinkedIn is "New York", regardless to where you really are. (Please do acquire a local number too)

> You can also access your location setting directly from your profile:
>
> 1. Click the (Ω) **Me** icon at top of your LinkedIn homepage.
> 2. Click **View profile**.
> 3. Click the ✎ **Edit** icon in your introduction card.
> 4. In the **Edit intro** pop-up window, scroll down to **Country**.
> 5. Select your country from the dropdown. This is a required field.
> 6. Depending on the country you select, you'll be given the option to add your:
>   - Province/State
>   - City/District
> 7. Click **Save**.

https://www.linkedin.com/help/linkedin/answer/38594/changing-the-location-on-your-profile?lang=en

> ⌄ **Updating the industry information on your profile**
>
> To update the industry from the Settings & Privacy page:
>
> 1. Click the (Ω) **Me** icon at the top of your LinkedIn homepage.
> 2. Select **Settings & Privacy** from the dropdown.
> 3. Under the **Site preferences** section of the **Account** tab, click **Change** next to **Name, location, and industry**.
> 4. In the **Edit Intro** pop-up window, select an option from the **Industry** dropdown.
> 5. Click **Save**.
>
> You can also update your industry from your profile:
>
> 1. Click the (Ω) **Me** icon at the top of your LinkedIn homepage.
> 2. Click **View profile**.
> 3. Click the ✎ **Edit** icon in your introduction card.
> 4. Select an option from the **Industry** dropdown.
> 5. Click **Save**.

https://www.linkedin.com/help/linkedin/answer/3077/changing-industry-or-company-information-on-your-profile?lang=en

2. MIGRATE THE CONTENT OF YOUR NEW RESUME INTO YOUR LINKEDIN PROFILE

Add responsibilities and achievements under each role. If you feel this is too long, consider leaving just the achievements after adding the context sentence ('My role was to...').

To add the Experience section and a position:

1. Click the ⓜ **Me** icon at the top of your LinkedIn homepage.
2. Click **View profile**.
3. Click **Add profile section** in your introduction card.
4. Under the **Background** dropdown, click the ➕ **Add** icon next to **Work experience**.
5. In the **Add experience** pop-up window, enter your information into the fields provided.
6. Click **Save**.

---

https://www.linkedin.com/help/testing/answer/1646/adding-editing-or-removing-a-position-in-your-profile-s-experience-section?lang=en

a. **Make sure you have an up-to-date current position** *(with a description)*
   In the event that you are currently unemployed, you can add a freelance position that would reflect the current work you're doing for others (free or paid work). Just make sure it is in line with the type of role / sector that you're after.

b. **Make sure you have at least 2 past positions.**
   If you have just finished your studies, feel free to add your internships and / or any relevant part time job you may have had while studying. By 'relevant', I mean something in line with the type of work you're after.

→ *By having at least 2 positions and a current one (with no end date – 'present'), LinkedIn Search Algorithm will treat your profile in priority.*

3. EDUCATION

Add your degrees and certifications. Consider adding also internal trainings you have had with past employers. Trained professionals will always reassure employers more than untrained ones.

⌄ **Adding the Education section to your profile**

To add an education section:

1. Click the ⓧ **Me** icon at the top of your LinkedIn homepage.
2. Click **View profile**.
3. Click the **Add new profile** section on the right rail.
4. From the **Background** dropdown, click the ➕ **Add** icon next to **Education**.
5. Type your education information into each applicable field.
6. Click **Save**.

Once you've added an education entry to your profile, you can continue to add more entries, or edit or remove existing entries.

https://www.linkedin.com/help/testing/answer/381/adding-editing-or-removing-education-entries-on-your-profile?lang=en

4. SKILLS (MINIMUM OF THREE)

You can put as many skills as you want but a minimum of 3 is necessary to be taken seriously by their algorithm... I recommend you list all of your skills.

⌄ **Adding skills to your profile**

If you don't have any skills listed on your profile, the **Skills & Endorsements** section won't appear. To add this section and a skill:

1. Click the ⍟ **Me** icon at the top of your LinkedIn homepage.
2. Click **View profile**.
3. Click **Add new profile section** on the right rail.
4. Select **Skills** from the dropdown.
5. Type the name of a skill in the **Skill** text box and select it from the dropdown list that appears. Once selected, it will automatically be added to your list of skills.

Once the **Skills & Endorsements** section has been added to your profile, you can include more skills at any time. To add more skills:

1. Click the ⍟ **Me** icon at the top of your LinkedIn homepage.
2. Click **View profile**.
3. Scroll to the **Skills & Endorsements** section and click **Add a new skill**.
4. In the pop-up window, type the name of a skill in the text box and select it from the dropdown list that appears. If your skill doesn't appear, type the full skill name in the field provided, then click it to add.

   - You can also add skills from the **Suggested skills based off your profile** options that are provided.

5. Click **Add**

Note: You can add upto 50 skills to your profile.

https://www.linkedin.com/help/testing/answer/4976/adding-and-removing-skills-on-your-profile?lang=en

5. USE A GREAT PROFILE PHOTO: *400 X 400 + A COVER PHOTO (MIN SIZE: 1400 X 425)*

Adding a photo increases your chances to come up in the search results by 11 times! But not ANY photo... Make sure it is a professional setting and that the picture is head and shoulders with an inviting smile.

→ *You have a great picture of you but the background is not great? Consider using a photo editor. You can find this service starting at 5 USD with websites like www.fiverr.com or www.upwork.com.*

Just go to google image and search for the type of ID Picture you want for your LinkedIn profile. Then, send it to the freelancer you will chose and ask him to do the same background with your picture.

To add or change your profile photo:

1. Click **the** Me icon at **the** top of **your LinkedIn** homepage.
2. Click View **profile**.
3. Click **on your profile photo in your** introduction card.
4. **In the Profile photo** pop-up window, you can:
5. Click Apply.

https://www.linkedin.com/help/testing/answer/1615/adding-or-changing-your-linkedin-profile-photo?lang=en

6. CRAFT YOUR HEADER / TAGLINE + USE GREAT KEYWORDS: 120 CHARACTERS MAX

After your name, this is the place where LinkedIn algorithm will look first when a recruiter (or anyone else) enters a few keywords in the search box.
I highly advise you make the tagline about others. Ask yourself the following question: How do others benefit from my expertise? Please notice how the below tagline is full of keywords (attracting / marketing) and how it is serving others:

→ *Ambitious Recruitment Consultant that always exceeds her sales targets and loves her work. Looking for my next role!*

→ *IT Project Manager | PMP and Prince 2 certified | Strong Track record in delivering Projects 100% on time and on budget.*

→ *Passionate C level Executive with a strong track record of drastically boosting companies' growth and profitability.*

→ *Digital Marketing expert; helping businesses generate new customers online through SEO & SEM. Need new leads? Call me!*

→ *Top rated programmer with a passion for coding in Java, C++, Shell, Ruby, SQL and ASP. Python and Pascal certified.*

→ *Rock Star Account Manager with a strong track record in growing my clients' portfolio and a passion for customer service*

→ *Office Administrator and PA with a passion for designing support systems that boosts everyone's productivity.*

To edit your professional headline:

1. Click **the** Me icon at top of **your LinkedIn** homepage.
2. Click View **profile**.
3. Click **the** Edit icon **in your** introduction card.
4. **In the** Edit intro pop-up window, make **your** changes **in the Headline** text box.
5. Click Save.

---

https://www.linkedin.com/help/linkedin/answer/2901/editing-your-headline?lang=en

7. MAKE SURE YOU HAVE AT LEAST 50 CONNECTIONS

If you're new to LinkedIn and do not have enough connection, you can connect your inboxes and send an invitation to your personal contacts. Even if you have more than 50 connections, I recommend you do that as the more contacts you have, the more people you will be able to find when you search for professionals.

Importing your address book

1. Click the ⬚ **My Network** icon at the top of your LinkedIn homepage.
2. Click **See all** below **Your connections** on the left rail.
3. Click ⬚ **Manage synced and imported contacts** on the top of the right rail.
4. Click **More options** below **Add personal contacts** on the right rail.
5. Enter your email address in the field or, choose a service provider from the list on the right. If your email provider is not supported, you can still invite people to connect by email.
6. Click **Continue**.
7. Contacts who are already on LinkedIn will be shown. Click **Add Connections** to send invitations or click **Skip** if you don't want to invite anyone. Contacts who are not yet on LinkedIn will be displayed next. You may see phone number contacts listed if you've imported your mobile contacts previously (these contacts will receive a SMS text invitation to join). Click the **Skip** link if you don't want to invite anyone or click **Add to Network** to invite them to join.

---

https://www.linkedin.com/help/testing/answer/4214/importing-and-inviting-your-email-contacts?lang=en

8. MAKE YOUR EMAIL PUBLIC AND ADD YOUR BLOG / SOCIAL MEDIA ACCOUNTS

Make it easy for recruiters to contact you. Make sure your email is public. If you're worried about spams, consider creating a new email address just for that purpose (and visit it from time to time)

Visibility of Your Email Address on LinkedIn

By default, the primary email address you've registered with LinkedIn is only visible on your profile to your direct **connections on LinkedIn**. It will also be visible to people who are your email contacts or vice versa.

You can change who can see your email address on your profile from your **Settings & Privacy** page.

To change who can see your email address on your profile:

1. Click the ⓡ **Me** icon at the top of your LinkedIn homepage.
2. Select **Settings & Privacy** from the dropdown.
3. Click the **Privacy** tab at the top of the page.
4. Under the **How others see your profile and network information** section, click **Change** next to **Who can see your email address**.
5. Select one of the following:

   - **Only you** – No one can see your email address.
   - **1st-degree connections** – Only those directly connected to you can see your email address.
   - **1st and 2nd-degree connections** – Only those directly connected to you and those connected to your connections can see your email address.
   - **Everyone on LinkedIn** – Any LinkedIn member viewing your profile can see your email address.

6. Your changes will be automatically saved.

https://www.linkedin.com/help/linkedin/answer/261/visibility-of-your-email-address-on-linkedin?lang=en

9. RECOMMENDATIONS + ENDORSEMENTS

Recommendations are a key added value to your LinkedIn profile. It's the one place where you could have ready available testimonials from ex employers or clients. Social proof is powerful testament of your qualities and expertise. The best way to ask for a recommendation is NOT to send a recommendation request via LinkedIn. I highly advise you contact the person by phone or by email first to explain what you want.

For example, if you're into management, the best thing to do would be to explain to your contacts that you would like a recommendation specifically on the managerial aspects. Contacting people in advance will help you secure more recommendations. But explaining what you want them to highlight will ensure the testimonials you acquire truly add value to your profile (and keywords). If you send them an email, you can send them the recommendation link (please see "EXTRA TIP #1" below) so that they do not spend time searching how to do that. Make it as easy as possible for them, to increase your conversion.

⌄ Requesting a recommendation from your profile

To request a recommendation from your profile:

1. Click the (⍜) **Me** icon at the top of your LinkedIn homepage.
2. Select **View profile**.
3. Scroll down to the **Recommendations** section and click **Ask to be recommended**.
4. Type the name of the connection you'd like to ask for a recommendation in the **Who do you want to ask?** field.
5. Select the name from the dropdown that appears.
6. Fill out the **Relationship** and **Position at the time** fields of the recommendations pop-up window, and click **Next**.
7. You can include a personalized message with your request by changing the text in the message field.
8. Click **Send**.

---

https://www.linkedin.com/help/linkedin/answer/96/requesting-a-recommendation?lang=en

EXTRA TIP #1: CREATE A PUBLIC LINKEDIN PROFILE URL *(ALSO CALLED THE VANITY URL)*

When editing your LinkedIn profile (click on your picture), you can amend your profile URL to reflect your full name only (By default, LinkedIn will add a random number to your profile URL).

To change your public profile URL:

1. Click the 🔘 **Me** icon at the top of your LinkedIn homepage.
2. Click **View profile**.
3. On your profile page, click **Edit public profile & URL** on the right rail.
4. Under **Edit URL** in the right rail, click the 🖉 **Edit** icon next to your public profile URL.
   - It'll be an address that looks like **www.linkedin.com/in/yourname**.
5. Type the last part of your new custom URL in the text box.
6. Click **Save**.

https://www.linkedin.com/help/linkedin/answer/87/customizing-your-public-profile-url?lang=en

→ **TIP: Add your new LinkedIn Public Profile URL to your email signature!**

EXTRA TIP #2: REMOVING OTHER PROFILES SUGGESTIONS ON YOUR OWN PROFILE PAGE

By default, LinkedIn will be suggesting other similar profiles on the right hand side of your profile page. I advise that you remove that as you would not benefit from promoting other profiles than yours.

Removing or Adding the "People Also Viewed" Box

The **People Also Viewed** box shows some of the other profiles that viewers of a LinkedIn profile have also looked at. You may see it on your own profile or on someone else's profile. You can show or hide this feature from your profile through the Privacy tab of your **Settings & Privacy** page.

1. Click the ⓠ **Me** icon at top of your LinkedIn homepage.
2. Click **Settings & Privacy**.
3. Select the **Privacy** tab.
4. Under the **Profile privacy** section, click **Change** next to **Viewers of this profile also viewed**.
5. Toggle to the left or right to select **No** or **Yes** respectively.
   - Changes will be saved automatically.

https://www.linkedin.com/help/testing/answer/2848/removing-or-adding-the-people-also-viewed-box?lang=en

While you're tweaking your privacy settings, please go through each option thoroughly. I have had many clients that overlooked this part and realized too late that their profile was not visible to people outside their 1st degree connections for example, or that some parts of their profile were restricted for recruiters...
      <u>This must not happen to you</u>!

With her resume in hand, Lisa spent the rest of the day registering and updating her profile on several databases, from job portals to LinkedIn to recruitment companies. It was a tedious process, but a necessary one.

As she was updating her LinkedIn profile, she was frustrated that it wasn't as well-formatted as her resume. LinkedIn did not offer any options for bullet points, symbols, or text formatting, and therefore wasn't as easy to read as her resume.

She thought about her customer service circle and decided that there must be a way to make her profile stand out a little more. After going on Google, she typed in the phrase: *'formatting my linkedin profile with bullet points.'*

There were a myriad of articles available. One of them was from Donna Serdula, a LinkedIn Optimization expert who wrote a simple and yet complete article on how to add bullet points and symbols by simply copying them from her article and pasting them on her LinkedIn profile.

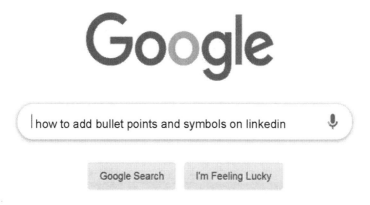

Lisa's profile was already standing out from the crowd after that, and she even added a few symbols to her tagline:

★★★Business Development Expert with a Solid Track Record of Exceeding Targets★★★

Encouraged, she also tried to see if there was any chance she could put some of the text of her LinkedIn profile in italics, bold, or underlined. After reading a few articles online, she discovered that the best Google Search would be to use the phrase: *'Unicode Text Converter'*.

Again, she found a multitude of websites. In most of them, all she had to do was to type any word or phrase in a content box and the same content would be offered in various formats. She then just had to copy-paste the right format on her LinkedIn profile.

All in all, it was possibly the coolest thing she had ever done to her LinkedIn profile.

The Recruiter Phone Call

As 2 PM approached, her stomach growled and reminded her she hadn't eaten yet. That's when her phone rang. It was an unfamiliar landline number, and when she answered the call, she found herself talking to a recruitment agent from *Iris Search*.

"Hello. Lisa speaking."

"Oh, hi there, Lisa. My name is Andy Smith, from *Iris Search*. We're a recruitment company that specializes in the placement of candidates in the sales sector. Is this a good time for you to speak?"

"Yes, it is," replied Lisa.

"Great!" said Andy. "The reason for my call is that I found your profile on Salesjobs.ae and it seems to match a role that we have with one of our clients, a leading CRM solutions provider. Are you currently open to new career opportunities?"

"Yes, I am" said Lisa, realizing that he was probably looking at an old version of her resume; she hadn't sent her new resume to that recruitment firm.

"Excellent!" said Andy. "We currently have a 'Sales consultant' role that I would like to speak to you about."

Andy went on to explain the role, which Lisa found very similar to her role at *Cloudcom*, except that the company was selling Customer Relations Management solutions instead of conference call software.

"I was wondering how your role at *Cloudcom* compared to this one?"

"That's pretty much what I've been doing at *Cloudcom* for the last three years," she answered comfortably.

"Great, that's what I thought," commented Andy. "My client is really looking for high achievers, obviously, and I was wondering if you could highlight a few key achievements with your role at *Cloudcom*. I wasn't able to find this on your resume, I'm afraid."

"Sure," said Lisa. Since she still had her latest resume open on her computer, she decided to read the achievement section. "I acquired, secured, and developed 35 new clients from scratch, generating almost one million dirhams in the last three years.

"In fact, since I started I was already exceeding my target within less than six months on the job, and I made the fastest first deal in the company's history. I've also turned a new team member into a top performer in less than three months by mentoring and training her."

"Impressive," Andy commented.

"Thank you," said Lisa. The coach had been right about her resume being 50 percent of her interview.

"Based on how you spoke, though," Andy continued, "it sounds as if you aren't working there any longer."

Lisa paused, taken off guard. She hadn't prepared an answer for that. Taking a deep breath, she remembered that whatever she said next, it would have to be something a recruiter wouldn't find repelling. She had to be honest, but flattering.

"That's right," she said. "I left *Cloudcom* a week ago." Sensing that Andy would want to know why, her mind started racing trying to find a 'good' answer.

"I see..." said Andy. "Can I ask you why?"

She thought of the three circles, thoughts still racing.

"To be frank with you, *Cloudcom* is a small set up in Dubai, and while I loved working there and I'm grateful for everything I learned I couldn't see a clear career path.

"I was reporting to the regional head, and he's doing a fantastic job at that, so there was no room for me to grow. With time, this hampered my motivation and we decided with my manager that perhaps it would be better to look for a company where I could branch out."

"Okay," commented Andy. "Did your results reflect that drop in motivation?"

She had been doing well, but that question left Lisa feeling cornered.

"That's correct," admitted Lisa. With no time to plan out an answer, all she had were what the coach told her about biting the bullet and her instincts. "During the past six months, my lack of motivation did hamper my results. Looking back, I'm not pleased with that and it wasn't fair to me or my manager.

"Although I've been a top performer in every job I've had and I'm absolutely certain I can generate substantial revenue in every sales role, the last six months were disappointing. It was a huge learning curve for me, and I will never let this happen again, and my next employer will benefit from my renewed determination."

"Well, thank you, Lisa," said Andy "It's not everyday that a job seeker is honest and takes responsibility for a termination. I'm not sure if this will be enough for me to get you an interview, and if I present your profile to my client, they'll probably want to know why you had such short experience at *Watch the Time*."

"That's fair," Lisa replied. "I was a top performer there until I was called directly by the Regional Head at *Cloudcom* for a role with them. The opportunity came when I was already looking to leave retail, so I resigned from my role at *Watch the Time* to join *Cloudcom*."

Those sessions with the coach really had helped more than just her resume.

"Working in a shop is very different from working in an office," Andy acknowledged. "Just so you know, it's common practice for employers to check your LinkedIn profile once they receive your resume. If I were you, I would try to get recommendations on your last two roles. Can you do that?"

"Sure, that was already on my to-do list for today," replied Lisa, though that wasn't strictly the truth.

"Great. Have you asked your previous employer how they'll represent the separation if a recruiter were to check references? Just to be sure the two of you actually say the same thing."

"Not yet, I'll definitely get in touch with him. Thank you, Andy."

"No problem. Can I ask you what your salary expectation would be?"

"My salary at Cloudcom was AED 8,000, plus commissions. I would be looking for a package around that figure."

Immediately after saying that, she wanted to kick herself. She couldn't exactly ask Andy about the client's budget right then and there, but she also knew that if the salary on offer was more than what she was earning at *Cloudcom*, she shot herself in the foot by revealing her last salary.

"Great," replied Andy. "That's all I need for now. I'll introduce your resume to my client, and if it's selected for an interview, I'll get back to you with more details."

"Alright, thanks." Just like that, Lisa's resume was going to be read by an employer. "Before you send my profile," she interjected, "I have actually just finalized a new version of my resume. Would you like me to send you a copy?"

"That would be great, thank you. I'm going to send you an email, you can reply to it with your updated resume ASAP."

"With pleasure," she agreed.

"Perfect. You should receive it in the next five minutes."

"Thanks again."

"You're welcome. Bye, Lisa."

"Bye, Andy," she replied.

As the two hung up, Lisa was pleased, despite flubbing the salary portion. She would have appreciated more time to prepare, but she was pleased all the same. She had chosen her words carefully. She had been honest. She was able to dress up the less glamorous aspects of her resume.

Writing a great resume had helped tremendously with the impromptu job interview.

Speaking to Mark at Cloudcom

After hanging up with Andy, she prepared herself a coffee and a salad that she ate in front of her laptop. It was already 4:05 PM when Lisa finished optimizing her LinkedIn profile.

Just as the Three Circles Coach described, she was able to find great video tutorials online about specific points she wasn't sure about. The recommendation section, however, was empty. She knew that she would have to get a few testimonials, especially from her experience at *Cloudcom* and *Watch the Time*, just to reassure employers about the way those jobs ended.

At that moment, she got a text notification on her mobile. It was a final reminder for her outstanding mobile bill. Lisa was certain that she would have received her last salary already, but that wasn't the case.

She went online to check her bank balance, but it was the same amount as last week: AED 347. It was enough to do her grocery shopping, but certainly not enough to pay for her outstanding utility and mobile bills.

She decided it was time to call Mark and see what had happened.

As she pressed the call button on her mobile, Lisa felt a spike of anxiety. Mark had always been friendly at work, but she wasn't sure how he would be now that the two were no longer working together. After a few rings, she heard his familiar voice.

"Mark speaking."

"Hi Mark, it's Lisa. Is this a good time?"

"Oh, hi Lisa, good to hear from you. How are you?"

"I'm good, thanks. How is it going for you guys?" she asked, knowing she wouldn't like the answer.

"It's going well, thank you. What can I do for you?" replied Mark, audibly distracted.

"I have a few things I wanted to discuss. I'll try to be brief."

"Sure, not a problem."

"Thank you. Listen, I'm not sure if you're aware, but I haven't received my salary for the last month."

Mark sighed, obviously aware of the situation.

"Yes, I know. I've tried to get this sorted out, but the CFO in London wants to pay all your dues at the end of this month."

"What?" Lisa asked sharply.

"I know," Mark sighed. "It's a new company policy, but I realize it's not fair for you. I'm supposed to speak to the general manager in London a little later today, I will definitely raise the issue again. I'm so sorry for this."

"Mark, I have bills to pay," she reminded him. "Even if I didn't, what I have wouldn't stretch another three weeks."

"I know, I know. Listen, can I call you after my call with the general manager? I promise to fight for that."

"Sure, fine, but I really need this, Mark."

"I'll do my best, I promise."

"Thank you."

"Lisa, someone is waiting to speak to me in my office. Can we cover the rest of your points when I call you later?"

"Alright, I'll just wait for your call, then."

"Thank you. Speak to you later."

Mark hung up before Lisa had a chance to say goodbye.

Since Lisa hadn't had a chance to ask Mark for a recommendation and was therefore not able to finish optimizing her LinkedIn profile, she used her time to upload and create her profile in the main job portals in Dubai.

After an hour, Mark had yet to call back, but Lisa was pleased with the fact that she was almost ready to start sending job applications. There was still one thing she wanted to do, though, and that was Leonard's resume. She texted Leonard to see if he would be free for a Skype call. Leonard was available, as she expected.

When they connected online, they briefly chatted, as they hadn't spoken since the last family reunion on the Fourth of July. However, still waiting for Mark's call, Lisa was quick to get down to business.

"So, I've recently gone through a little coaching on how to write a resume and I wanted to see how we could improve yours."

"Thank you so much for thinking of me, but I've tried everything. I had my resume reviewed by a consultant from the local employment agency. "I don't see how it could get better, but I guess we can try."

"Let's do this, then," said Lisa, not willing to listen to him spiral downwards. Countless times, she heard Leonard saying the economy, the market, his career gap, and his unfortunate fame at the time of the union strike were at fault. Lisa knew better now.

And in her mind, there was no way that every employer would still remember Leonard's media exposure from nine years ago. There had to be a few that didn't know about it.

Lisa nudged and prodded Leonard into quantifying his previous work experience and his achievements. They were completely absent from his resume.

Using a table again, she was able to supercharge Leonard's resume with great sentences, each starting with powerful action verbs. Lisa noticed that she was much faster at writing Leonard's resume than she had been with hers, though she was unsure if it was because she knew the call from Mark could be coming any minute.

She created a special section she called 'Training,' listing all the different training that Leonard had acquired with his past employers, including not only the formal ones but also the ones he had as part of his day-to-day job.

Tackling the gap on Leonard's resume, she realized that he had done a lot of manual work during his unemployment period, as the coach had assumed. Leonard had helped friends and neighbors, some of them elderly or disabled, in all sorts of tasks, such as repairing home appliances, moving and packing, painting, and even computer maintenance.

Following the coach's advice, she listed them all under one hypothetical job that she called 'Handyman'.

Handyman *(Households & Computer related)*   **April 09 – Present**
Volunteer work   *Freelance*

➔ *Helped dozens of elderly or incapacitated persons with various manual works such as electrical & plumbing maintenance, IT & Internet assistance and house moves and paintings jobs.*

Responsibilities
- Repainted the houses of 4 elderly persons from A to Z in a record time.
- Organised the entire move out of 7 neighbours and friends.
- Installed and repaired 15 computers & internet connections *(3 in the last year alone)*
- Repaired various aging household items such as wardrobes, stove, taps and plumbing, electricity switches…

Achievements:
- ✓ Saved 1000's of dollars for several elderly or incapacitated persons in the region
- ✓ Produced an outstanding work on par with what professionals would have done
- ✓ Delivered a world class service everywhere I went in terms of cleanliness and results.
- ✓ Developed a reputation for being the go-to person for any manual work and computer related maintenance tasks in the region.

Lisa wasn't sure why his local employment agency consultant wouldn't have thought of doing this. "Aren't these people trained to help job seekers find work?" she wondered after broaching the topic.

"Well, that's not really a job, is it?" replied Leonard,

"What's your definition of a job?" asked Lisa, wearing her coaching hat.

"Well, for me a job is when you're employed by someone that actually pays you," replied Leonard.

"Did none of your friends or neighbors offer you money?"

"A few," conceded Leonard. "I suppose you're right. I just never saw it like that. My head was too wrapped around the conventional idea of a job."

"There you go, then!" interrupted Lisa, clearly in a rush.

"Listen, Lisa, thank you. The way my resume looks now means a lot to me."

"I think your resume is great, Leonard. I'm glad we did this."

"Me, too," said Leonard. "And I want you to know that if this doesn't work—"

"Why wouldn't it work?" she interrupted again.

"Well, I'm not sure if you've noticed, but I kind of got used to being labeled as unemployable."

"No one is unemployable. You have a great heart and so many skills that have helped countless people."

"I hope so," said Leonard. "But honestly, don't worry if it doesn't work. You improved my self-esteem, if nothing else. I think I'm good at what I do, even if it's sporadic work I was able to get here and there."

Lisa's phone suddenly rang, Mark's number on the caller ID.

"You go ahead and answer that," Leonard assured her.

"Thank you. Let me know how it goes, okay?"

"I will. Thanks again, Lisa."

"Don't mention it."

Leonard hung up and Lisa quickly answered her phone.

"Hey, Mark."

"Hey, Lisa, sorry for earlier. Things were busy."

"No problem. Did you have a chance to speak to Steve in London?"

"I did, and it's sorted. They're going to pay you in full tomorrow."

"Oh, thank you," Lisa breathed, relieved. "You're a star."

"You're welcome. Sorry about all of this."

"No harm done."

"So, how is your job search going?" he asked, more relaxed than he was before.

"Well, I ended up working with the Three Circles Coach and we completely rewrote my resume."

"Wow, how did it go?"

"It was transformative. I learned so much about me and the direction I want to take."

"That's great. I'm assuming he explained the three circles?"

"Of course. I haven't mastered them yet, but I understand them in a deep way now. Beyond that, he helped me take responsibility for what happened to me. It actually helped me a lot when I was talking to a recruiter earlier. Especially when he asked me what happened at *Cloudcom*."

"That must have felt like a pit trap."

"Only a little. I just told him the truth and he appreciated that, I think."

"Good for you."

"Thank you. In fact, that's related to what I wanted to discuss with you. A potential employer might want to check references with you, and I wanted to make sure that what I would say would be in line with what you would say. Would you have any advice?"

"Not really, as long as you don't ask me to lie. I would simply outline the good work you have done for us and how you somehow stopped fighting. The way I would normally put it is that we both agreed that this role was not really for you. Do you see any issue with that?"

"No, that's actually what I said earlier to the recruiter."

"Good, then."

"Mark, there is one thing that could tremendously help me reassure employers about my abilities and I'm not sure I could ask your help with that..."

"What do you have in mind?"

"OK." Lisa took a breath as she mustered her courage. "Would you write me a recommendation on LinkedIn?"

He hesitated. "I don't know if I could do that, Lisa."

"I understand," replied Lisa.

"Don't get me wrong, you've done a great job for us in the past, but I wouldn't want it to look like I'm hiding something about you."

"I thought about that, and I might have a solution, if you're open to hearing it, of course."

"I'm all ears," replied Mark.

"So, I know that the real value of a recommendation would be to highlight some of my skill set, but in our specific case, would it be possible to simply highlight the type of person I am? What you see as my soft skills, things like that."

Mark did not say anything for a while. Finally, he sighed.

"Alright, just let me think of something that I would feel comfortable with, and I'll send it to you for your review. If you think this is okay then that would work for me."

"That's great, thank you."

"I'll try to send you something today, I know you probably want to get this sorted," offered Mark. "Was there anything else you wanted to ask me?"

"No, you've been very helpful."

"Thank you. Listen, I'm going to write a few lines for your recommendation before I go home," he suggested. "I wish you all the best with your job search, and I'm glad you're working with the Three Circles Coach."

"Thank you so much, for everything."

"You're welcome. Let me know how your job search goes, okay?"

"I will."

"Bye now."

"Have a good evening."

Twenty minutes later, Mark sent an email to Lisa.

Hey Lisa,

So here's what I can write:

'Lisa was great to work with. She was well-liked by her clients and colleagues alike. She started with no experience in our industry and was able to quickly show early signs of success. I wish her the best of luck in her future career.'

Let me know if this works,
Mark.

It was more than Lisa could have wished for, and she was glad she asked Mark.

In her notebook, she wrote:

AT THE TIME OF RESIGNING (OR BEING TERMINATED),
THERE ARE 2 THINGS TO ASK:

1. ASK WHAT INFORMATION AN EX-EMPLOYER WOULD GIVE TO A POTENTIAL RECRUITER DURING A REFERENCE CHECK. *(TO MAKE SURE WHAT I SAY IS IN LINE WITH WHAT HE SAYS.)*

2. ASK FOR A RECOMMENDATION ON LINKEDIN OR AN EXPERIENCE LETTER. *(ALWAYS LEAVE ON GOOD TERMS TO INCREASE YOUR CHANCES REGARDLESS OF THE SITUATION.)*

After sending a 'thank you' email to Mark and agreeing on what he suggested, she went out to spend the bit of cash she had left to buy some groceries.

After dinner, Lisa went to bed feeling more serene. It had been a productive day. But as she mentally went over the day's events, she realized that she hadn't actually sent Leonard his resume.

She got up, and his resume was still open on her computer. She saved it and sent it to him quickly. Her LinkedIn tab was still open, and she noticed that Mark had already sent her the recommendation. She felt proud of how her LinkedIn profile was presented, and with Mark's recommendation, she felt a sense of relief.

It felt like her job search was finally about to start, and that as soon as she started sending a few job applications, she would be interviewing for great roles. Wishful thinking, perhaps.

No Results

The next few days were great, at first. Lisa received everything that *Cloudcom* owed her at once, representing two months of salary and her end of service benefit.

After repaying Sabrina for the loan she took to pay for the coach's package, she knew that she needed to keep half of it in reserve as, even if she were to find a job soon, she would have to complete the month before receiving her first paycheck. It was also a safety net in the event she needed to buy a ticket to leave Dubai.

The remaining half would be used for various bills. Life in Dubai was expensive, and her bills alone meant that she only had enough money to stay in Dubai for three weeks. The relief of receiving her salary from *Cloudcom* quickly disappeared, anxiety taking its place. "Three weeks to find work..." she said to herself.

If she had hoped she could use the Three Circles Coach's service, that option was no longer there. It would cost her everything she had put aside, and she couldn't risk it all.

Now that her home back in Virginia was going to be rented out, and the fact that she couldn't count on any financial support from her mom, it meant that she had to be extra cautious with her money.

Still very confident that her newly created resume would do the trick, she spent the next three days sending around 50 job applications. On the third day, she realized that there were no new jobs being published and that she had pretty much applied to all that were available online.

Apart from the usual automated notifications letting her know that her profile was not selected for the time being, Lisa's hopes of generating job interviews were steadily vanishing.

On the third day, she received a text from Leonard, saying that the guys at Leonard's local employment agency loved his new resume so much that they asked if they could use part of it as a template for other job seekers, especially the part where he presented his career gap. Lisa was pleased with the news, of course, and Leonard seemed excited.

The text ended this way:

> Who would have thought, right? Not sure where this will go, but I'm definitely visiting a few temporary agencies with my new resume. THANK YOU!

Lisa smiled as she read it. She wanted to reply, but she was interrupted by an incoming call from Sabrina. She heard the sound of a car engine in the background.

"Hey, Lisa!"

"Hey, hun," said Lisa.

"How are you doing?"

"Not great. I haven't received a single call. If this doesn't change, I might have to consider going back to New York."

"Don't you think it's a little early?" asked Sabrina.

"Maybe, but time isn't really on my side."

"Maybe I could stop by and we can talk about your job search a little. I'm no expert, but perhaps another perspective can help."

Even if she didn't think it would help, Sabrina was the only social life Lisa had left, and she wasn't going to turn down the company.

They agreed to meet at the same coffee place where they met last time, and they greeted each other at the cafe with a hug.

"So, how can I help?" asked Sabrina with a smile.

"I'm not sure," replied Lisa. "Maybe I should start by explaining the three circles of a job search..."

"Sure."

It only took a few minutes for Sabrina to grasp the three circles.

"It's like you're selling your services and trying to find your own clients, I love the concept," she commented.

"That's actually what the coach said," Lisa replied. "But my biggest problem is time. Including my final salary from Cloudcom, I just can't stay in Dubai for more than three weeks," she admitted.

"I don't think that's your biggest problem," said Sabrina.

"What do you mean?"

"Working with top executives, I've organized many job interviews for them, and there is a fundamental difference between how job seekers and how employers think."

"I know that," said Lisa.

"So why do you think like a job seeker? Doesn't that contradict the 'service to others' circle?"

"What do you mean?"

"Well, if you think like an employer, you shouldn't think in terms of time, but in terms of risk," Sabrina replied. "As a job seeker, your main problem is time. You want to find work as soon as possible. But an employer's main problem is the risk of hiring the wrong person, so they take their time. Can you see the problem?"

"So, I'm doomed," Lisa translated flatly.

Sabrina chuckled.

"No, I'm just saying that you should start thinking like them and develop an approach that convinces them to get in touch with you sooner."

"Any recommendations?" asked Lisa.

"Well, all the top executives that I served usually waited for HR to present them a list of, say, five candidates to interview. It sounds to me like you focused on sending your profile online to HR via the 'apply now' button for the job adverts. I'm not even sure if your resume goes to a real person's inbox when you do that."

"But I checked my resume against different adverts," Lisa protested. "It's packed with the right keywords, so I should come up in their search results when they skim through the list of applicants."

"Correct me if I'm wrong, but putting keywords in your resume has made your marketing circle larger, right?"

"I guess so," replied Lisa.

"But somehow your problem is that it's not crossing with the sales circle, which would mean job interviews for you. So even if writing a great resume and adding keywords has grown your marketing circle, you need to find a way to make it bigger. Not sure how, but we need to add some marketing stuff somehow."

Sabrina paused for a moment to think.

"I think you're onto something here, but what else can I do?" asked Lisa.

"The one thing I know for sure with HR is that their job is to eliminate the wrong applications and wait until they have enough profiles to present to the line manager. The two words to remember here are *'eliminate'* and *'wait.'* Definitely not the right strategy if you want to accelerate things."

"Okay, but I don't see what else I can do here."

"I remember a few instances where job applicants were able to send an email directly to the head of department I was supporting. If the resume was great, the head of department would ask me and HR to organize an interview."

"But that's not something I can do," said Lisa. "I mean, it's a great idea, but employers don't usually leave their email addresses on LinkedIn."

"Oh, that's a job for Youssef. He's good at that. You two should have a conversation, he'll definitely help."

"Okay," said Lisa half-convinced. "But wouldn't that be perceived as out of line if I try to contact them directly?"

"Lisa, it's an email, not a crime."

They couldn't help but laugh.

"Alright, I guess speaking to your husband won't hurt," Lisa agreed.

"It can't hurt! I mean, if you just do what every job seeker out there is doing, you're probably not going to be much luckier. I'm sure your resume is great and it might have been selected already. Your problem is the waiting that HR does, going through hundreds of resumes," said Sabrina.

"You need to go straight to the decision-makers. And if I were you, I would try to find ways to grow my marketing circle with more methods, which Youssef can definitely help you with."

"I think you're right. And since I would have already applied online for HR to see, I can't be accused of bypassing HR."

Sabrina promised to speak to Youssef once she got home, and they continued to talk for another half hour.

Once at her apartment, Lisa went straight to her notepad and wrote:

HR'S JOB IS TO ELIMINATE CANDIDATES IN ORDER TO PRESENT THE BEST SHORTLIST

AN EMPLOYER'S RISK IS HIRING THE WRONG PROFILE $\longrightarrow$ SO THEY TAKE THEIR TIME

A JOB SEEKER'S RISK IS NOT FINDING WORK ON TIME $\longrightarrow$ SO THEY GET FRUSTRATED AND SEND TONS OF APPLICATIONS

EMPLOYERS AND RECRUITERS ARE FROM 2 DIFFERENT PLANETS, AS THEY THINK FROM 2 DIFFERENT PARADIGMS:

$\longrightarrow$ HIRING THE WRONG PERSON VS. NOT FINDING WORK ON TIME

With the excitement of finally being able to apply to jobs, she had forgotten to always analyze her job search with the three circles in mind. If something was wrong, it was probably one or several circles that were not big enough to cross with the others.

Her resume was done with the three circles in mind, but now she needed to make sure that it was read by humans as many times as she could.

Lisa's talk with Sabrina had opened her eyes. She needed to up her game, and she definitely needed to add some more tricks to her marketing circle and boost her visibility.

'*The more my resume is read by the right decision-makers, the more job interviews I'll get.*"

And with that, she resolved to take matters into her own hands.

Finding Hidden Jobs Online

The following day, Lisa received a text from Sabrina, saying that Youssef would be free over Skype at noon. *'This will be much easier than meeting him somewhere,'* Lisa thought.

She felt like she had applied to every available job out there and there were no new jobs, either. She would spend the morning finding out if there was a way to access hidden jobs online.

As she was doing her research on Google, she found an amazing article from a website called *'The Undercover Recruiter,'* listing specific phrases that could be typed into Google using the main Applicant Tracking Systems that companies were using.

Each ATS offered a customized job portal that was usually added to employers' websites.

It explained how ATS's were hosting jobs on their servers and connecting them to the career sections of their clients' websites.

These career pages would never appear on Google's first pages, especially with the aggressive Search Engine Optimization—or SEO—campaigns job portals were doing to ensure they occupied the first pages of Google's Search Results.

The article was written by Maebellyne Ventura and offered the following Google search phrases for the main ATS's in the market:

→ The Google search to find hidden jobs published via the aplitrack ATS was:
   site:aplitrak.com intitle:*"the role you're looking for"* **AND** *city*

→ The Google search to find hidden jobs published via the Bullhorn ATS was:
   site:bullhornreach.com/job intitle:*"the role you're looking for"* **AND** *city*

→ The Google search to find jobs published via the Smart Recruiter ATS was:

site:smartrecruiters.com intitle:*"the role you're looking for"* AND *city*

→ The Google search to find jobs published via the Taleo ATS was:
site:taleo.net intitle:*"the role you're looking for"* AND *city*

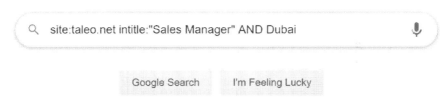

Trying each one, she found that Taleo offered the most results, probably due to its presence in the market Lisa was in.

Lisa quickly realized that since these jobs would not necessarily appear on mainstream job portals, she was going to have much less competition! Excited, she pushed onward, looking to see if there were any other ways to access hidden job opportunities.

She also found that she could simply set up a Google alert for new jobs, so that she would receive a notification every time something was published with the job titles she was after.

She bookmarked the following Google Support page that indicated exactly how to set up an alert:

https://support.google.com/websearch/answer/4815696?hl=en

Lisa felt like she was definitely gearing up for her job search. Using the free tools she found was going to make her job search much more effective. '*It's as if I found a shortcut and skipped traffic,*' she thought.

Since she knew job sites were actively campaigning on Google to occupy the first few pages of the search engine, she wondered if there was a way to eliminate the main job sites from her Google Search, so that she could see if other jobs were out there.

After a quick search, she was able to locate Google Search's 'settings' just below the search bar on the right hand side, but only visible once a search result was conducted. As she clicked on it, she located the *'Advanced Search'* option.

There, she was able to tell Google exactly what she wanted and what she didn't want, and of course, she made sure the usual websites she was coming across were removed from her search result, after making sure she selected the country she was targeting results for.

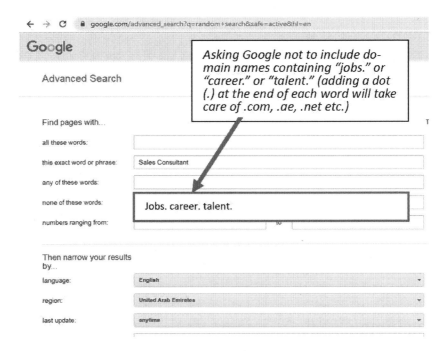

Not willing to stop before she exhausted all the possibilities to find hidden jobs online, she forged ahead by typing *'finding hidden jobs using social media'* into Google. There again, she found many great articles on the topic.

Social media was a gold mine of hidden job opportunities.

On LinkedIn, she joined a few groups where some of them actually had jobs advertised only on those groups. All she had to do was send a request to join each group.

But her best discovery was job bots. Job bots were small programs that worked with Facebook Messenger that searched the web for jobs on the user's behalf.

The best part was that they seemed to be detached from search engine algorithms and job portal rankings. This meant that Lisa could access jobs that were fairly hidden, and often directly from employers' websites.

On her Facebook Messenger search bar, she found more job bots by simply typing the term "job bot." Some were by industry, and some by region.

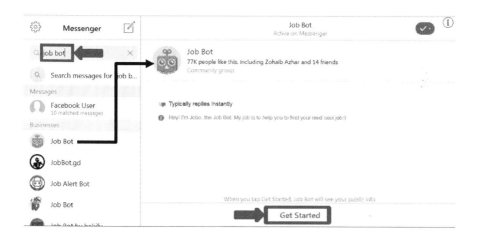

With the ATS's Google search string and the job bots on Messenger, Lisa unearthed dozens of new jobs she hadn't seen before. She was eager to send her resume, but she wanted to wait for her call with Youssef to see how she could be more strategic about it.

Just sending her application via the normal HR process was not enough if she wanted to accelerate her job search results.

The Marketing Session With Youssef

Lisa received a text from Youssef ten minutes before noon. He was free for their call and included his Skype ID in the text message. They connected on Skype shortly after.

"Hey, Youssef."

"Hello, Lisa."

"Thanks for taking the time to speak to me. I know you're busy."

"No problem. Sabrina explained the three circles theory, and I have to say, it's impressive. I'm keeping it in mind in my own work, now." He sounded cheerful.

"Glad you liked it."

"So, how can I help?"

"I need to find a way to send an email to decision-makers that I'm not connected to on LinkedIn."

"Oh, that's fairly easy," said Youssef brightly.

"Really? How?"

"There are many tools that offer that. Have you ever tried to search Google for the phrase *finding anyone's email address for free?*"

Lisa typed the phrase as soon as she heard it:

"Not really. Are all these free tools?"

"You'll find both. My favorite ones are www.hunter.io and www.voila-norbert.com. I think you can search for fifty emails a month for free, and you can get a paid account if you need more. Or you can try other tools, as they also have free trials."

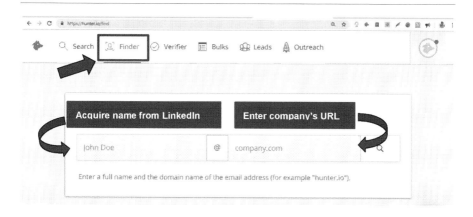

"Most of them will give you a confidence score that will help you assess whether the email is likely to be the right one or not. You can also verify these emails by using other free services. Just go on Google and type the phrase..."

He trailed off, and Lisa could hear him typing before the following phrases showed up:

'free email verifier'
OR
'free email tester'

"Type these phrases in any search engine and you'll find tons of tools that can verify the validity of most emails."

"That's good to know, but it still seems like sending a job application email to heads of departments, directors, or CEOs could be seen as inappropriate. Don't you think this approach could backfire?"

"Who else do you want to send them to if you don't address your email to decision-makers?"

"I was thinking that I could use these tools to send them to HR personnel, actually."

"I wouldn't bother if I were you. I mean, I would advise you send them through their portal to avoid being accused of skipping their recruitment team, but I would definitely send proper job applications to decision-makers directly."

It made sense, but it wasn't as if she had much to lose by also sending her application to the head of recruitment or the head of HR. She needed as many eyes on her resume as possible.

She remembered the coach saying that the number one objective of a job search was to get as many people reading her resume as possible. The more her resume was read, the more phone calls she would get.

"Thank you, Youssef."

"My pleasure. Oh, and before I forget, most of these tools will ask you to first register with your corporate email. Since you're out of work at the moment, feel free to ask a friend who has a work email if she can help."

"I'll probably ask Sabrina about that."

"I'm sure she'll be fine with it. And if for any reason she has some sort of company policy that would prevent her from helping, you can also find decision makers' emails the old fashion way, by guessing the person's email based on the email format of other employees in the company.

"You can type the following phrase on Google:

'email * * companydomain.com.'

"This will help you determine what format other employees in the same company have and 'guess' the person's email according to that format.

"Most of the time it is the same format. Like this." More typing, and the example showed up in the chat: **firstname.lastname@domain.com**. "Or similar formats."

Lisa was taking notes, and she couldn't wait to try these out.

"Alternatively, adding just the domain name of the company on hunter.io or voilanorbert.com will also give you many emails of employees in the same company. Just guess the person's email based on the email structure that is used for other employees," added Youssef.

"Thank you. It sounds easy enough; I can't wait to try these out."

"Just keep in mind that some companies block these tools."

"Is there any other way to send decision makers a direct email, then?"

"I usually use LinkedIn."

"Yeah, I thought about that, but I only have a free account. I can't send InMails on LinkedIn unless it's a person I'm already connected with or I subscribe to one of LinkedIn's packages. To be frank, I can't afford extra expenses right now," sighed Lisa.

"There's a way to send free InMails on LinkedIn, actually, even if you're not connected to the person. I can show you."

"That would be great!" she enthused.

After sharing his screen, Youssef opened a LinkedIn page and logged in.

"LinkedIn InMail is LinkedIn's version of an email. It offers most of the same features, but they're usually not free, unless you send an InMail to a person who shares a group with you," he began.

"To find employees in a specific company, just click on the search bar and select *'People'* from the drop down menu."

"Once you do that, just go to *'Filter'* on the top right of the page."

"There are many filters, but there are at least two you can select: *'Location'* and *'Current companies.'* Under *'Location'* you can type the country or the city you're targeting."

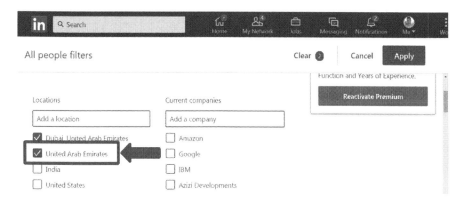

"Now, type the company you're targeting under the *'Current companies'* section. Once you're done, just click on *'Apply'* on the top right corner," Youssef explained.

"Now, locate the LinkedIn profile of the person you would like to get in touch with and open it. Find out which group she's subscribed to; this is usually located at the end of their profile, under the *'Interests'* section," he continued.

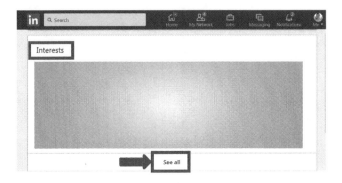

"Groups are usually hidden, so you will have to click on *'See all'* in the bottom of the *'Interests'* section, and a window will pop up."

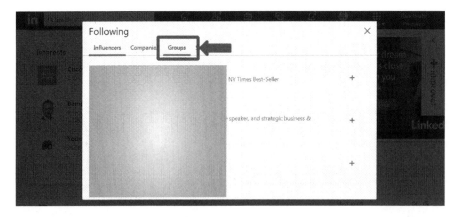

"Now go to the *'Groups'* tab. That's where you'll find the groups they're subscribed to. From there, locate a group that you're also a member of and open it in a different internet tab.

If you're not sure which group you have in common, you can open several groups in different tabs. Otherwise you can simply request to join the group they're part of."

After doing that, Youssef closed the pop out window and went back to the top of the person's profile.

"Before you go into these group tabs, make sure you select the name of the person's profile and *copy* it on your computer clipboard."

Once Youssef copied the full name of the person, he opened one of the group tabs.

"On the top right corner of the group page, locate the number of members that the group has and click on it to access the group's directory."

"In the search box, type or paste the full name of the person."

"Once you find them in the directory, notice a *'Message'* button on the same line."

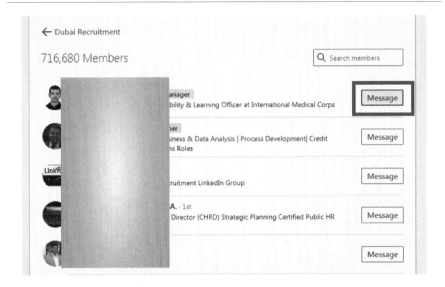

"If you click on it, you'll be able to send an InMail to the person and even attach your resume by clicking on the clipboard icon in the bottom of the message window that just popped up."

Lisa was speechless. How on earth could she have not known that? It would have helped her a lot during her sales role at *Cloudcom*.

"Youssef, that's amazing. Just give me a minute."

Youssef was quiet as Lisa wrote the steps down in her notebook.

THERE ARE MANY OPTIONS TO FIND PEOPLE'S PROFESSIONAL EMAILS.

1. BY USING FREE TOOLS SUCH AS HUNTER.IO

   – MOST OF THEM WILL REQUIRE ME TO REGISTER WITH A COMPANY EMAIL. I WILL
   ASK SABRINA IF SHE CAN HELP (OTHERWISE I'LL TRY TO GUESS HIS EMAIL BY
   FINDING OTHER EMPLOYEES EMAILS FROM THE SAME COMPANY.
   (TYPE THIS ON GOOGLE: "EMAIL * * COMPANYWEBSITE.COM")

2. IF EMAIL-FINDING TOOLS DON'T WORK FOR A SPECIFIC CONTACT, I CAN SEND A
   MESSAGE TO ANYONE ON LINKEDIN, EVEN IF I'M NOT CONNECTED WITH THEM!

   – I FIND A GROUP WE SHARE IN COMMON (OR JOIN ONE THAT HE'S A MEMBER
   OF) AND I FOLLOW THESE STEPS:
   OPEN THE GROUP $\longrightarrow$ LOCATE AND CLICK ON THE NUMBER OF MEMBERS TO
   ACCESS THE GROUP'S MEMBERS DIRECTORY $\longrightarrow$ COPY PASTE THE FULL NAME
   OF THE PERSON IN THE SEARCH BOX $\longrightarrow$ AND SEND HIM A DIRECT MESSAGE
   WITH MY JOB APPLICATION

Youssef waited until her pen stopped scratching over the paper before he asked, "Would you like to know how to find out if your recipient opened your email or not?"

"Do you mean that I should ask for a read receipt?"

"No, I'm talking about a tool that would track each opened email, so you know if they read it."

"That would be great, yeah. It'll let me know how many people could have actually read my resume."

"It's actually quite simple, but people just don't think of doing it. Just go on Google, and if you're using Gmail for example, type in: 'Free Email Tracker for Gmail'. You'll find many of them.

"The more employers read your job application emails, the more times your resume will be opened, and the more you will receive inquiries. So tracking your email open rate will give you a critical insight.

"In marketing, that's how you monitor the efficiency of your campaigns. You don't just wait, hope, or assume anything, you measure and monitor."

Lisa couldn't help but do a quick search while Youssef was talking, and found many free tools, just as he explained.

Google

| Free Email Tracker for Gmail   🎤 |

[Google Search]   [I'm Feeling Lucky]

"Are you sure that the recipients won't be asked to send me a read receipt with these tools?"

"I'm positive."

"That is amazing. I knew I was right to speak to you."

"Anytime. Do you know what subject line you'll be using?"

"Not yet. Does that matter?"

"You bet!" said Youssef. "It's the subject line that makes the recipient open your email!"

"I guess you're right," commented Lisa. "I never open an email when I see a spammy subject line."

"So what subject line would you use?"

"Maybe '*Lisa Dutoit—Business Development Specialist Role.*'"

"It's not bad, but how about: '*Attn: John Smith—Business Development Specialist Role.*' Just use the recipient's name instead of *John Smith.*"

"Why would that be better than the one I suggested?"

"Putting his name in the subject line will make him curious, and curiosity is a powerful force. Why is this e-mail specifically meant for him, and not anyone else? Wouldn't you be more inclined to open an email with your name in the subject line?"

Lisa thought for a moment before she conceded, "You're probably right."

"And if you see that your emails aren't being opened with that subject line, you can always try..." Lisa heard Youssef typing before she saw the following subject line appear on her screen: '*RE: Business Development Specialist role.*'

"It looks like I'm responding to a message the decision maker would have sent me before," Lisa observed warily. "That's clever, but maybe a little too bold for me."

"That's what you want him to think, of course, but for you '*RE*' could be short for '*regarding*,'" Youssef explained.

The idea was sinking into Lisa's head. She knew that if she did not try to make her subject line stand out from the sea of applicants, her resume would never be read by enough people.

And that could be the difference between generating enough job interviews and not doing so. She had to admit, Youssef's approach was surely going to increase her resume views.

"All this is really impressive, Youssef. Thank you so much."

"You're welcome. I think with these tools your marketing circle is going to expand, while your competition will just keep doing what everyone else does."

"I can't wait!" replied Lisa, remembering she also had free tools to find hidden job opportunities.

"Good luck. Let me know if you need anything else."

"I will, thanks a lot."

"Bye now."

"Bye, Youssef."

The call ended, and Lisa grabbed her notebook. She needed to regroup.

WHEN SENDING MY JOB APPLICATIONS ONLINE, I MUST REACH OUT TO DECISION-MAKERS DIRECTLY AFTER I SEND MY APPLICATION THROUGH THE NORMAL PROCESS ('*APPLY NOW*' BUTTON)

KEY DECISION-MAKERS ARE HEADS OF DEPARTMENT, DIRECT MANAGERS FOR THE ROLE AT HAND, HEADS OF COMPANIES
(I CAN ALSO SEND MY APPLICATION TO HR PERSONNEL TO INCREASE THE NUMBER OF RESUME VIEWS, BUT I SHOULD NOT FOCUS ON THEM SINCE THEY'RE NOT DECISION-MAKERS)

1. AFTER FINDING THE PEOPLE I'M TARGETING ON LINKEDIN, I CAN FIND THEIR CORPORATE EMAIL BY USING TOOLS SUCH AS HUNTER.IO

2. I WILL SEND MY JOB APPLICATION EMAIL TO AT LEAST 2 DECISION-MAKERS TO MAXIMIZE MY CHANCES OF MY RESUME BEING READ OR INCREASE THE ODDS OF BEING DIRECTED TO THE RIGHT PERSON IF THESE ARE NOT THE RIGHT PEOPLE.

3. The best subject lines increase the chances of my emails being opened by these very busy executives:

   → 'Attn: Recipient's full name—Business Development Specialist Role'

   → 'RE: Business Development Specialist Role'

4. I can (and should) track the open rate of each email I send to employers, by using free email trackers—(do a Google search for 'free email tracker for Gmail'—or any other email provider)

5. In the event that I can't find someone's corporate email, I can send them an InMail via LinkedIn for free once I share the same group as them (need to join relevant groups to do that)

   → I find a group we share in common (or join one that he's a member of) and follow these steps:

   → I open the group → locate and click on the number of members to access the group's members directory

   → I then copy-paste the full name of the person in the search box → and send him a direct message with my job application!

6. Once I see that there are no new jobs being published in the mainstream job portals and LinkedIn, I can find hidden jobs by typing ATS search phrases on Google:

   A. site:taleo.net intitle: "the role you're looking for" AND city

   B. site:smartrecruiters.com intitle: "the role you're looking for" AND city

   C. site:aplitrak.com intitle: "the role you're looking for" AND city

   D. site:bullhornreach.com/job intitle: "the role you're looking for" AND city

7. I can also find hidden jobs by typing 'job bot' on Facebook messenger.

With all these techniques, Lisa wasn't sure where to start. She had already sent a lot of job applications via the *'APPLY NOW'* buttons online. Since she had not received any feedback, she decided to go back to each one of them and contact decision-makers directly.

In order to keep track of who she sent her applications to, when, and whether or not they were read, she created a Google Spreadsheet to be sure she could access it from anywhere, including her smartphone. She typed the following URL and logged in with her Gmail account:

https://docs.google.com/spreadsheets/u/0/

After creating a job application follow-up document, she felt a sense of clarity she didn't have before. The spreadsheet acted like a dashboard that offered structure in her job search.

Job Title	Company	Job Ad URL	Applied online on	Sent to the following contact emails	Contact Job Title / Designation	Email/InMail Opened on (Date)
Sales Consultant	ACME CORP	www.jobboard.com/page1234	MM/DD/YEAR			
Account Manager	ABC CORP	www.indeed.com/ref176	MM/DD/YEAR			
Business Development Specialist	TECHKNOW LTD	www.linkedin.com/page1234	MM/DD/YEAR			
Sales Representative	IRIS TRAINING	www.indeed.com/ref198	MM/DD/YEAR			
Business Development Manager	THE BUTTERFLY	www.jobsite.com/ID675	MM/DD/YEAR			
International Business Developer	SIMON & CO	www.linkedin.com/?page568	MM/DD/YEAR			
Client Generation Specialist	CRM & MORE	www.jobboard.com/ID675	MM/DD/YEAR			

A few hours later, after going through each application she had already made and searching for the emails of key decision-makers, Lisa managed to send her profile to most of them.

For the first time, she had a work-in-progress spreadsheet that she could analyze and connect with what the coach told her about the three circles.

At that moment, she had a revelation. Her job search was becoming a very meticulous process. She took her notebook and started jotting down some notes:

→ THE RESUME IS FULL OF KEYWORDS AND INCREASES MY CHANCES TO BE FOUND ON ANY DATABASES, WHETHER I APPLY TO A SPECIFIC JOB OR WHETHER I REGISTER ON JOB PORTALS AND LINKEDIN.
BUT THAT WON'T WORK 100%. HR PERSONNEL ARE HERE TO ELIMINATE AND WAIT UNTIL THEY HAVE THE RIGHT RESUMES. PLUS, MY PROFILE CAN'T COME UP ON EVERY KEYWORD SEARCH. IT DEPENDS ON WHAT KEYWORDS EACH INDIVIDUAL RECRUITER WOULD USE.

→ THAT'S WHY I SHOULD ALSO SEND MY JOB APPLICATION TO DECISION-MAKERS DIRECTLY TO AT LEAST FILL THESE GAPS AND ACCELERATE THINGS FOR ME.

Inspired, she was able to draw a diagram for her job search:

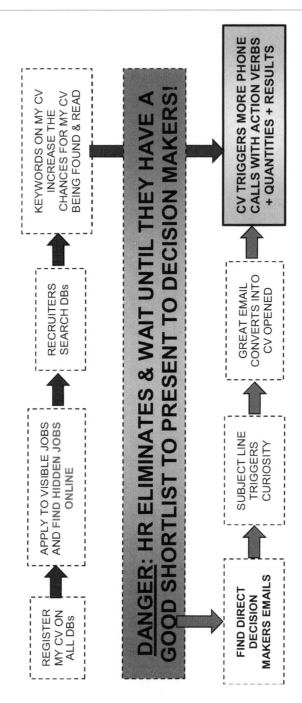

She could easily visualize how all these techniques made her marketing circle even bigger.

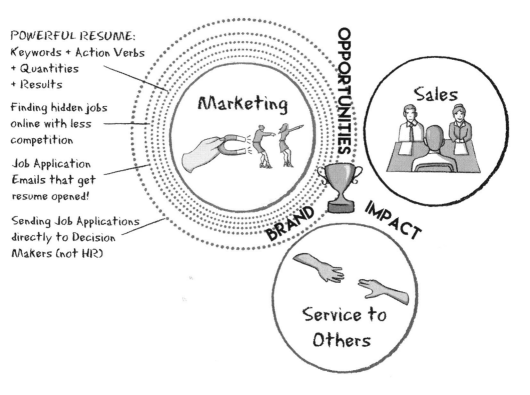

POWERFUL RESUME:
Keywords + Action Verbs
+ Quantities
+ Results

Finding hidden jobs
online with less
competition

Job Application
Emails that get
resume opened!

Sending Job Applications
directly to Decision
Makers (not HR)

Although Lisa wasn't able to find every email she wanted, she was still able to send InMails via LinkedIn Groups. Her main focus from then on was not receiving phone calls, but getting her resume read by as many relevant people as possible.

She decided to thoroughly track her email open rate as an indication of how many employers were actually opening her resume. This didn't mean that anyone opening her emails would necessarily read her resume, but she knew it was a close indication nevertheless.

It was 4:30 PM, and all in all it was a very productive day. Lisa felt like she went up to the next level with her marketing strategy. '*The Three Circles Coach would be impressed*,' she thought.

Just as she was thinking that nothing more would happen that day, an email came through, entitled: 'Job Interview Request.' Lisa's heart raced with excitement as she opened the email.

Dear Lisa,

I hope you're well.

After reviewing your profile for the role of "Sales Associate," we would like to invite you for an interview at our premises.

- Date & Time: Tomorrow at 5 PM.
- Role: Sales Associate for the BMO Division.
- Location: Business Bay, Building #4, 2nd floor.

Please find attached our location map.

Awaiting your confirmation for the same.

Deepthi Khan
Talent Acquisition Officer
DL: +971 4 777 7777
deepthi.k@biganco.com

Lisa couldn't believe her eyes. Her marketing efforts were finally starting to pay off.

Opening her spreadsheet, she quickly located the role she applied to three days ago. But two hours ago, she'd sent a job application to the head of Sales directly using what she learned earlier that day and he apparently opened her application, according to her email tracker notification. "It works!" she blurted out.

She was glad she saved the job advert link, as she would use it to prepare herself. She didn't have much information about the person she would be meeting, nor about the role itself, but it was great news nevertheless.

Lisa promptly replied to confirm her attendance. She did want to ask questions as to who she would be meeting, but she decided not to, worried she would somehow irritate Deepthi Khan with her questions. Besides, she would find out tomorrow anyway.

As she opened the company's website, she tried to learn as much about them as she could. *Big&Co* was a large construction company. Based on the job advert, a sales associate would essentially be promoting and selling their off-plan projects in Dubai.

'*It's all there,*' she thought as she looked at her resume again. '*I can do this.*'

Thirty minutes later, her phone rang. It was Andy, the recruitment agent from a few days ago. Lisa picked up the call, keeping in mind that she needed to switch to her *'customer service'* circle.

"Hello, Lisa speaking."

"Hi there, Lisa. This is Andy from Iris Search."

"Hey Andy, good to hear from you."

"Same here. Listen, I just got an interview request for the role I told you about. Are you still interested?"

"That's great, of course I am!" Lisa enthused.

"Great. However, the line manager that would like to interview you is going on holiday for three weeks after tomorrow, and asked if you could come for an interview tomorrow at 3 PM."

"That should be okay!" said Lisa without hesitation.

"Great! Let me confirm it with them before they leave work for the day, and I'll send you the details of your interview straight after, okay?"

"Sure, not a problem, thanks."

"You're welcome. This is a great opportunity, I'm sure you can do this."

"I hope so, Andy. Thank you!"

"And please don't hesitate to reach out if you have any questions."

"I will."

"Okay, bye now."

"Bye, Andy."

Lisa's heart raced. Two interviews in one day. *'The Three Circles Coach would be so proud!'* she thought.

But as she waited for Andy's email, she didn't have much to do other than worry. *'How can I prepare for two interviews with so little time?'*

Determined to do anything in her power to pass these interviews, Lisa went on Google and typed several search strings, such as *'How to prepare for a job interview'* or *'Job interview questions for a business development specialist.'*

There was a *lot* of information online. But somehow, none of it was offering an easy, step-by-step method to prepare for job interviews. There was a lot of content giving tips on a variety of things, like keeping eye contact, dress code, or even how to do a handshake.

There were also thousands of tips on how to answer specific questions, usually accompanied with scripts from the authors.

Since she found it impossible to predict which questions she would be asked tomorrow, she wasn't sure what to do with all the information.

It was at that moment that Andy's email came through, confirming her interview the following day at 3:00 PM. It read as follows:

Hey Lisa,

Congratulations on securing an interview with the prestigious *'The CRM Guys.'* They started in Dubai five years ago with just two partners, Rupesh Singh and Patrick Haddad. Rupesh is an Indian engineer who developed several applications for other companies before developing their CRM products.

He met Patrick at his previous company. Born and bred in Lebanon, Patrick Haddad came to Dubai almost at the same time as Rupesh. Patrick was the Head of Business Development in the same company when the two met and clicked almost immediately.

After spending his career selling IT & Telco solutions in the region, Patrick approached Rupesh one day and discussed a possible partnership to set up a CRM solution that they could sell to SMEs in the region.

There were already some big names in the region at that time, but very few were actually providing an affordable CRM solution for SMEs. And that's how *'The CRM Guys'* was born.

You will be interviewed by Patrick Haddad himself, who still looks after the Sales & Marketing Dept. while Rupesh oversees R&D and Technical Support.

- Interview date and time: Tomorrow at 3 PM
- DIFC - Building 4, 3rd floor

Here's the location map: https://googlemap.com/x3Xs_%dkjhak

I'm also attaching the job description for the Sales Consultant role. The goal of tomorrow's interview is for them to see how you could help them generate more sales and CRM implementation projects.

I'm still in the office for another 30 minutes, so please do not hesitate if you have any questions, Lisa. My contact details are in my signature below.

In the meantime, all the best with your preparation.

Best regards,
Andy.

Lisa was excited and anxious at the same time. The company sounded great, and she liked the fact that it was one of the founders that would interview her. But at the same time, it was daunting. She opened the job description and read it carefully.

Most job descriptions were boring and lifeless, and this one was no exception. It included vague words and phrases that did not mean much without understanding the context. Phrases like:

- Generate new sales in line with the Sales and Marketing objectives.
- Communicate and coordinate with various stakeholders *(internal & external)*
- Create sales reports
- Achieve KPIs and targets

... and so on.

After going through the entire job description, she didn't feel like she was anywhere near being ready for tomorrow's interview. At the same time, she knew she couldn't just improvise. She needed a method to prepare effectively, and in the absence of the Three Circles Coach, she wasn't sure what she could do.

Lisa decided to dial Andy's number to ask for some advice. He had to have helped plenty of candidates in the past. If anyone had any tips, it had to be him.

Little did she know, Andy had much more than just tips.

SECTION 2:
THE SALES CIRCLE

The 5 S's of Every Job Interview

"Good evening, Iris Search. Andy speaking."

"Hi again, Andy. It's Lisa."

"Hey, how can I help you?"

"You mentioned that I could call you if I had any questions. Are you free now?"

"Of course, ask away," replied Andy.

"Thank you. I actually only have one question, if that's okay. I've gone through the job description and I was wondering if you could offer some advice on how to prepare for this interview effectively? I tried looking for help online, but that just made me even more anxious."

"Oh really? Why?"

"Well, there is a sea of information that ranges from the way we should dress and shake hands to the way we should answer specific questions that I'm not even sure I should prepare for..."

"I see your point. You don't want to spend your time preparing for questions you won't be asked."

"Exactly. Sorry, I know it's probably time for you to leave work, but I was wondering if you had some slightly more specific help."

"As a matter of fact, I do."

Lisa breathed out a relieved sigh. She didn't mind working hard, but knowing what direction to go would be helpful. She reached for her pen and her notepad.

"Okay," Andy began, "the first thing to remember is that nobody can predict the questions at the interview, but there is a pattern. Once you understand it, you'll be rocking!"

Lisa smiled as he continued. "But first, there are three questions that you can expect almost for sure. *Tell me about yourself,*' first of all. You'll probably hear *'What do you know about our company?'* and *'What do you understand about the job description?'*"

Andy paused, and Lisa used it as a chance to quickly write the questions down.

"According to a study," Andy explained, "by 'Classes and Careers', 33 percent of employers reported knowing within the first **90 seconds** of an interview if they would hire someone.

"So the first question—*'Tell me a little about you'*—is critical in that regard. I'm sure you can find tons of videos on YouTube about how to handle it."

"Sure."

"Now," he continued, "when it comes to the second question, that's a classic. Employers will ask you what you know about their company. Numbers like their size, the number of employees or offices they have, their market, the date they were created... etc. are important of course, but don't forget to take note of the type of clients they serve, especially if they're prestigious. Also try to find out if they have received any accolade, awards, or positive press coverage.

"But I always advise my candidates to go beyond the website, I highly recommend you understand how they make money.

"In other words, what's their business model? What are their services or products? What is their competitive advantage? How do they market themselves? Do you see what I mean?"

"I'm with you so far," replied Lisa.

"Perfect! Now, the third question is not necessarily going to be asked, but..." Andy paused. "It's crucial that you can understand the job description in a simple yet effective way.

"Unlike what most job seekers think, a job description is not a description of a series of tasks. It's actually a solution devised by the client to tackle a gap or a challenge they currently have. If you try to explain the job description as a series of tasks, you will fail to see the point and your entire interview will go off course." Andy stopped talking for a while, as if he wanted to choose his words carefully.

"For an employer, your skills are more like a service that he would buy to help him tackle a problem. The job description is like a product or a service card. You've got to distinguish between the features and the benefits of that product."

"Enlighten me," she requested.

"Features are what your product can do; they're the technical side of things. Benefits are what your product can achieve for someone; they're the effects people actually see," he explained. "Do you remember the ad from Apple when they launched the iPod Mini?"

"Not really," Lisa confessed.

"Instead of saying that it had one gigabyte of memory space, they advertised it as 1,000 songs in your pocket. Can you see the difference between the feature and the benefit?"

"I get it," Lisa confirmed.

"And a job description is just a list of features that the right candidate should have. Now, studying the job description will let you extract the benefits for the employer, so you'll know exactly what they'll be looking for. Benefits sell, not features."

"But how am I supposed to know what the benefits are for an employer?"

"Very simple. Take your last job at *Cloudcom*, for example. Can you think of three benefits that your role provided to *Cloudcom*?"

"Do you mean my results?"

"No, your interviewer won't see those until he hires you. I'm talking about the value that your day-to-day work adds to the company."

"If I think about my skills as the product, then the benefits would be generating more sales, delivering great customer service, and trying to get as much repeat business as possible," said Lisa. It sounded just like her new resume.

"Bingo!" Andy exclaimed. "You see, it's not about what you do in terms of cold calls, contract negotiation, and so on. It's what you allow your employer to achieve through your day-to-day tasks.

"The features are the day-to-day tasks, and the benefits are what the employer can get from them. You've got to be able to prepare your job interviews to line up with the benefits that the employer is looking for, not the tasks," he carried on.

"For example, an accountant job interview is not measured on the basis of his accounting skills, but on the basis of providing a clear visual of where the company is at any point in time, of being the guardian of the employer's cash flow, and of putting in place a system that would allow these numbers to be accurate at all times.

"Some accountants even sell themselves on the basis that they can help the company reduce its tax expenditure. These are truly the benefits that employers are looking for."

"I'm following you so far."

"Great! More importantly, a job interview is very much like a sales meeting. The one thing that makes a sale possible is if the perceived value or the benefits a client will understand exceeds the effort or the price he will have to pay."

A sale can only happen if:

PERCEIVED VALUE > EFFORT / COST

[Specific benefits an employer can get] must exceed [Salary, Time, Training, Risk, Fear]

"I get it," replied Lisa, remembering the three circles and realizing that in order for her 'sales' circle to cross with her 'service to others' circle, she had to convince the employer that he would greatly benefit from her services.

"So how would you synthesize the job description in terms of benefits for the employer?" asked Andy.

"Like I said before: more sales, good customer service, and repeat business. That's pretty much what I was doing at *Cloudcom*."

"Excellent! In my sixteen years of experience, 99 percent of interview candidates *thought* they understood the job description but really didn't," Andy sighed.

"Most candidates read the job description without studying it. What you want to do is take each line of the job description and prepare an example in line with the corresponding skill or soft skill mentioned. Just saying you can do something doesn't mean anything without any examples."

"I'll prepare as many examples as I can," Lisa assured him quickly. "Thank you. Is there anything else you think I should prepare?"

"You bet!" said Andy. "How about I give you the five categories of questions you'll get at every job interview?"

"I didn't know that was a thing, so that would be great."

"Great!" said Andy. "I heard it online from a career coach. He called it the 'Five S's,'" he explained.

"Okay," Lisa coaxed, ready for more.

After a brief pause, Andy took a deep breath and began reciting something he must have said countless times before.

"S1 is for '*Stability.*' Employers want to make sure that if they invest in hiring and training someone, that person will stay long enough to recoup their investment.

"So you're going to get questions about why you left previous jobs or why you're leaving your current one. The answer needs to make sense, so try to stay away from answers that are vague, like 'Well, I was looking for growth,' because employers will think that if you couldn't grow in that role then maybe you didn't perform well.

"Same issue with answers like 'Well, I was looking for a new challenge.' This doesn't reflect stability."

"I need to be crystal clear about why I left my previous job in a way that would reassure my interviewer," Lisa paraphrased.

"That's right," replied Andy. "S2 is about the 'Skills' that are necessary for the role. That's where you'll have questions like 'How you would do this or that, how you would handle a situation with a client?' and such.

"I expect you'll also have questions about your KPIs, like 'how many cold calls or meetings have you done on average?' The interviewer will then cross the numbers to see if the results you mention on your resume are reflected with the KPIs you achieve on a daily, weekly, or monthly basis.

"He'll want to understand the methods you're using. In short, any question that would highlight your skill set will be under S2. On Google, feel free to type phrases like 'Job interview questions for a business development specialist,' or variations of that."

"So I'll need to get my numbers ready so he feels confident I know what I'm talking about," Lisa stated, remembering she had already done that when she wrote her resume.

"Exactly," Andy agreed. "S3 is for 'Soft Skills.' This is what a lot of candidates fail to understand. The one thing an employer will not be able to train you on is your soft skills, so this is a field that has seen the most development in interviewers' techniques. Have you heard of behavior-based questions?"

"Vaguely, yes."

"That's the key here. Behavior-based questions are there to analyze your behavior in specific situations. You might have some hypothetical questions, like 'Imagine if you're dealing with a customer who wants to go to the competition, what would you do?'

"Your ability to outline a structured approach to this situation will reveal your behavior and attitude in the face of challenges. Soft skills are about the intangible: your personality, your resilience, your mindset. An all-time favorite question from HR personnel is 'What are your strengths and weaknesses?' Have you ever been asked that?"

"So many times," Lisa laughed.

"Well, there you go. When discussing areas of improvement or weaknesses, they won't be trying to trick you. They're just trying to understand your soft skills and how you handle some weaknesses. We all have some, so it's important to be upfront with these.

"But please, avoid the fake weaknesses like *'I'm a workaholic'* or *'I'm a sore loser.'* They might be true but they could be seen as a way to manipulate the interviewer, and they're no fools. Instead, mention something you could be working on, like being disorganized, being too emotional sometimes, or anything real."

"But wouldn't that be shooting myself in the foot?"

"Not if you're doing all you can to tackle it. That's truly what they're after, not the weakness itself. We all have some, and they do too. What they want to see is that you're aware of them, and that you're handling them."

"Basically, being upfront with my weaknesses will show honesty, and that's a soft skill by itself. And then showing them how I'm improving shows resolve and other soft skills, right?"

"Correct," said Andy.

"I always felt uncomfortable with this question, but it doesn't seem like such a big deal now. And I would definitely want to know if I were in their shoes."

"Soft skills are really important. Remember, this is the only thing an employer won't be able to change. He can give you all the training in the world, but soft skills are usually hard coded with each and everyone of us. And I'll let you in on a little secret: there are three soft skills that employers are desperately looking for."

"Which ones?" asked Lisa, intrigued.

"The ability to take responsibility for mistakes or weaknesses, the ability to demonstrate problem-solving skills, and the ability to learn from mistakes.

"If you can show them that you take full responsibility for everything, that would be a great start, and showing that you took the initiative to fix things that went wrong without running to your manager for solutions will send a strong message to the person interviewing you. You will be seen as a problem-solver, not as a problem.

"Employers are not interested in hiring someone that will give them more problems. They expect people to bring solutions, so they will put you in various hypothetical situations to discover these soft skills. Never forget that it's not problems they're after, but problem-solving skills. And don't forget your ability to learn from mistakes.

"Mistakes are bound to happen, and every employer knows that. It is a necessary evil for someone to develop.

"But they will be extremely attracted to you if you can show them that even if you have made some mistakes, you made sure those mistakes never happened after that by taking responsibility, solving that problem, and learning from those mistakes."

"I think I understand the purpose of these questions," mused Lisa. "They're not after my weaknesses or my mistakes, they're after my behavior and my attitude when confronted with these situations."

"You got it," Andy enthused.

"So what's the fourth S?"

"S4 is about 'Success.' They will ask you questions about your results, and I commend you for writing a resume that is full of that. Just make sure you know your numbers by heart when they ask about your targets or anything related to your achievements."

"... Is that it?"

"Yes," chuckled Andy. "I would normally explain what I mean by results, but in your case, your resume already reflects them beautifully."

"So what's the last S, then?" asked Lisa.

"S5 is about 'Salary,'" he stated simply.

"Do you have any advice on how to tackle that?" Lisa probed when he didn't elaborate.

"Not really," he admitted. "There are different schools of thought, but if I were you, I would just mention that you discussed the salary aspect with me and that it would be easier if these questions are discussed with me. Just pass the ball to me, and I'll handle it for you."

Lisa couldn't say she was comfortable with the idea of not having any control over her own salary.

"Can I ask why I wouldn't negotiate directly with them?"

"That's one of the perks of being represented by an agent. Having someone like me negotiating on your behalf means that you will get as much as possible for this role. But more importantly, there is a certain way to do it, and you won't be able to get ready for it with all the preparations you already have to do."

"Okay," she agreed reluctantly.

"You mentioned that you wanted AED 8,000 per month plus commission, right?" asked Andy.

"Yes I did, but..." She trailed off. As nice as Andy was, he was still working for his client, and she had no proof he would do all he could to get the best deal for her. "Do you think that I could get more if things go well at the interview?"

"I think so. I'll ask for more, but the better you do during the first four S's of your interview, the more negotiation power we'll have."

"Thanks, I understand. But can I ask you a question?"

"Go ahead."

"I'm confident that you'll try to get the maximum amount possible for this role, but what's in it for you? Why would you negotiate the highest salary for me?"

"That's a fair question," he acknowledged. "It's in my interest as well," he explained. "The way most recruitment companies work is that they agree on a fixed percentage of the annual salary of every candidate we place permanently.

"So the employer will pay us, say, fifteen or twenty percent of your first year's annual salary if you get hired. And since the percentage is fixed by our contract with the employer, the only way for me to earn more would be to get you as much as possible."

"Oh. Okay," Lisa sighed, relieved.

"Trust me, negotiating someone else's salary is way easier than negotiating my own," chuckled Andy. "I've been doing this for years. Just focus on preparing for your interview, okay?"

"I will. Thanks for all your advice, Andy. Wish me luck."

"I don't think you need it, but good luck, Lisa. If you don't have any questions, I'm gonna have to go now."

"No more questions. I'll prepare the best I can and I'll call you after my interview."

"Great, I look forward to it! have a good evening."

"Bye, Andy." Lisa hung up the phone.

In so many ways, the conversation was a huge eye opener for Lisa.

The five S's approach helped her understand what she needed to prepare. But more importantly, she finally understood the employer's mindset. '*There are no trick questions,*' she mused to herself. '*Only relevant questions.*'

She picked up her pen and notepad again. The talk with Andy was key, and she thanked herself for giving him a call as she wrote:

3 QUESTIONS THAT I CAN EXPECT FROM MOST INTERVIEWERS:

1. 'TELL ME ABOUT YOURSELF.'

2. 'WHAT DO YOU KNOW ABOUT OUR COMPANY?'

3. 'WHAT DO YOU UNDERSTAND ABOUT THE JOB DESCRIPTION?'

THE 3 BENEFITS OF MY ROLE FOR ANY EMPLOYER ARE:

1. ACHIEVE MY SALES TARGETS

2. BUILD STRONG RELATIONSHIPS WITH MY CLIENTS THROUGH GREAT CUSTOMER SERVICE

3. RETAIN CLIENTS IN THE LONG RUN TO GENERATE REPEAT BUSINESS OPPORTUNITIES

THE 5 S's OF JOB INTERVIEWS ARE 5 CATEGORIES OF QUESTIONS THAT EVERY EMPLOYER WILL GO THROUGH:

S1: STABILITY: THE 'WHY' I LEFT/AM LEAVING EMPLOYERS. OR "HOW I SEE THE NEXT 5 YEARS"

S2: SKILLS: THE 'HOW WOULD YOU DO XXX' QUESTIONS. HERE, I MUST PREPARE NUMBERS ABOUT MY KPIs, MY TARGETS, MY METHODS, MY TECHNIQUES, THE TOOLS THAT I USE, THE SYSTEMS I HAVE PUT IN PLACE, EVERYTHING THAT WOULD REASSURE AN EMPLOYER ABOUT MY SKILL SET.

S3: SOFT SKILLS:

EXAMPLE:

→ WHAT ARE YOUR WEAKNESSES?

→ TELL ME ABOUT A TIME YOU HAVE MADE A MISTAKE.

→ CAN YOU DESCRIBE A TIME YOU HAD TO DEAL WITH A DIFFICULT CUSTOMER/COLLEAGUE/MANAGER/SITUATION/ETC.?

3 MOST IMPORTANT SOFT SKILLS ARE:

— TAKING RESPONSIBILITY

— PROBLEM SOLVING

— LEARNING FROM MISTAKES/SITUATIONS

S4: SUCCESS: QUANTIFIED RESULTS OR CLIENT/EMPLOYER RECOGNITIONS

S5: SALARY: WILL BE HANDLED BY ANDY

IMPORTANT: ALWAYS PREPARE EXAMPLES THAT RELATE TO AS MANY SKILLS/SOFT SKILLS MENTIONED IN THE JOB DESCRIPTION. THIS IS THE DIFFERENCE BETWEEN READING A JOB DESCRIPTION AND STUDYING IT.

→ DON'T TELL THEM, SHOW THEM WITH EXAMPLES!

Now that Lisa knew what types of questions she needed to prepare for, she wrote all the answers to relevant job interview questions she found online. It helped her memorize them, and Lisa found great things online that she took notes from.

The more she was creating her scripts, the more confident she felt. Tedious though it was, her in-depth preparation would only need to happen once. The other roles would be about fine-tuning what she had already done.

Soon, she'd be ready to give the best interview of her life.

Tackling the Early Questions at the Job Interview

After jotting down some examples for most of the points outlined in the job description, Lisa also prepared some answers to typical questions in line with the first four S's that Andy described. By then, it was almost 11:00 PM, but she didn't feel tired at all.

After a quick search online, Lisa found a great video on how to answer the '*Tell me a little about you?*' question.

https://www.youtube.com/watch?reload=9&v=OW-yxxPMtro

In the video, which had millions of views, Antony Stagg proposed a smart structure he called E.E.S., short for Education—Experience—Strength.

He advocated, and rightly so she thought, that it was not a question to be taken lightly, as it constituted the first job interview question and, if answered correctly, could give the employer the right first impression.

Lisa took notes on the E.E.S. structure and tried to write a script for each section, starting with her education background, continuing with her employment background, and finishing off with two personal and relevant strengths for the role. Having a structure in mind helped her channel her anxiety.

She continued with her preparations until she was done. When she finished, it was already 11:55 PM. Closing her computer, she prepared her outfit for the following day and went to bed.

The Day of the 2 Job Interviews

At 8:30 AM, as Lisa's alarm clock rang, she immediately felt stressed.

The first thought that Lisa had was to have another round of preparation since her first interview was only at 3 PM and *The CRM Guys* was not very far from where she lived. She got up and had a quick shower before preparing two slices of toast to have with her coffee.

She was satisfied with the answers she wrote the night before, but a thought persisted in her mind: *'What if it's not the same questions that I prepared for?'*

Lisa was fighting with her inner voice that seemed to do everything to make her doubt herself. Above all, she was worried about how she would answer questions about why she was no longer working at *Cloudcom*.

"Shut up, Lisa, you're awesome!" she said out loud. "You have done exactly what they're looking for, you're a hard worker, and you have results that prove that."

Sipping her coffee, she reviewed her notes from the night before, but she still didn't feel ready. The more she read the answers to the questions she prepared, the more she felt she hadn't memorized them.

She couldn't stop preparing for today's interviews, her mind creating an ever ending sequence of doubts and new interview questions she should also research. At 2:15 PM, she was in her car, remembering that her car loan would be due soon. *The CRM Guys* were located in Dubai International Financial Center, probably due to the fact that their software was widely used by the financial Industry.

As she drove towards Dubai International Financial Centre, she was too stressed to listen to the radio, and the sound of her engine helped her relax and focus.

Once she arrived at the DIFC parking, she tried to follow the instructions given by Andy. But she quickly found that she parked in the wrong parking area and had to walk ten minutes to get in front of the entrance on the seventh floor.

Not wanting to be late, she hurried along the stairs and through the alleys of the DIFC. Lisa still arrived at 2:55 PM, a little out of breath.

As the sliding door opened, she was greeted with a smile by the receptionist.

"Good morning, I have an interview with Patrick Haddad at 3:00 PM," Lisa said.

"Please have a seat." replied the receptionist, indicating a seating area to her right, next to another sliding door that led to an open space.

"Thank you."

Although she managed to catch her breath, her heart was still racing and her hands were clammy. Lisa tried to calm down and discreetly wipe her hands with a napkin.

As the sliding door opened, she saw Patrick Haddad accompanying a smartly dressed and beautiful Arab lady to the door, ignoring Lisa on his way.

The two were laughing and it was clear that the lady was another candidate for the same role. Lisa felt small and unimportant, and she didn't speak any Arabic. It was probably a great asset that the other woman had.

"I will let Andy know soon," said Patrick, laughing, before making his way back to reception. Lisa was shocked. She was apparently not the only candidate that Andy presented for this role.

As Patrick Haddad came back to the reception area, he said something inaudible to the receptionist, who waved towards Lisa.

Patrick made his way over.

"Hello Lisa, I'm Patrick," he said with a smile and an Arabic accent.

"Hi Patrick, great to meet you." She smiled back.

"Likewise," said Patrick. "Would you like to follow me?"

"Sure," complied Lisa.

As he scanned his employee card to open the sliding door, Patrick showed her to the meeting room where the interview would be conducted. On the way there, she heard laughter from someone on the phone, while a few employees turned around to watch the two enter the meeting room.

It was a small, minimalist meeting room, with a long table and eight chairs, with a whiteboard and a flip chart that both had notes and graphs she couldn't figure out.

"Please have a seat, Lisa," Patrick said, waving at an empty chair opposite to where he would be sitting.

"Thank you," she replied as she sat down, while Patrick took a seat across from her.

"Would you like something to drink?" asked Patrick.

"No, I'm okay, thank you," replied Lisa.

"Great, so..." he began with a deep breath. "Tell me a little bit about you, Lisa," he said with a smile.

"Sure." Lisa remembered the E.E.S structure for Education, Experience, and Strength. "I'm 28 years old and I graduated from the University of Virginia, which is attached to one of the top 20 business schools in the United States.

"I started my career in the Luxury Retail sector, where I quickly progressed to become one of the top sales associates in New York and Dubai.

"After that, I pursued an opportunity to sell conference call solutions to businesses in the region, where I quickly adapted to a more consultative B2B sales approach.

"One of the achievements I am most proud of was breaking the company's record on the fastest deal made for a new junior. As for key strengths, I *must* highlight my ability to learn fast, which served me well when I tackled the Dubai market and the B2B sales approach at *Cloudcom*.

"Another strength is my resilience in the face of market conditions and competition. The combination of these two skills and my previous track record are what I believe would help me perform fantastically at your company."

"Thank you." It looked like he was paying attention finally. "So, what do you know about our company?" he continued.

Cautiously, Lisa allowed herself to relax slightly.

"Well, based on my research, you founded *The CRM Guys* back in 2008, and you essentially offer CRM solutions for mid-sized companies in the region. Today the company has grown to 27 employees, and you still cater to the SME market in the Middle East.

"From what I've gathered, you have two types of income streams. The first one is about implementing and customizing your CRM solutions at client premises. The second one is essentially based on recurring licensing and maintenance fees," Lisa offered, feeling more confident now.

"Not bad at all," said Patrick. "But your resume seems to say that you haven't sold CRM solutions before, am I right?"

The bit of calmness that Lisa gained was almost immediately lost and her mind started racing trying to find an answer.

One side of her brain was confused as to why Patrick would organize an interview with someone that clearly didn't have much experience in his company's specific niche. The other side was trying to find a solution to Patrick's question.

"That's true, you're right. But one thing I have always done is adapt and learn, and I'm sure I can learn this market quickly," she attempted.

"Okay," said Patrick, clearly unimpressed by Lisa's stock answer. Looking at Lisa's resume, he continued. "So tell me, why are you looking to change jobs?"

Taken aback by Patrick's question, her heart was racing again. Looking down at the table and trying to think of a reassuring answer, she panicked.

"I resigned from *Cloudcom* two weeks ago, so I'm pretty much available." Lisa hated herself for lying out of panic, and she knew that she had just exposed herself to another difficult question.

"Can I ask you why?" said Patrick, frowning.

"This was actually something I've been contemplating for a few months now. *Cloudcom* is a small office in Dubai and career progression was not really on the cards despite my great results.

"So after a while, I started losing my motivation and instead of allowing the company to suffer or look for a job behind my employer's back, I spoke to my manager and we both agreed that perhaps this opportunity wasn't the right one for me."

"Hmm..." Patrick looked silently at her resume, frowning.

He was silent for what seemed an eternity. Looking down at the table, Lisa noticed her hands were shaking and opted to put them under the table, which made her posture curled up now. Clearly seeing that things were not developing in her favor, she attempted to regain control of the situation.

"Patrick, if I may, I know you're looking for someone who can achieve sales targets, deliver a superior level of customer service while building strong client relationships to retain customers in the long run, and generate more repeat business opportunities and client referrals through these relationships.

"That's exactly what I have been doing across every role I have had, including at *Cloudcom*." It was the script she had prepared the night before for the '*what do you understand from the job description?*' question.

"I understand that, but I'm a little bit concerned that you lost your motivation and ended up resigning from your previous employer, to be honest," said Patrick, looking at her resume again.

"I appreciate your concern, and to be honest, I would probably be worried, too, if I were you. The truth is that I realize now that I am in charge of my own motivation, not my employer, and not my environment.

"I truly loved working at *Cloudcom* and I learned a lot from my manager there. This incident in my career was a huge learning experience for me and it has made me more resilient. I'm now certain that a company like yours will benefit from this learning experience."

"But it looks like you didn't stay long at your previous role either, according to your resume. You didn't even complete five months at '*Watch the Time.*'"

"That's correct. I was called directly by the manager at *Cloudcom*, and this was a career shift towards the B2B sales sector."

"Okay, let's move on..." said Patrick, seemingly unfazed by Lisa's answer. "Can you tell me about your daily tasks and KPIs at *Cloudcom*?"

"Sure. My role at *Cloudcom* was essentially revolving around three aspects. Cold calling and business lead generation, client on-boarding and relationships, and trying to expand my client portfolio by promoting more updates and modules to their business."

"That's fine, but can you describe how a standard day looked?" asked Patrick, sounding impatient.

"I called an average of 30 to 40 companies a day, most of them cold calls to try to secure demos and meetings. I went to up to four meetings a week at different client premises, typically in the UAE and Saudi Arabia, my two biggest markets."

"Thank you. What was your monthly or quarterly target?"

"I had to sign up at least two new clients per month."

"And how did you do in relation to this target?"

"Before my demotivation phase, I was one of the top performers in the sales team, with an average of 3.8 new clients per month throughout the year." Lisa immediately regretted using the word 'demotivation' again.

"Thank you, Lisa," commented Patrick, still disconcertingly unfazed. "Can you describe a meeting where you had really difficult people to persuade?"

"Sure," said Lisa, trying to recall a relevant meeting for Patrick's question. She knew that this was a behavioral question to get a glimpse of her attitude and soft skills at large. She did prepare a similar question the night before and after a few seconds decided that it was relevant enough:

"One of the most challenging meetings was with the CEO and the CTO of a company during a demo meeting. It was one of the first meetings I was handling alone, and they had very specific business and technical questions that I found myself not able to answer.

"They were fair questions, such as *'What was the minimum internet speed to make sure our software works in every country?'* or *'Can some governments block our conference call software and make communications impossible?'* and other questions that I honestly did not have the answers to.

"So I did what I usually do in these cases; I took notes and promised to get back to them the same day or the day after. But the CTO started challenging me on the fact that I apparently didn't know my product, since I couldn't answer his specific questions.

"I tried to tell him that these were very specific questions and that I would for sure have an answer for them in the same day. But I could see they weren't impressed, and I started feeling embarrassed. That's when the CEO stood up and left, saying it was a waste of time. Even the CTO seemed a bit embarrassed."

Patrick was silent for an uncomfortably long moment, and Lisa realized that perhaps she should have chosen a different story, with an ending that would reflect a positive result despite the challenge she went through. Instead, it was just a story with a sad ending. *'No one would want to hear a story like this,'* she thought.

She blew it, and she knew it even before Patrick Haddad said, "Thank you for your time today, Lisa. Before we end this meeting, do you have any questions?"

Lisa thought for an instant and realized the working hours for the role were not discussed. She decided to ask, trying to sound like it wasn't the most important point of her interest.

"Yes, maybe one. We haven't discussed the working hours for this role. Would you like to leave this for a later time in the process?"

"This will be discussed with the candidate we will be selecting for the role," Patrick replied, sounding almost irritated by Lisa's question.

"Great." Lisa smiled uncomfortably. "Do you know when you will be making a decision?"

"We will let the agency know in the next few days, and I'm sure Andy will update you accordingly. Do you have any more questions?"

"Not for the moment. Thank you so much for your time today, Patrick. I hope to hear from you soon."

"The pleasure was mine," he replied with a smile as he stood up to indicate the end of the meeting.

After accompanying Lisa to the reception area, he thanked her for her time with much less enthusiasm than the previous candidate. Lisa smiled and made her way to the elevator.

Alone in the elevator, the first thing Lisa felt was remorse. She knew her interview didn't go as she wanted. Almost mechanically, she took out her phone and noticed three new messages.

One was from Sabrina, at 2:30 AM, wishing her luck with her interview. The second was from Andy, wishing her luck and asking her to call him after she finished with Patrick. The last message was from her mom, which read as follows:

> Leonard was just hired on a 3-month temp job! If things go well, it could become a permanent job. What have you done to him?! :-)

Lisa was shocked. It seemed that for whatever reason, the whole world was successful but her! She couldn't get herself to be happy for Leonard. She prepared herself so much for this role... "That's okay, you still have one interview. You can do this," she said out loud, as she started her walk back towards her car.

She was in Business Bay 25 minutes later, following the Google Map she was sent the day before. She would reach her destination in the next five minutes, which would make her 30 minutes too early still.

Finding a space to park was difficult, as the basement parking was only for employees. After a few minutes of roaming the area, she found a space a short walk from the building. *Big&Co's* offices were not as prestigious as the *The CRM Guys'*, but decent nevertheless.

Arriving on the second floor, she proceeded to the reception area and a similar process as at *The CRM Guys* ensued. Only this time, the room was full of people, most of them standing as the seats were all occupied.

The atmosphere was heavy with silence. Glancing quickly at everyone, it was clear they were all there for an interview. *'I hope there's more than one job...'* thought Lisa.

One by one, each candidate was escorted by the receptionist to the relevant meeting room. After almost an hour of waiting, Lisa's turn finally arrived.

Following the receptionist through a corridor of offices and meeting rooms, she finally arrived at the room her job interview would be conducted in. As soon as she was seated, the receptionist left and Lisa heard her stopping at one of the offices to let someone know Lisa was waiting.

One minute later, a middle-aged man came and shook Lisa's hand with a broad smile. With a Scottish accent, he introduced himself as Jim, the head of Sales at *Big&Co*. That's when she realized that the person she was meeting was actually the one she sent a direct email to, after hearing nothing from her application online.

"Hello, Jim. Nice to meet you," replied Lisa.

"So, what brings you to the job interview today?"

"Well, I understand from your job description that you're looking for results-driven sales people to help you sell off plan apartments for your ongoing construction projects. And having been in sales my whole career, I think I would be great for this role."

"Thank you, but you've never sold properties before, have you?"

"No, I haven't, but to be frank with you, selling is selling. I might need a couple of weeks to understand your products, but after that, I think that my hard work and resilience will pay off like it always has."

"Okay," said Jim with a smile. "So, why are you leaving your current employer?"

"I left already, actually. After several years with a solid track record of selling conference call software, I now would like to get into the property market," said Lisa.

"Can I ask you why you resigned from your previous work?"

Lisa thought it would be best not to correct Jim about his use of the word resigning.

"*Cloudcom* is a great company and I learned a lot there, but the fact that it is a small set up meant that there wasn't much room for progression. After several years of being one of the top performers there, I figured it might be time to work for a larger company that could offer more opportunities for growth, providing, of course, that I exceed my target."

"Alright, please allow me to be transparent with the package on offer for this role."

"Sure," said Lisa, taken aback by the way the interview was progressing.

"Should you pass the interview process, you would be offered a salary of AED 4,000 per month with one percent commission on each sale you'll make."

"Thank you for sharing that. May I ask the size of your average sale?"

"Sure. It's around AED one million, so one percent would be AED 10,000 per sale.

"That's actually not bad," mused Lisa.

"It's not. But let me tell you something, people usually don't make sales before they complete their first 3 months."

"Okay," Lisa acknowledged levelly.

"Do you have any questions about the role?"

"No, I think that's fine," said Lisa, worried she would create the same reaction that she did at *The CRM Guys*. But this also seemed wrong...

"Really?" commented Jim. He sounded skeptical. "Well then, someone will be in touch soon." As he said that, he stood up to indicate the end of the interview.

Lisa noticed that he wasn't impressed with the fact that she didn't have any questions, but there wasn't much more she could ask, she thought.

"Thank you for your time, Jim. Do you know how long you will need before you make a decision?"

"Not sure. We still have a few candidates to interview this week and next week. Someone will be in touch soon."

"Okay, no problem. Thanks again for your time," said Lisa as the two were walking down the corridor.

"Pleasure," replied Jim. "Do you know how to find the exit?"

"I do," she confirmed.

"Well, good luck, Lisa," Jim offered as he extended his hand towards Lisa. Lisa shook his hand.

As Lisa walked down the corridor, she heard Jim's voice again.

"Oh, one last thing, Lisa," said Jim. "How did you get my email address?"

"Oh," said Lisa, pausing as it occurred to her that her methods made her look like something of a busybody. "I actually just tried different combinations, and I guess I got lucky. I hope you don't mind," she answered, hoping it sounded innocuous.

"No, not at all, I was just curious. Have a great day."

"You, too," she replied, relieved.

Lasting a whopping five minutes, that was definitely Lisa's fastest interview ever... and she knew it wasn't a good sign. Although Jim did not make her feel it as much as Patrick had, she knew that she couldn't have passed that job interview, either.

On top of that, she saw how Jim had expected questions from her. *'It probably sounded like I didn't care...'*

Even if she got the job, she could not accept a role that paid AED 4,000 per month. Her previous salary at Cloudcom was double that and she still barely had anything left at the end of the month...

Passing by the reception area, she noticed two more candidates waiting for their interviews. She said goodbye to the receptionist without hearing anything back and waited for the elevator. The idea that perhaps Dubai was not for her was starting to sound more convincing.

She started envisioning a return to New York, and her first thought was that she should book a flight to New York that day to take advantage of the best rates.

On one hand, she knew that she could get more job interviews, and if she prepared better, she could still have a chance of staying in Dubai. But taking the competition into account, it was a gamble nevertheless to find work in the next two weeks.

After that, her car loan and student loans would be due again. She was running out of time and money.

'Not planning ahead would be stupid,' she thought. *'A last minute flight would cost me an arm and a leg.'* It already wouldn't be cheap.

After walking back to her car, she sat at the steering wheel, incapable of making a move. She had a decision to make, and she needed to make it that day. It was 5:20 PM and she knew Tina, her friend from *Cerrutini*, would already be awake preparing for her 10:00 AM shift.

She sent her a text to see if she would be free via Skype. Starting the engine of her car, she made her way home. Stopping at a red light, she checked her phone again to find Tina calling her via Skype. Her phone was still on silent from her interview and she was glad she checked it at that moment.

She needed to talk to someone, and Tina had never just been someone.

Lisa picked up the call and put her phone on speaker mode with the volume up so she could drive at the same time.

"Hello babe!" shouted Tina, her voice exuberant but her expression blank as she put on makeup.

"Tina, I'm so glad I'm speaking to you..." Lisa suddenly burst in tears.

"Oh, Lisa, are you okay?" Tina asked, more subdued.

"I am, I'm sorry..." Lisa tried to compose herself. "I'm okay, I just needed to speak to someone."

"What's going on? I'm freaking out!"

"Things have been a little tricky lately. I lost my job and I still haven't been able to find work here."

"Okay," Tina prompted, waiting to hear more.

"I might be coming back to New York in a couple of weeks. The market here is not..."

Lisa heard the Three Circles Coach's voice in her head at that moment. She didn't want to sound like a victim, but there she was, crying and blaming the market for her situation.

"Listen, Lisa," Tina interrupted her thoughts, "mi casa es su casa for as long as you need. You know this."

"Thank you, Tina."

"Now, do you want to tell me what happened?"

"The fact that I got fired is a party pooper for most interviews I will ever get," Lisa explained glumly, "and even if it wasn't the case, the competition is fierce."

"Can't you just tell them that you resigned?"

"They can check references, and my previous manager won't lie about this."

"So tell them you're still there. They won't be checking references if you're still there, will they?"

"I thought about it, but my VISA was already cancelled, they can easily find out that I'm no longer employed there."

"I'm sorry. You probably thought of all this already. But hey! I think this is great news, between you and me." Tina paused. "I miss having you in New York. And I'm sure that with your international experience, you would find a great job here."

"Thank you. It means a lot to me."

"Not a problem, I mean it. And remember, mi casa es su casa, amiga!"

As Tina was already late for work, the two agreed to speak later, after Lisa booked her ticket to New York.

As she arrived at her empty flat, the same feeling of being an outcast took hold of her. It was yet another day where everyone in Dubai seemed to be working or going somewhere, and she wasn't. She was right back to square one.

She dreaded turning on her computer and seeing nothing but automated rejection emails from her past applications.

Instead, she opted to call Andy and explain what happened. Apparently, Patrick had already called Andy to tell him that he would not be shortlisting Lisa.

"I'm sorry it didn't work out, Lisa."

"That's okay. You tried to help, but it's really hard to reassure an employer after what happened with *Cloudcom*."

"I know," commented Andy. "But I still think you're a great candidate, and I promise to call you if I have something else for you. Deal?"

Lisa smiled. "Deal," she agreed, even if she knew the odds of that happening before she left were slim.

After the two hung up, she wondered how much the flights to New York were. After a quick search online, she found a great flight departing in a little more than two weeks.

The site indicated there were only three seats left at that price, but Lisa dithered over the decision to buy. The flight was not refundable. She decided to check her emails first, to see if there was anything remotely positive before pulling her debit card out.

As if he had sensed something, the Three Circles Coach had sent her an email an hour ago, asking how her job search was progressing. Lisa decided to reply after she secured one of the last seats for the flight to New York. It was a good deal and she didn't want to miss out, especially with her current financials.

Just before her confirmation, the screen of her mobile lit up. It was Sabrina calling, but the site showed only two seats left by then. She went ahead and booked her flight, deciding to call Sabrina back afterwards.

Calling Sabrina back, her friend was keen to know how her interviews went.

"Hey, you job interview magnet!"

"It was awful," replied Lisa immediately, shifting her friend's mood at once.

"Oh, I'm sorry, was it that bad?"

"Worse," Lisa groaned.

After Lisa told her what happened, she announced to her friend that she had just booked her flight.

"Oh no..."

"I know, but I had to make a decision. I've pushed it as far as I could, but I have to be sensible." After all, even a job hunt that was going well could still take more time than she had.

"Lisa, let me cut you a deal," Sabrina requested after a moment of quiet.

"Okay," Lisa agreed, bemused.

"Now that you've booked your flight, promise me that you'll still do everything to find work here. Because if you pass the first interview, I'm happy to lend you some money to finish the process."

"No, Sabrina!" Lisa snapped, before she sighed. "Sorry, just... I'm tired of not having money and being an extra weight for you or anyone else. I'm a grown-up with no money. I'm a total failure, and I think I need a new beginning. Besides, I've applied to most available jobs already, even the hidden ones."

"Okay," sighed Sabrina, sounding reluctant. "But you know that option is on the table, okay?"

"I know. Thank you. It means a lot."

After the pair hung up, Lisa replied to the Three Circles Coach as follows:

Dear coach,

Thank you so much for following up. I just had my first 2 interviews, but they did not go well at all, unfortunately.

I wish we could have more sessions together, but I'm in such a shape financially that I'm not even sure how to pay my car loan this month.

I'll keep pushing, and if things don't work out, I have already booked a return flight to New York in 2 weeks, where I'll try my luck there.

Thank you so much for caring,
Lisa.

PS: Leonard found work, for the first time in 9 years. Your resume writing formula rocks. Thank you for challenging me on my assumptions.

As she opened her work-in-progress spreadsheet, Lisa noticed that many job applications she had sent directly to decision-makers were still unopened. She knew her emails could have landed in their spam folders, but it was disheartening all the same.

"On the other hand, one of her applications had apparently been opened more than twenty times by the same person. "That's weird," she mused.

And then it occurred to her that it must have been due to her email being forwarded internally to several people, and since the original tracking link was always in the email, that's how her open rates multiplied for that one single contact.

Updating her spreadsheet with her recent job interviews, she decided to spend the rest of the afternoon searching for more job adverts, although she knew the chances of finding any new ones were slim.

That was when a Skype call window popped up; it was the Three Circles Coach.

The Courtesy Call from the Coach

"Hello, coach."

"Hello, Lisa. I just read your reply and I wanted to check in," the coach admitted. "How are you doing?"

"I'm good, I guess, all things considered."

"So what happened since our last session?" he pressed.

"Well, in terms of my marketing circle, I think you'd be proud. I was able to find hidden jobs online and send my applications directly to decision-makers, so I skipped some competition and even converted one of these applications into an interview. I was able to secure two interviews for today."

"Impressive," the coach commented. "And...?"

"Unfortunately, neither of them went well. There's an issue with my sales circle, but I don't know what."

"That's normal," he replied.

"What do you mean?" she asked, perplexed.

"You've gotta walk and fall before you run," he explained. "So what's your plan of action now?"

"Well, I'm in a bit of a situation financially and I've applied to most jobs online, even the hidden ones. So today I decided to book my flight to New York before the prices go crazy.

"I'll be leaving in two weeks, unless I find work before that. My plan in the next two weeks is to just keep generating interviews with the marketing techniques that I have and see what happens."

"How do you feel now that you've bought a ticket?"

Lisa didn't answer immediately. It had been such a hectic day, she'd hardly had time to think about it. Eventually, she replied, "I feel more serene, somehow. I'd be gutted to leave Dubai, but at least my return flight acts as a safety net in case I don't make it."

"Interesting..." commented the coach without adding another word.

Well, that didn't sound encouraging. Sighing, Lisa said, "Well, let's have it."

After a brief pause, the coach offered, "You might not like what I'm about to say."

"I already know that," she pointed out.

"I think you're acting like a coward," stated the coach bluntly.

"Wait a minute—" She didn't get a chance to say anything else.

"I haven't finished," he interrupted. "I didn't say you were a coward, I said you're acting like one. Listen, **things *always* get worse before they get better.** There's no escaping it. You've been running a marathon job search, and now that you're five miles away from the finish line, you're planning for failure?"

"I'm not planning for failure," corrected Lisa. "I'll keep running regardless, but I had to secure myself. I couldn't just wait for things to happen or not," replied Lisa.

"I'm sorry if I misunderstood, but it seemed to me that the first thing you did after these interviews was plan for retreat. Did I get this wrong?"

"I am not planning for retreat, coach, it's just in case—"

"Yes, I know, a plan B, right?"

"Yes, of course, I really don't see anything wrong with that..."

"What's wrong is that you've started putting too much thought and energy towards plan B, and that's thought and energy you are taking from plan A. Let me ask you something," the coach pursued. "How are you planning to make plan A happen?"

"I've been working on it, the pieces just haven't all come together yet."

"*That's* my point right there. You've planned for retreat before planning for success. The challenge with that approach is that now, losing is an option for you. And trust me, I've seen this too many times not to warn you today.

"What makes people fail at their job search is not the competition or the obstacles they have, it's them relying on plan B.

"Whether it's a place to go to or social allowance they'll receive during their unemployment, plan B's bring people back into their comfort zone. When people feel comfortable, they get complacent, and apathy is guaranteed to make it so your job search never goes anywhere."

"I can assure you that's not the case. I'm determined to make it happen."

The Three Circles Coach was silent again. Lisa was starting to regret answering the call.

"Lisa, have you heard the story of an army that came to a foreign land to conquer it and found itself facing an army ten times its size, ready to do anything to defend their land?"

"No, I haven't," Lisa sighed.

"When Tariq ibn Ziyad, the commander of the Muslim army, came to conquer the Iberian peninsula, nowadays Spain and Portugal, he found a gigantic army of Visigoth which numbered at 100,000 men. Compared to his 13,000 men, they were no match for the Visigoth.

"As soon as this huge army was sighted, Ziyad saw fear taking root in his ranks. What he did that day has changed history forever. He ordered his ships to be burnt, leaving no escape for his men. The choice was simple: win or die. Do you know what happened?"

Lisa remained silent, sensing it was a rhetorical question.

"Against all odds, they won, and Spain became a beacon for Art and Science in the 8th century onward, which later contributed greatly to Europe's renaissance.

"You see, you need to feel the heat if you're going to get anywhere. As long as you have ships waiting for you to take you home safely, then you can still afford to be apathetic, and apathy will take you back to New York faster than that ticket ever will. You're writing your story today, but how will it end? Have you made a decision yet?"

Lisa was silent. On one hand, she already bought her ticket, but on the other, the coach had a point. She knew she was less stressed after getting the ticket, as if she had taken a few steps closer to her comfort zone.

"It's already done, coach," she pointed out.

"I know, but your mindset is still under your control. In the face of defeat, it is no time for giving up or taking the easy way out, Lisa. It's time for a fight, and it could be your last stand."

"You have a point," Lisa conceded. "I *did* feel more comfortable with the idea of not finding work once I knew I had a departure date."

"You're staying in Dubai if that's what you really want. Your competition is weak, they will give up and think about plan B. Not you. It's time to dig deep. Your sales circle is weak, and you've got to find a solution. If you just stay at the same level for the next two weeks, you might as well leave today."

"So what do you suggest I do?" asked Lisa.

"That's for you to decide; I'm not here to tell you what to do. You've left a life raft, that's fine; you now have a crazy deadline. Now count your other ships and burn them. Embrace a tiny bit more pain now that you're only five miles away from the finish line.

"All you need is one great interview. Just one. And you can generate interviews. You have a good resume and many ways to get employers to read it. The only thing left in the equation is courage. Burn your ships, or they will cause you to fail."

Lisa heard a mobile ringtone in the background. It wasn't hers, so it had to be the coach's.

"I gotta go, Lisa. I know you can do this. Let me know how it goes, okay?"

And just like that, the Three Circles Coach hung up. Lisa never knew what to expect from his calls.

"Burn my ships..." she mused out loud. "Burn my ships... Think, Lisa, think... What would I do if I were stuck here with no plan B?"

The first thing that came to her mind was that Sabrina could lend her some money, of course. 'I could hire the Three Circles Coach again,' she thought, 'and give this last round a proper fight.' Going into debt with Sabrina again was a bearable pain, considering her renewed vision.

The bit of money she had left in her account would be solely for her groceries and mobile bill. She knew that DEWA, the main utility provider in Dubai, would not cut off her electricity if she didn't pay that month. It wasn't great receiving warnings, but it was a mild discomfort compared to the prospect of leaving Dubai.

As for her car loan, she could sell her car, which might even get her extra cash if she did it well. 'Youssef can help me write an ad for my car, and I'll use the extra cash to pay for my next rent, or... no, I can try to negotiate my notice with my landlord now, and share a flat with cheaper rent and more flexibility.'

"Why didn't I think about all this before?" she wondered aloud, before quietly singing, "*Burn, baby burn...*" under her breath.

As always when Lisa needed to put a plan together, she grabbed her note-book:

1. SPEAK TO SABRINA ABOUT BORROWING MONEY FOR THE COACH'S PACKAGE AND TO YOUSSEF ABOUT THE AD TO SELL MY CAR FOR AS MUCH MONEY AS POSSIBLE (AND ASAP).

2. SPEAK TO MY LANDLORD → TELL HIM THE TRUTH; I LOST MY JOB AND I WON'T BE ABLE TO PAY MY RENT. (EXPECT THAT HE KEEPS MY DEPOSIT → BUT I'LL RECOUP THE LOSS WITH CHEAPER/MORE FLEXIBLE FLATSHARE.)

3. PURCHASE THE COACH'S PACKAGE.

4. FIND WORK BEFORE MY DEPARTURE DATE OR FACE AN IMPOSSIBLE CHOICE.

Whether she left or stayed in Dubai, Lisa realized that she had to sell her car and speak to her landlord anyway. But the third and the fourth point made her feel like the men in Tariq ibn Ziyad's army. She had to make it happen fast, and she knew that once she purchased the coach's package, she would be at the point of no return.

Later that day, Sabrina was thrilled Lisa had decided to climb back into the ring. "It's the first time I've heard someone so happy to lend me money," Lisa joked, and Sabrina assured her that Youssef would be writing a great ad that evening.

Her conversation with the landlord was far from pleasant, but she highlighted the fact that he treated her fairly and it wouldn't be fair for her to ask for a delayed payment.

The landlord understood that, but decided to keep her deposit never-theless to cover up for her short notice. The two agreed that Lisa could leave anytime in the next two weeks, but no later.

After that, Lisa was finally back in front of her computer. She sent an email to the coach, asking him if he would be free to start tomorrow, once Sabrina's transfer hit her account.

The Three Circles Coach replied with a simple, *'Yes! Glad you've decided to fight. Let's speak tomorrow at 9 AM your time.'*

The rest of her evening was spent searching for new roles online, visible and hidden, but it seemed not much had changed in less than a day. There were no new roles being advertised, and it was a daunting realization.

She wasn't sure what to expect from the Three Circles Coach, or if her plan would even work.

But despite everything else, Lisa went to bed more excited than anxious. She had no clue how all this would end. '*I think I've gone mad,*' she thought.

She was scared, but somehow... it felt great.

1st Booster Shot: The Follow-Up Process

At 9 AM the following morning, the Three Circles Coach called as agreed.

"Good morning, Lisa!"

"Good morning, coach."

"We have a lot to talk about, so let's get right into it."

"You know I haven't purchased the package yet. I'll be doing that at lunch time, is that okay?"

"Of course, I trust you."

"Thank you."

"So, first things first. Do you have any interviews planned in the next few days?"

"Not yet, but I'm working on it."

"So that's what I want our session today to be about. Let's see if we can beef up your marketing circle to put all the chances on our side."

"Okay," agreed Lisa. "But I don't think much more could be done."

"We'll see about that. Would you like to start by telling me where you're at with your marketing efforts?"

"Sure."

Lisa updated the Three Circles Coach on everything she had discovered and implemented from her own research online and Youssef's advice. When Lisa finished outlining her marketing strategy, she truly sounded like a CEO marketing her services.

She also showed him her work-in-progress spreadsheet, which the coach seemed particularly interested in.

"You've done some in-depth work. I'm sure your competition doesn't do five percent of what you're already doing. I also love the fact that you're sending your application to several decision-makers directly and that you're tracking your open rates. That's very smart."

"Thank you. I'm not sure much more can be done beyond this, though," said Lisa.

"The answer will be on your spreadsheet, actually. Please let me have a look."

"Sure."

After a few seconds, the Three Circles Coach delivered the verdict.

"Your search is about 30 percent effective," he declared.

"What do you mean?" asked Lisa, bewildered.

"Looking at your spreadsheet, the majority of your contacts are not opening your emails. In fact, if the information you filled up on your spreadsheet is correct, either they opened your email and asked you for an interview, which is **less than five percent**.

"Or, they opened your email and rejected your application, which represents **25 percent**. *Or,* you are ignored, and that's **roughly 70 percent**. What are you doing about that?"

"I tried to change the subject line, but it hasn't worked. I think my emails are going to their spam."

"Or maybe the email addresses are wrong, or they're on holiday. Either way, I want you to add two columns to your spreadsheet. 'Last follow-up date' and 'last follow-up email.' It's time you have a follow-up process in place," announced the coach.

"Are you sure I won't sound desperate?"

"Not if it's done properly. In my experience, job seekers have 70 to 95 percent of their applications ignored. And do you know what they do about these?"

"Nothing?"

"Exactly. They wait and hope for the best. Meanwhile, employers forget about them and job seekers get frustrated and lose motivation because they don't hear back." He sounded a bit pointed there.

Lisa cleared her throat. "What if I just wind up annoying them?"

"That's why the majority of job seekers don't have a proper follow-up process: *fear*," commented the Three Circles Coach. "Their mind makes up imaginary scenarios that may never happen. It usually starts with '*what if?*' Fear is responsible for more failures and lost opportunities than anything else in the world."

"But it could happen, couldn't it?"

"Lisa, let's think about this rationally for a second. Do you actually see an employer receiving your follow-up and saying '*What?! How dare she follow up? Let's disqualify her immediately!*'"

Lisa laughed at how ridiculous it sounded. "No," she replied. "Of course not."

"So what's the worst that can happen?"

"He can reject my application, I guess, but in that case my profile wouldn't have been suitable anyway. I get it, coach."

"That's right. Your job is to move these ignored applications towards the *'yes'* or *'no'* status."

"What if no one replies to my follow-ups?"

"You send another one a few days later."

"So, when should I stop sending follow-up emails?"

"When you get a definitive 'yes' or 'no'. Otherwise, **never**."

In Lisa's mind, waiting for a reply allowed her to keep some hope. But the Three Circles Coach was clearly anti-waiting. When his protégé didn't respond, the Three Circles Coach added, "Lisa, the only people who can stop your follow-up emails are employers. All they have to do is to reply to you with a 'yes,' 'no,' or 'wait a little longer.'

"It's your job to follow up if you really want the role. It's their job to reply to your email or face your follow-up process."

"Why can't employers and recruiters just reply to each application?" Lisa grumbled.

"Because they're not accountable to job seekers, they're accountable to their bosses and recruitment objectives. They get assessed for meeting those objectives, not giving feedback to everyone.

"Although ATS's and technology make it easier nowadays to update the application status of each candidate, only a few companies actually realize the importance of that process for their brand."

"So, companies don't care about updating all job applicants."

"They mildly care. Look, they're not the enemy here. Somehow employers and recruiters got comfortable with the fact that everytime they didn't update a candidate, the latter understood that he was not selected for the role. It's always been implicit."

"So why shouldn't I wait, then?"

"Waiting is the employer's job; your job is to get results. The more of those you get, the more opportunities you get. The challenge on your spreadsheet is that you're not crossing things out. Every job application stays and stares at you, reminding you that things are not moving. That's bad for your morale.

"You want to cross things out and replace the old with the new. **Progress creates motivation.** Don't allow things to stall, or you'll think nothing is moving and employers are not recruiting, and the market sucks blablabla..."

As usual, Lisa was taking notes:

I MUST HAVE A FOLLOW-UP PROCESS.

I WILL NOT STOP FOLLOWING UP UNTIL I GET A YES OR A NO.

THE WORST THAT CAN HAPPEN IS THAT I GET A NO, NOBODY WOULD DISQUALIFY ME FOR FOLLOWING UP ON MY APPLICATION.

THE NAME OF THE GAME IS TO GET YES'S AND NO'S SO I CAN CROSS OUT THE NO'S AND KEEP MOVING WITH NEW APPLICATIONS.

MOTIVATION IS PROGRESS. I AM RESPONSIBLE FOR MY OWN MOTIVATION.

WAITING WILL GIVE ME AN IMPRESSION OF STANDSTILL AS THE LIST OF APPLICATIONS GROWS AND WILL ULTIMATELY KILL MY MOTIVATION.

WAITING WILL INCREASE THE CHANCES OF EMPLOYERS FORGETTING ABOUT ME.

As she wrote it down, she had a thought:

"How appropriate do you think it would be if I started telling everyone I follow up with that I'll be leaving the country soon?"

"I think you should, but I wouldn't put it as you *leaving* the country because it could make employers think you'd no longer be able to come back. Perhaps it would be better to mention that you'd be going away for two or three weeks."

"That's great," said Lisa. "That's long enough to disturb a recruitment process, but not long enough to be disqualified for not being available, especially if I give them warnings ahead of time.

"The key would be to *give* them an update on my situation instead of *asking* them for feedback; that will keep my 'customer service' circle working for me."

"I think you've got something there. I'd like you to prepare a sequence of follow-up emails with that key idea in mind. If your profile is interesting, they'll want to see you before you leave."

"Great. I'll do that as soon as we hang up."

"Then let's hang up now. It's important you rescue a few applications before they move on to another candidate."

Before hanging up, they agreed to meet at the same time the following day. Meanwhile, Lisa dove straight into it. She had some shaking up to do.

Keeping the three circles in mind, she knew that her email should tend towards helping, informing, and updating employers, as opposed to the selfish reason of trying to get feedback. '*I need to keep in mind my customer service circle,*' she thought.

Using her possible departure as a reason for following up made her not feel desperate. In fact, with a solid reason, following up was completely legitimate.

After an hour, she was able to write three follow up templates:

FLW UP #1: 1 WEEK AFTER JOB APPLICATION - FWD PREVIOUS EMAIL + RESUME → Change the subject line to:

RE: Attn: [first name last name] - [job title] role

Dear [hiring/line manager's name],

I hope this email finds you well!

As I'll soon be traveling for 3 weeks, I was wondering if you had a chance to review my job application for the role of XXXX. *(You will find my application with my resume attached below.)*

The job description completely aligns with my profile, as this is exactly what I have been doing for the past XXXX years, mainly at [company name #1], [company name #2], and [company name #3].

I hope we have a chance to organize a face-to-face interview before my departure, as I'm sure it will be more effective than via Skype/Phone.

Please do not hesitate if you require any further information for the time being.

Thank you in advance,

[Your name]
[Your Mobile Number]
www.linkedin.com/in/firstname-lastname

FLW UP #2: 3 DAYS AFTER FLW UP #1 - FWD SAME PREVIOUS EMAIL + ATTACH YOUR RESUME.

Dear [hiring/line manager's name],

I hope you won't mind this reminder for my email below. As my departure date approaches, is there any additional information I can provide to help you in your decision-making process?

Should you decide to invite me for an interview, do you prefer that it happens before my departure in 10 days, or once I return?

I will be traveling for 3 weeks, and I want to ensure that this does not interfere with your hiring process.

Please let me know what suits you best.

Kind regards,

[Your name]
[Your Mobile Number]
www.linkedin.com/in/firstname-lastname

To download this template for free, please go to:
www.nameyourcareer.com/jobsearchtemplates

FLW UP #3: 2 DAYS AFTER FLW UP #2 - FWD SAME PREVIOUS EMAIL + ATTACH YOUR RESUME.

Dear [hiring/line manager's name],

Would you be so kind as to help me ensure that the e-mails below have been safely received? I do not want to be a bother and will gladly follow your directions.

I am an applicant for the XXXX role, and I believe my qualifications make me an ideal fit.

However, I will be traveling for three weeks starting on MM/DD/YYYY, so I wanted to ensure that your team has a chance to interview me before I depart.

Concerning my job application for the XXXX role, you will find that my profile is a great fit and that I have a successful track record in similar roles, as shown on my resume.

(I have reattached my resume for your review.)

Hoping to hear from you soon,

[Your name]
[Your Mobile Number]
www.linkedin.com/in/firstname-lastname

To download this template for free, please go to:
www.nameyourcareer.com/jobsearchtemplates

Lisa was quite pleased with her process and sent the templates to the coach for his review. She wasn't sure what a fourth follow-up email could look like, but she had enough to get started on her follow-ups.

She went ahead with the coach's recommendation of starting her follow-up process.

After an hour, she received a reply from the Three Circles Coach, where he advised the following email:

FLW UP #4: **CONTACT HIS BOSS (OR SOMEONE HIGHER) AND COPY THE PERSON THAT HAS BEEN UNRESPONSIVE.** (+attach your resume)

Dear [hiring/line manager's boss's name],

I was wondering if you could help?

I have been sending the below emails to Mr/Mrs/Ms. [first name last name], but I have received no response. I suspect that my e-mails may be landing in his/her spam folder, and I am unsure how else to contact him/her.

Would you be comfortable forwarding him/her the below emails, or providing me with a phone number I may be able to call to confirm that they've been received?

The role of [job title—ref#] is a striking match with my profile and I'm trying to ensure that my upcoming travel plans won't affect your recruitment process.

I will be leaving the country for three weeks starting on MM/DD/YYYY, so I wanted to ensure that Mr/Mrs/Ms. [first name last name] is aware of this, and has the opportunity to speak with me before I go.

Thank you so much in advance for your help,

Best regards,

[Your name]
[Your Mobile Number]
www.linkedin.com/in/firstname-lastname

To download this template for free, please go to:
www.nameyourcareer.com/jobsearchtemplates

Since it had already been one job application and three follow-up emails, Lisa liked the fact that she would be adding a new person on her follow-up list. The fact that the original decision-maker was kept on copy of the email she would send to his boss meant that she was not doing this behind his back and, at the same time, showed her resolve.

After reading the fourth template, she added the two columns to her spreadsheet that the Three Circles Coach recommended:

Job Title	Company	Job Ad URL	Applied online on	Sent to the following contact emails	Contact Job Title	Email / InMail Opened on	Last email FLW UP #	LAST FLW DATE
Sales Consultant	ACME CORP	www.jobboard.com /page1234	MM/DD/YR					

To download this template for free, please go to: www.nameyourcareer.com/jobsearchtemplates

As much as Lisa wished for an employer to reply that day, the only calls she received were from people interested in seeing her car. Things were moving quickly, and Lisa could feel it.

At the end of the day, after using all the search techniques she knew, she was only able to find one new role. But all in all, her chances relied on the follow-up emails.

"I hope it works," she sighed. "And quickly."

No longer busy, Lisa finally remembered she hadn't congratulated Leonard for his new role. After sending him a text message, he replied:

> Hi Lisa, I'm starting next week. I'm so stressed, LOL. What if they don't like me? It's actually great to feel this again. Thank you ever SO much Lisa.

2nd Booster Shot: Unsolicited Job Applications and Laser Focused Job Search

The following morning, Lisa's session with the Three Circles Coach started a few minutes early, as if he was as anxious as she was.

"How did it go yesterday?" he asked once the niceties were out of the way.

"Good, I guess."

"You don't seem convinced."

"I'm just a little worried, coach. After sending the first batch of follow-up emails and updating my spreadsheet, I looked to see what other jobs were published, and I only found one. It feels like I've already applied to everything."

"Oh, Lisa, you've only scratched the surface!" exclaimed the coach. "Up to 85 percent of jobs never get listed anywhere!"

"That many?" It sounded like an exaggeration to reassure her.

"Of course. Listing a job is often a last resort. Employers start by spreading the word through their network and asking for referrals."

"If you're talking about networking, I've already sent a resume to people I know, but nothing came of it."

"We will talk about networking soon. Have you thought about unsolicited job applications?"

Lisa thought for a moment.

"Not really. But who should I send them to?"

"There must be tons of Sales Managers and decision-makers in the software industry in Dubai," said the coach. "And that's definitely a point in common that you have with them, no?"

"Of course!" exclaimed Lisa. "I can find their email addresses to send them a job application, but they have no roles advertised. What email would you send them?"

"Almost the same as your job application email. Just change the first sentence."

Lisa could hear him typing, and he shared his screen to show a text file:

> Instead of:
> "My name is XXXXXXX and I have come across your job advert for the Business Development Executive role at (ABC Company)."
> → You can say:
> "My name is XXXXXXX and I have come across your profile on LinkedIn."

Lisa liked how simple it was. She couldn't resist conducting a quick LinkedIn search on the spot. With a quick glance, she estimated there were at least 100 contacts that had sales or business development leadership roles in the software industry. It was as if she found buried treasure. *'I'm sure a few have a vacancy,'* she thought.

"Are you still with me?" said the coach when she didn't respond.

"Yeah, sorry. I was just checking how many contacts I could reach through LinkedIn."

"I'm sure there are plenty. And in case your LinkedIn wouldn't show certain contacts, you can list all the companies in that industry and search for contacts from the company names.

"Remember, you have a solid point in common with these companies. They won't need to train you much; your skills are very much transferable."

"It sounds great, but..." said Lisa suddenly realizing something: "I have not subscribed to a LinkedIn Premium account, so chances are I will soon reach LinkedIn's free limit and I won't be able to search new decision makers to send job applications to. Do you have any hack around that?" she asked, regretting that she hadn't asked Youssef earlier.

"There sure is!" Said the coach much to Lisa's surprise. "Log out from LinkedIn and go on Google, then type the following phrase on the search box." She heard him typing as he was saying this:

site:ae.linkedin.com (HR OR Human OR "Talent Acquisition" OR Recruitment) AND (CRM OR "Conference Call" OR "Software")

"What is this?"

"It's a phrase you can type on Google. The 'ae' just in front of linkedin.com forces Google to only show you people located specifically in the United Arab Emirates. You can change this by using any country code.

As she pasted the search on Google, she found a myriad of HR contacts in companies that she hasn't seen before, with most of them in her industry.

As she clicked on these contacts, she noticed that she had access to their general profile without being logged into LinkedIn, which meant that she could try to find their email ID without the risk of reaching her free limit.

"Wow... thank you." said Lisa, figuring she could also find line managers and heads of departments by simply replacing the words in the first bracket, the model being self-explanatory.

"You're welcome," said the coach. "While we're on that topic, try to use different words when you search for jobs online, especially with the job bot tool you're using on messenger. What keywords do you normally type?"

"'Business development,' 'sales,' or 'account management,'" replied Lisa, "and it works."

"I'm sure it does, but you're still competing with anyone in these areas when you do that. What if you focus your search on something more specific, like 'software sales' or 'conference call?'"

"I hadn't thought of that," said Lisa, trying a few searches as she was speaking.

"This is called a laser focused search; that's how you eliminate even more competition."

Lisa was reading the search results.

"Wait a minute, I've never seen these jobs before..."

"There you go," said the coach. "And while you're at it, has your LinkedIn profile been seen by anyone recently?"

"Quite often since I updated my profile to reflect the work we've done on my resume," Lisa replied.

"Good. Then every day, make sure you send the following template to the ones that look like recruiters or decision-makers," said the coach as he was typing:

> Hi [first name],
>
> I noticed that you viewed my profile yesterday. Thank you. I'm always open to hearing about a great opportunity. Also, if I can be helpful to you with any of your searches, please don't hesitate to ask.
>
> Kind regards,
> Lisa.

"I found this template in an article from Kat Boogaard, and I've been recommending it since then to all my clients. You can send them this by InMail messages or as a note once you invite them to connect with you," explained the coach.

"That's great, thank you," said Lisa.

"Sure, anytime," he replied, "there's one last thing I wanted to discuss with you today Lisa..."

She was all ears sensing this was going to be important.

"How do you keep yourself motivated during your job search?"

"Well, that's the thing that has been going up and down lately." She replied. "Usually if I have interviews or phone calls, I get a boost of motivation, but if I hear nothing for too long, I certainly start feeling down..."

"Sounds to me that your motivation is dependent upon external factors, isn't it?"

"Well, yes of course, getting phone calls or job interviews just shows progress. And I remember you said that motivation is the feeling of progress, wasn't it?"

"Progress generates motivation, yes, but my problem is that you've handed the key to your motivation to recruiters and employers and that is a dangerous game to play. I think you have already experienced it... You must own your motivation." he added.

"I see what you mean, but how can I stay motivated if I am getting no results?"

"Well, by not focusing on the results of your job applications. Instead, focus on the strength of your marketing funnel."

"My marketing funnel?"

"Yes." said the coach as he shared his screen, revealing a funnel with different stages.

"If you focus on tracking your numbers week by week, your attention and therefore your energy will go towards something you can control. How would you feel if you were to see that every week more and more employers are opening your emails?"

"It'd feel great," said Lisa as she was starting to understand how to be motivated by her own process. "So what you're saying is that it's the results that I create through my applications and my follow up emails that I should focus on; not whether or not someone would get back to me, is that right?"

"Absolutely!" exclaimed the coach, "it really doesn't matter who gets back to you, as long as you're working on your conversion rates from one stage in the funnel to the next." He added. "The more your email tracker will show that your job application emails are being opened, the more you'll get those shots of motivation.

"The more people read your resume week in week out, the more that motivation is sustained, and the more you unfold your follow up process, the better your conversion rate towards getting replies from employers. And so on and so forth... do you see what I mean? You are the master of your own motivation."

"Completely," replied Lisa, "but it's just an extra pain to track things..."

"Well, you're going to have to choose between two evils then Lisa... Either you track your numbers, measure your performance and try to generate progress from your own process; or hope that employers will call you enough times to keep you motivated."

Lisa thought for a moment. "I see your point, coach. But I've made a decision to fight now, whether I'm motivated or not."

"That's good to hear," commented the coach "but if you go demotivated for too long, your attitude, energy, body language and tone of voice will betray you during an interview. Make no mistake, you cannot feed your brain and heart with stress, anxiety, negativity, lack of confidence... etc. and at the same time expect your attitude to remain positive. You will always become your greatest emotion Lisa. I have seen it so many times. People 'not being themselves' during an interview and sounding too desperate for example...

"They get rejected and hate themselves for being like that. Most job seekers don't understand it, but that's the work of constant frustration, anxiety and stress over an extended period of time. Their attitude becomes their emotions and employers pick it up very easily during the interview stage.

"The worst thing is that it sometimes creates a vicious loop because the more they fail the few interviews they get, the more anxious and frustrated they are about their job search. And that cycle repeats itself indefinitely until luck strikes or the job seeker accepts something lower than what he is really worth. In more extreme cases, that cycle can put people into a very long period of unemployment where professionals no longer have the strength to fight, as it appears to them that the more they look for work, the more they get rejected. I call this phenomenon the *'job seeker's emotional cycle to hell'*"

Lisa couldn't help but think about Leonard and how it must have been so difficult to be trapped in that vicious cycle, while everyone would point fingers at you.

"That's why I want to warn you..." the coach continued "do not hand over the keys to your motivation to employers. They will disappoint you. Your own process should motivate you. And you can easily make this happen if you just track your performance. Like great athletes, put your attention on the match and the score, not on whether or not the NBA or the NFL will call you to offer you a contract. The real fight is always within Lisa, so be in the moment. Your power is always in the present."

The coach paused to allow Lisa to process this. Lisa assumed it was partly what happened during her previous interviews. Without knowing it, the fear of not finding a job and the frustration she had accumulated over months of job search, had become part of her. She also remembered what Sabrina said about her job search, that things only got better for her job search when Youssef and her got better. It was logical to her now. She hurried up writing before the coach continued:

I CAN'T SUBJECT MY MIND TO NEGATIVE THOUGHTS AND EMOTIONS
OVER AN EXTENDED AMOUNT OF TIME,
AND EXPECT MY ATTITUDE TO NOT BECOME NEGATIVE
AS WELL DURING JOB INTERVIEWS.

EMPLOYERS ARE AFRAID TO MAKE THE WRONG HIRING DECISION, AND IF I BRING MY OWN
FEARS TO THE TABLE, 2 NEGATIVES WILL NEVER GO TOGETHER.

"I see what you mean; I need to look after my mindset so that my energy and attitude are always at the highest level during interviews." she commented. "Thank you coach."

"You're welcome. I suggest we stop for today so you have time to send a few unsolicited job applications and start engaging with the people who are viewing your profile. What do you think?"

She agreed, and they decided to reconvene on the following day at 9:00 AM.

Lisa opened her Internet browser like a kid ripping through a birthday present. *'And I thought I had already done an in-depth job search!'*

In her notebook, she wrote the following:

UP TO 85% OF JOBS NEVER GET PUBLISHED/LISTED

LIST OUT ALL THE COMPANIES THAT RELATE TO MY INDUSTRY AND FIND THE DECISION-MAKERS ON LINKEDIN

CREATE A NEW TAB ON THE SPREADSHEET ENTITLED "UNSOLICITED"

SEND JOB APPLICATION EMAIL TAILORED TO AN UNSOLICITED JOB APPLICATION.

I NEED TO TRACK MY PROGRESS AND ALLOW MY PROCESS TO BE THE SOURCE OF MY OWN MOTIVATION!

I WILL NOT FALL INTO THE 'JOB SEEKER'S EMOTIONAL CYCLE TO HELL'!

Lisa prepared her unsolicited job application email template, as per the coach's recommendations.

Dear XXXXXXXXXX,

My name is Lisa Dutoit and I have come across your profile on LinkedIn.

I was wondering if you'd be interested in meeting with a young and ambitious Business Development Professional in the software industry who considers the following as the most important keys to my success:

- Relentless at exceeding my targets in every role I've had.
- Non-stop cold calling attitude and weekly client meetings.
- Effective at increasing repeat business from my customers.

I have attached my resume, where you will find my achievements in these areas throughout my 3 years of experience in the **Software Sales Sector**.

If you feel these achievements are in line with your expectations, I would be eager to meet you to discuss how I could add value to (ABC Company).

In the meantime, please feel free to call me should you have any questions, of course. My mobile number is 050 670 0000.

Thank you in advance for the time you will dedicate to my application.

Best Regards,
Lisa Dutoit
050 670 0000
https://linkedin.com/lisa-dutoit

The Art of Networking

"Hey, coach"

"Morning, Lisa. How was your day yesterday?"

"Alright. Nothing new when it comes to my follow-ups or my unsolicited applications, but I'm pushing along."

"Just keep it up," said the coach, unfazed by Lisa's lack of results.

"You don't seem too concerned," commented Lisa

"You just need a few days to build momentum. Besides, I'm sure you haven't sent unsolicited applications to every company in the software industry."

"No, there are over a hundred."

"Let me know once you send your second follow-up emails, and keep it up with the unsolicited applications," repeated the coach before he swiftly moved on. "Today, I'd like to review your networking activities."

"Well, apart from when I sent my resume to my friends, I haven't really done any networking. Considering the results I got, I don't think my network is good enough for me to rely on it."

The Three Circles Coach remained silent for a few seconds before he said, "Lisa, if you just sent your resume to your acquaintances hoping they'll take that risk towards their own friends and employers, you're being naive. Asking things from people seldom works if they don't see what's in it for them."

"How about the pleasure of helping a friend in need?" Lisa grumbled. "I would have done it for them."

"That's charity, not networking. And you're not part of their professional network out of friendship," the coach sighed.

"A professional network is like a private club for people who are ready to help one another professionally. For this to happen, you better have helped them before you ask for help yourself."

"So, I don't really have a professional network, since I haven't helped anyone find work?"

"That's not what I said. I think you don't have a reliable network because you've never cared about building one," explained the coach.

"I'm not sure how I could have built my network, other than just knowing people..."

"By supporting the people you want in your network. Contacts, advice, information, and so on. By using your 'customer service' circle."

Lisa was silent, mulling over the point for a moment.

"So, I don't have a proper professional network. Now what?"

"Build one, of course. Better late than never."

"Do you really think it's necessary?"

"I don't know about you, but if I had a job to fill, I would always trust the recommendations of people I know, rather than hoping the random applicants I'll get online would fit the role."

"Okay, I get it," sighed Lisa. "But doesn't building a network take time?"

"Of course, but there are some hacks that I'll be sharing with you. First, let's define 'networking.' Do you have any idea?"

Instead of guessing, Lisa googled the term 'networking' and found a definition from Ivan Misner in an article he wrote. She read the definition out.

"The process of developing and activating your relationships to increase your business, enhance your knowledge, expand your sphere of influence, or serve the community."

"Great. Now let me ask you something. What are the two conditions you need for your networking activities to work?"

"Two conditions?" Lisa repeated dubiously.

"Simple: the two conditions you'll need to keep in mind for being effective at reaching out to someone for the first time. Firstly, you need at least one point in common with the person you're approaching. Secondly, you must give something before you ask for anything."

"I don't think I'm in a position to give much," Lisa pointed out.

"Of course you are. You can introduce people to one another, you can share some of your expertise, you can do someone a favor, you can remember someone's birthday or special date, you can even compliment or praise someone.

"All these things cost nothing and take nothing from you, but they require you take a genuine interest in what others want."

"I think I understand why people hate networking. Most people feel like beggars, asking for things from people, and to add insult to injury, they feel rejected when they don't get it.

"But what you're saying is completely different: you're advocating that developing a network is about helping others, by taking a genuine interest in the people I want in my network. But how do you switch to asking them something?"

"Thanks to the principle of reciprocity," he replied. "It's the principle that when you do something for someone, he will feel compelled to reciprocate in one way or in another. For example, a waiter who takes special care of his customers will be more likely to receive tips.

"Same thing with great employers when they really look after their employees, they can expect more loyalty and engagement from them. Or when you offer a birthday gift to someone, that person will be likely to give you something back for your birthday."

"I get it," Lisa assured him as she took notes:

MY JOB SEARCH CAN HUGELY BENEFIT FROM NETWORKING SINCE UP TO 85% OF JOBS ARE NEVER LISTED ANYWHERE

THE 2 CONDITIONS TO MEET BEFORE SOMEONE CAN POTENTIALLY HELP ME ARE:

1. HAVE A POINT/A CONTACT IN COMMON WITH THE PERSON

2. HELP THEM FIRST, IN A WAY THAT IS MEANINGFUL TO THEM (AND OFTEN INEXPENSIVE TO ME → THINK CONNECTING PEOPLE, SHARING INFORMATION, EXPERTISE, RECOGNITION, PRAISE, ETC.)

IF I SPEND TIME HELPING OTHERS, I COULD COUNT THEM IN MY NETWORK AND THE PRINCIPLE OF RECIPROCITY COULD KICK IN IF I NEED HELP FROM THEM.

"Did you say you have some hacks for me?" she asked when she finished taking notes.

"Sure," the coach obliged. "Let's begin with your four F's," he suggested. "They stand for: *Family, Friends, Family of Friends,* and *Friends of Family.*

"The idea here is to do an inventory of their network before you ask for anything. The purpose of this is to make an anonymous list of your four F's first degree network in Dubai, by listing only their job titles and the industry they work in."

"But why would they give me that? What's in it for them?"

"Great question. The deal is that if they add their contacts in Dubai anonymously on a spreadsheet, they would get the master spreadsheet with everyone of your four F's contacts in return. Do you see the value now?"

"Absolutely. That adds up to a lot of contacts for not a lot of effort. My issue is that you said these contacts would be anonymous on the spreadsheet. Only their job titles and the industry they're in would be listed, right?"

"Right. They wouldn't have their names or their contact details, but the master spreadsheet would allow them to know who input them and then your four F's could contact one another to get introduced accordingly."

"Got it," said Lisa "What would this spreadsheet look like?"

"Here's the template that I send to my private clients," he offered, sharing his screen.

Name of the 4 F contact	Job Title	Mobile #	Email	Job Title of the people he knows in Dubai	Industry they work in
4 F #1 The Three Circles Coach	Career & Business Coach	+971 XX XXX XXXX	help@name yourcareer.com	Head of Engineering	Defense
				Logistics Coordinator	E-commerce
				Sales Manager	Pharma-ceutical
				Marketing Executive	Retail
				HR Officer	Banking
				CEO / Entre-preneur	Recruitment

To download this template for free, please go to:
www.nameyourcareer.com/jobsearchtemplates

The coach was silent as Lisa reviewed the spreadsheet.

"The idea is that you acquire everyone's top ten contacts in Dubai," explained the coach after a moment.

"Imagine if one of your four F's contacts was to add ten of his contacts, which would remain anonymous and thus confidential, then in exchange he could get 100 potential contacts once you share the master spreadsheet with ten of your four F's contacts. You can see how this could serve you and your four F's contacts."

"I do," she confirmed. "I'll definitely send this across to my friends."

"Great. But let me give you a tip that could change the result of this. Make sure you call them to explain the benefits of doing this. Don't just send an email or a message, it won't work. Remember, in order for this marketing tool to work, you've got to sell it."

"Sure. Now, suppose that one of the contacts I receive is of interest to me. Then what?"

"Then you ask the person you both know for an introduction. The idea is to see if you could organize a coffee or phone call. This is called an informational interview. They're used when you're trying to gather information about a specific topic, like the market, a career path, or anything that the other person is knowledgeable about.

"This puts the person you're interviewing in the position of being an expert. Obviously, make sure to offer your support should he need to be in touch with some of your contacts or anything else. That's how you'll start building a relationship, and ultimately grow your professional network."

Lisa didn't immediately reply, hastily scribbling down notes:

NETWORKING HACK #1:

1. CALL MY 4 F'S *(FAMILY—FRIENDS—FAMILY OF FRIENDS—FRIENDS OF FAMILY)* AND ASK THEM TO INPUT 10 CONTACTS OF THEIRS ON THE SPREADSHEET—ONLY MENTIONING THEIR JOB TITLE AND THE INDUSTRY THEY'RE IN.

2. MERGE EVERYONE'S SPREADSHEETS INTO A MASTERSHEET AND SEND IT BACK TO THEM.

THE 3 CIRCLES:

> ATTRACT/MARKETING: "RECEIVE DOZENS OF CONTACTS FROM MY 2ND DEGREE NETWORK FOR FREE THAT COULD HELP YOU IN YOUR BUSINESS, JOB SEARCH, AND / OR CAREER."
>
> SELL/CONVINCE: TELL MY FOUR 4 F'S THAT ALL THEY HAVE TO DO IS TO PUT 10 ANONYMOUS CONTACTS → RECEIVE 100 CONTACTS
>
> SERVE/CUSTOMER SERVICE: MERGE ALL SPREADSHEETS AND SEND MASTERSHEET TO ALL WHO PARTICIPATED.

"Is there any other networking hack?" Lisa asked once she finished writing.

"Sure," the coach obliged. "The second hack is something that many job seekers seldom explore. Tell me, how many people in Dubai have studied in the same school as you?"

"I have no idea."

"Well, how many people are there in Dubai who grew up in Virginia, like you did?"

"Not a clue."

"I could ask the same question about people that have worked in the same company as you. This is called common background, and you can find these people by doing a quick search on LinkedIn.

"With the search filters, you can select, for example, people who went to the same school as you and are located in the United Arab Emirates."

"But I don't necessarily know them. How would I approach them?"

"Of course you don't know them; the goal is to get to know them. Since you've already established that you have a point in common, now you can try to serve them in some capacity.

"Remember, the two conditions to build a network are to have a point in common and to serve them first. Your purpose is to secure an informational interview, not to ask them for a job."

"So how would you approach them?"

"Here's a template that some of my clients send via LinkedIn, I think the original template comes from an article from Lindsey Pollak."

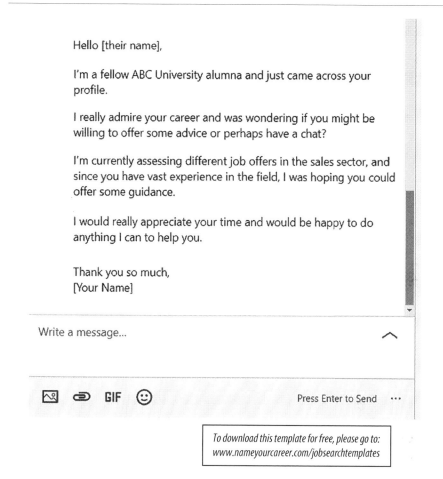

Hello [their name],

I'm a fellow ABC University alumna and just came across your profile.

I really admire your career and was wondering if you might be willing to offer some advice or perhaps have a chat?

I'm currently assessing different job offers in the sales sector, and since you have vast experience in the field, I was hoping you could offer some guidance.

I would really appreciate your time and would be happy to do anything I can to help you.

Thank you so much,
[Your Name]

Write a message...

GIF ☺   Press Enter to Send   ···

To download this template for free, please go to:
www.nameyourcareer.com/jobsearchtemplates

"Remember, recognizing someone's career is a great way to start this kind of relationship," he offered.

"But what if they don't reply?"

"Who cares? Remember to not be results-driven, Lisa. Just follow the recipe. Out of ten messages like these, some people will get back to you and some won't."

"I get it, it's a numbers game. I can't wait to try this out, thank you."

"You're welcome. Are you ready for the third hack?"

"Just a moment," she replied, before hastily taking notes:

NETWORKING HACK #2:

1. RUN A SEARCH ON LINKEDIN TO IDENTIFY PEOPLE WITH THE SAME BACKGROUND AS ME (SCHOOL, PLACE OR ORIGIN, COMPANIES WE WORKED FOR, ETC.) AND THAT CURRENTLY LIVE IN THE UAE.

2. SEND THEM THE TEMPLATE THE COACH SHOWED ME AND TRY TO SECURE INFORMATIONAL INTERVIEWS (PHONE OR FACE-TO-FACE)

"Okay, I'm ready."

"I call the next hack the 'Networking events hack,'" the coach explained.

"I think I'm already familiar with networking events. Going to networking events isn't really a hack, though."

"I know. The way you'll do it will be a hack. First, let's see how you can find networking events."

"Sure."

"You'll need to try different networking events in order to find one or a few that are valuable for you, so knowing how to find most networking events in your city is critical."

"I agree."

"An easy way to find them is via social media. Just go to a few prominent Facebook groups and ask for a recommendation on where you can find networking events in town and when they're happening. Meetup.com is also a great platform to start with.

"Each Meetup group focuses on a specific niche, so you can join any of them and meet new people face-to-face. But bear in mind, meetup events are not for networking, they're for gatherings. Once you go to a few, it'll be easy for you to start knowing the people that attend."

"I'm sure soon I'll have a list of events I can start going to. But honestly, there's a reason I haven't gone to any for a while," Lisa admitted. "There is so much competition, and for an introvert like me, it's even worse. Besides, I didn't like the needy atmosphere that the event I've been to had. It just made me feel I was in the same bag."

"Okay, so let's change the rules of the game a little bit," said the coach. "How about if you offer to volunteer at these events and help organizers?

"As one of the organizers, you could naturally be introduced to others as such, and you would be much more visible yourself. More importantly, you could approach key people by serving them like organizers do."

"I can definitely do that. Organizers tend to some of the most visible people in an event."

"That's right. But you'll still have to rehearse a proper elevator pitch. Do you have one already?"

Just the phrase 'elevator pitch' made Lisa anxious. "I've never had to prepare one. Do you have an example?"

"Sure," replied the coach. "Why don't we do a role play?"

"Okay," replied Lisa, taken off guard.

"Great. Let's suppose that you're a random person and I have no idea who you are."

"Okay."

"Rule number one," said the coach. "Be the first to take an interest in people. Now, let's say I've just introduced myself and asked your name, please go ahead and reply to me."

"I'm Lisa, hi. Nice to meet you."

"Hi, Lisa. Can I help you out with anything?"

"Well, I'm actually looking for a job."

"In what field?"

"In the Software Sales sector; I'm a business developer."

"Great! I actually have a friend who works for Blablabla Software Company. Not sure if he could help, but maybe he can connect you with people who can."

"That would be amazing, thank you."

"Now, Lisa..." the coach paused from the role play. "I'll take my phone and I'll send an email to my friend, Cc'ing you. You should receive the notification at the same time. Let's go back to the role play," he instructed.

"So, Lisa, I just sent an email to my friend and you should have received it, too." At the same time, an email notification from the Three Circles Coach popped up on her screen. It read as follows:

Hey John,

I hope you're well. I wanted to introduce you to Lisa (Cc'ed). I met her at a networking event recently and she happens to be in the same industry as you, working as a business developer.

I advised her to get in touch with you to see if the two of you could exchange some contacts.

Either way, I'll let you two get acquainted.

Speak soon,
The Three Circles Coach

"How did you write such a long email while you were talking?" Lisa asked, forgetting the scene for the moment.

"It's a template. I just replaced the blanks in the text," replied the coach. "How would that feel if you were at that event and you really received that email?"

"I would feel like you're honest and actually introduced me to someone. I actually would find it hard to just say thanks and leave after that. Can we go back to the role play?" asked Lisa.

The coach obliged easily. "Of course."

"*Thank you so much. Can I ask you what do you do?*"

"*I actually help companies save money on their IT projects.*"

"*So are you an IT Project Manager?*"

"Lisa, before you continue, did you notice how I introduced myself?"

"Yes, you said that you help companies save money on their IT project. It's not really a job title, it's a benefit statement for potential employers, which still makes me curious as to what job you do, but at the same time I'm also curious because I'd like to understand how you save money on IT projects."

"So you see, you probed further to know more, and that's where I wanted you to go. Because then you gave me permission to give you my elevator pitch."

"It felt pretty natural."

"Exactly. If it feels scripted or rehearsed, people will have their defenses up."

"So, how would you answer my question? I asked you if you were a project manager."

"OK, I will now deliver my four P's and my reason for coming to the event as my elevator pitch. The four P's are Past experience, then my Passion, followed by a recent Performance, and finally my Purpose today."

"So are you an IT Project Manager?"

"Yes, most of my background is in managing complex IT Projects; I've got around twelve years of experience. I've always had a knack for rescuing projects that were running late or out of budget. Right now, I've just finalized two projects that I conducted at the same time, where I helped the company save AED 1.2 Million in various resources.

"I actually came to this event to see who would want to achieve similar results with their IT projects. How many people do you know in the IT field?" The coach paused for a second. *"Do you see what I did there?"*

"Completely. Your past helped me understand how senior you are. Your passion added positive energy about your profile. Your performance was a result you delivered for your previous employer. And finally your purpose was your reason for being here."

"Did you notice how I made my purpose sound?"

"It was great! You didn't say you're looking for work, you said you're looking for people that want the same results as your previous employer. And then you asked me how many people I knew in the IT field, which offered me an opportunity to connect you with a contact of mine in the IT field."

"Spot on."

At that moment, Lisa's phone vibrated on the desk. It was one of those landline numbers.

"Go ahead and take it, we're done for today anyway," the coach offered. "You can mute your microphone if you want, and I'll wait to see if you have any questions."

"Sure," said Lisa, as she rushed to pick up before the other person hung up.

Her microphone was still on, but she didn't mind the coach listening.

Organizing an Interview the Right Way

"Hello, Lisa speaking."

"Hi there, Lisa, my name is Viviane. I'm a talent acquisition officer here at *Louis Vuittel*. The reason for my call is that we came across your profile on salescareers.ae and your profile matches a role that we currently have in one of our stores.

"Would you be free for an interview tomorrow at 9:00 AM with the store manager?"

Lisa hated the sound of it. She did not want to go back to the retail sector, but at the same time, she *was* out of work.

"Tomorrow at 9:00 AM," she repeated. "Yes, that should be fine."

"Perfect."

"Will you be sending me the address of the store?"

"It will be at our headquarters, actually. I'll send you a location map now. Can you please confirm your attendance once you receive my email?"

"With pleasure, I look forward to it."

After the two hung up, Lisa opened her inbox and nearly forgot the Three Circles Coach was still listening.

"Lisa?"

"Oh, right, sorry. I completely forgot that you were still here."

"Not a problem," replied the coach. "Was that an interview request?"

"Yes, it was," sighed Lisa.

"You don't sound very positive about this," he observed.

"Well, it's in retail; it's to go back to selling in a store. I don't think I'll be attending. There's no point wasting my time or theirs."

"Interesting," mused the coach. "Why do you feel it would be a waste of time?"

"I'd rather leave Dubai than work in a store again. It would feel like I'm back to square one."

"But you're not going back to selling at a store. You'd just be going for an interview to meet people."

"Yes, but what's the point if I already know I'm not going back to that career path?"

"Okay, please listen carefully," said the coach, almost sounding solemn. **"An interview is either a lesson or a blessing.** You either use it as practice or you get a great job.

"Besides, you'll be speaking to people who have an overview of all the roles available at that company. Don't you think it could be great to see if you could fit any other role they have?"

"I suppose you're right," sighed Lisa.

"You go to *every* interview you can. You need practice, and you don't know how your meeting will turn out," said the Three Circles Coach.

"Okay, I agree."

"However, I'm concerned with something," said the coach. Lisa frowned in anticipation. "Why have you agreed to go to an interview tomorrow? Do you think you'll have enough time to prepare for it?"

"I know it's a little bit short notice," said Lisa, "but I'm always worried that if I don't say yes to what they suggest, I would be starting off our relationship on the wrong foot."

"What would definitely start your relationship off on the wrong foot is if you go there unprepared. Were your last two interviews also last minute?"

"Yes—no—I mean, I've prepared as much as I can, but I have accepted interviews for the next day, yes."

"Hmm..."

"What?"

"Lisa, I would like you to call the person again and give yourself at least two days to prepare. Do you know who will be interviewing you?"

"No, not really."

"Do you know if this would be a panel interview or a one-on-one interview?"

"No," said Lisa, realizing that she couldn't really prepare well if she didn't know all of the info in advance.

"Will she be sending you the job description?"

"I'm sure I can find it on their website."

"No, that's a job advert. A job description is often much more complete than the job advert. Do you think it would be interesting for you to have the full job description, and therefore as much info about the role as possible?"

That was when Lisa realized how her job interviews had been starting off on the wrong foot straight away. "Don't you think that if I ask her all these questions, she'd be irritated?"

"No, I think she would see you're taking this seriously: that you're in this game to win it. And if you feel that she's irritated because you're asking these basic questions, then that's one bad point for them."

"What do you mean?"

"You are assessing them as well, aren't you?"

"In a way, I guess."

"If you just focus on being liked by them, how can you truly join a company that deserves you? You've got to have some standards. You must be assessing them, too. And if things don't work out because they're not up to your standards, then you've probably done yourself a huge favor.

"The job search will end either way, but you will bear the fruits of your decision, so make sure it's the right one for your career."

"So we're both assessing one another."

"Of course. If you feel they're getting irritated by your questions now, how do you feel it will be if you were to work there?"

"You're right. I shouldn't be afraid to ask them important questions. It's just that job interviews drain you, coach. I just want the right one; it's not really fun to go through them."

"Not fun?" repeated the coach. "That is such a strange way to describe this," he commented. "Let me tell you what's not fun: working for a lousy boss in a toxic environment, and having to come up with excuses as to why you're leaving this job yet again during your next job interviews," the coach continued.

"Lisa, a job search is maybe one of the biggest career opportunities you could ever have. Think about it, you're in a position to benchmark different companies, and by that the sectors they're in, the culture they have, and the potential boss you will have. There is nothing else that can give you that much choice in your career."

"You're right," Lisa sighed. "I better call that lady back to see what other info I can get."

"Sure, go ahead. And one last thing," said the coach. "Do you have any number you can call to notify them in case you're late or lost?"

"I won't be."

"I hope not, but you can't predict a disturbance on the metro or an accident on the road, can you?"

"I suppose you're right, but then I could call the company's general number, no?"

"These numbers are most of the time saturated with calls. Besides, that's not the real reason I ask my clients to secure a direct phone number in HR."

"What is it, then?"

"It's for after the interview. You want to be able to call them directly and follow up with them, otherwise you'll be stuck at following up by email. You'll soon thank yourself for getting these numbers, while others are waiting and hoping they might hear back soon."

"Got it, I'll ask now."

She muted her microphone and quickly called back Viviane, asking every question she could think of, until she was positive that she had wrung every bit of information out of Viviane as she could.

When Lisa hung up, she had much more information about the role at hand. She unmuted her microphone with the coach.

"Coach, I'm done."

"Great. How did it go?"

"So far so good. The lady I spoke to was helpful. I will be meeting the head of talent acquisition, John Macalister.

"Viviane said that she'll be sending me the full job description via email in a few minutes, and her mobile number in case I need anything. But the one thing I haven't done is to postpone it. I felt bad, since I already said yes."

"That's fine. Just try to give yourself more time next time to prepare."

"I will. But honestly, I really won't fight for this interview. It's not what I want to do at all."

"Then why do you want to go?"

"But you told me—"

"I told you to go for the interview, not to fail at it," interrupted the coach. "Either you go to convince them that you can really help them, or you can stay in tomorrow."

"I'm confused. I do not want this job, coach."

"Then you won't accept it if it's offered to you. But right now, it's not on the table. If you want to have the choice to say yes or no, you've got to do well tomorrow."

"Okay...?"

"Lisa, what I want for you tomorrow is that they fall in love with you, so much so that they would offer you something more in line with your expectations."

"Is that even possible?"

"Of course it is. It happens all the time, and the person that is interviewing you is aware of all the roles that there are," replied the coach.

"But how can I bring up the fact that I would not want this role?"

"Towards the end of the interview, when they're in love with you already."

Lisa chuckled. "How would you bring it up?"

"Towards the end, you can say, *'John, I would like to be honest with you. When Viviane called me, I wasn't sure I wanted to attend an interview for a role in a store, as this is really not where I could add the most value.*

"I don't regret coming to meet you and have a glimpse at how great the environment at Louis Vuittel is. Now that you know me a little better, are there any other roles that you feel could better fit my profile?'"

"I don't think they'll be upset if I say that," Lisa conceded.

"They won't. And if they are, that's one bad point for them, not you, remember?"

"I do," said Lisa. "Thank you."

"Now let me tell you a secret that experienced employers use to select the right candidate," said the coach. "Candidates are often on their best behavior during job interviews, that's normal. But experienced recruiters know that candidates can't remain at their best behavior on a daily basis if they were to join their company.

"So what employers will do is take that best behavior and say to themselves, 'ok, what if I only get 70 percent of that on a daily basis? Or what if something they discovered is, say, 30 percent worse? Would that still be in line with what I'm looking for?' So if they notice something wrong, they will magnify it because they know that little something they discovered was on a day you wanted to show your best self."

"Well, I think I'm starting to see why I didn't do well at my last job interviews," mused Lisa.

"I'm sure you are. Now, can I ask you a favor?"

"Of course."

"I need you to send me all the questions that were asked to you during your previous interviews. Once you do that, I would like to organize a mock interview, where I will be the interviewer and you the interviewee. Do you think you can send me all the questions in the next half hour?"

"Sure, but I don't think I will remember all the questions..."

"That's okay," said the coach, evidently not in the mood to debate. "We'll talk about all this in an hour. I have to run now."

Once the call ended, Lisa went straight to her notebook:

I SHOULD GO TO EVERY INTERVIEW, FOR EACH ONE IS EITHER TRAINING OR A BLESSING.

BEFORE ACCEPTING AN INTERVIEW, I NEED TO MAKE SURE I HAVE ENOUGH TIME TO PREPARE $\longrightarrow$ 2 DAYS?

- ASK FOR THE LOCATION MAP AND FIND THE PLACE ON GOOGLE MAPS BEFOREHAND TO ASSESS TRAVEL TIME.

- ASK FOR THE JOB DESCRIPTION (MORE COMPLETE THAN THE JOB ADVERT)

- FIND OUT WHAT TYPE OF INTERVIEW IT WILL BE. (ONE-ON-ONE, GROUP INTERVIEW, PSYCHOMETRIC TEST, ETC.)

- FIND OUT WHO WILL BE INTERVIEWING ME AND HIS TITLE

- ASK FOR A NUMBER IN CASE I'M LOST $\longrightarrow$ WILL BE VALUABLE WHEN I WANT TO FOLLOW UP AFTER MY INTERVIEW.

I SHOULD ALWAYS GO TO THE INTERVIEW WITH A WINNING MINDSET. THE IDEA IS THAT THEY "FALL IN LOVE" WITH MY PROFILE.

ONCE THEY DO, I WILL BE HONEST WITH THEM AND TELL THEM THAT THE ROLE AT HAND IS NOT MY FIRST CHOICE AND PROBE FOR SOMETHING ELSE.

$\longrightarrow$ I HAVE NOTHING TO LOSE!

IMPORTANT: AFTER EVERY INTERVIEW, WRITE DOWN ALL THE QUESTIONS ASKED AND CONSIDER BETTER ANSWERS (EACH INTERVIEW IS TRAINING FOR THE NEXT ONE $\longrightarrow$ BUILD A LIBRARY OF INTERVIEW QUESTIONS FOR MY TARGET JOB)

After that, while trying to compile the questions from her job interviews, Lisa was worried she had forgotten some. She wished she had done this exercise as soon as she got home. Nevertheless, she decided to categorize each one into one of the five S's categories Andy told her about.

Intro questions:

- ❖ Tell me a little bit about you.
- ❖ What do you know about our company?
- ❖ What brings you to the job interview today?

S1: Stability:

- ❖ Why are you looking to change jobs?
- ❖ According to your resume, you didn't complete five months at *Watch the Time*, what happened?

S2: Skills:

- ❖ Can you tell me about your daily tasks and KPIs at *Cloudcom*?
- ❖ Can you describe what a standard day looked like?
- ❖ Your resume seems to say that you haven't sold CRM solutions before.

S3: Soft Skills:

- ❖ Can you describe a meeting where you had really difficult people to persuade?

S4: Successes:

- ❖ What was your monthly or quarterly target?
  → How did you do with your targets?

- ❖ What would you say is your proudest professional achievement?

S5: Salary:

- ❖ What are your salary expectations?

Towards the end of the interview, employers usually ask:

- ❖ Do you have any questions?

After doing that, Lisa decided it was time to send the second follow-up email to all her contacts. Time was passing quickly, and her flight was ten days away.

The Three S's of an Interviewee

Thirty minutes after Lisa sent the interview questions to the coach, a chat message came in from him on Skype.

> Lisa, I'm about to call you, but I'll call as the interviewer, not as your coach, Can you let me know when you're ready?

> Sure

> OK, I will be recording our session this time so you can listen to it. Are you OK with that?

> No problem

As the two connected and began the mock interview, the coach asked similar questions to the ones Lisa had sent him and added a few new ones. The only thing Lisa could do was give pretty much the same answers she already had, though maybe a little better, since she was much more relaxed.

Once the coach had heard enough, he decided to end the role play.

"Okay, we can switch back to being you and me now."

"Sure," she sighed in relief. "What did you think?"

"I'll tell you once you listen to our recording, okay?"

"Okay," she agreed, bemused.

"You should have already received the recording in your chat box," explained the coach. "Can you send me a message once you've listened to it?"

"Alright," agreed Lisa.

"Great. I won't be available for the next two hours, but that will give you plenty of time to advance in your job search."

As the two hung up, Lisa was dreading listening to herself. The fact that the coach didn't praise her at all didn't bode well.

With less than ten days before her flight back to New York, she knew she was heading towards the impossible choice of staying and losing the flight ticket, or leaving and feeling like she was going back to square one.

As she began listening to the recording, she felt uncomfortable. She didn't know why, but somehow she knew she wouldn't have hired herself with the answers she was listening to.

It was something she felt but couldn't put her finger on. The tone of her voice was a little monotone, but she hoped it was because she was answering the same questions all over again.

As far as she could see, she did give the right answers most of the time, but there was something else missing. One thing for sure was that she didn't feel like the three circles were crossing, but she couldn't identify what needed to change.

It was already 2:00 PM when she finished listening to her recording, and although she had a pen in hand and was ready to write down the things she could improve, it seemed that the only thing that wasn't right in the recording was... herself.

Her interview was tomorrow at 9:30 AM, and she would be meeting with the person who had an overview of all vacancies in the company. Her anxiety spiked until it had to be called panic. The Three Circles Coach wasn't available for another hour, and she wondered what he would say to her.

People were at their best during job interviews, and experienced interviewers would ask themselves if 70 percent of everything they heard would be enough.

Considering that *was* already her best and she still hated it, Lisa couldn't see how she could impress *Louis Vuittel*, or anyone else for that matter, especially if they were to downgrade her by 30 percent.

"It's okay, Lisa, the coach knows what he's doing," she muttered to herself. "Fear is part of every success. I need to have faith."

Instead of following the coach's instructions and pushing on with her job applications and networking activities, Lisa decided to listen to the recording again, hoping she could somehow understand what she was doing wrong. The second attempt was no better than the first, though.

But she couldn't just give up as soon as she hit a speed bump. She couldn't allow herself to end up homeless in Dubai!

Her thoughts were suddenly interrupted by the Three Circles Coach calling. Lisa eagerly and anxiously picked up.

"Hey, coach."

"Hi, Lisa. Were you able to listen to your recording?"

"Twice, actually, and it was worse than I thought. I wish we hadn't recorded it."

The Three Circles Coach chuckled. "That's what great athletes do, Lisa," he explained. "They go through the pain of re-watching their race or their match, especially when they lose. It hurts, but they're ready to go through pain to achieve excellence. Are you still committed to that?" he asked.

"Of course, but that definitely knocked my self-confidence a bit," she confessed.

"That's okay. The important thing is that now I know why you haven't done well in your previous interviews, and I think you'll find it easy to fix."

"Easy? Really?" asked Lisa skeptically.

"It can be," he assured her. "But before we begin, who told you about the five S's methodology?"

"Andy, the recruitment agent that introduced me to *The CRM Guys.*"

"I saw this before, and although I think you should definitely use it to prepare for your interviews, it's incomplete," said the coach.

"Is it?"

"Yes. The five S's are the five categories of questions that employers will ask you. Those are *their* S's. What about *your* S's? Do you have a methodology for answering these questions?"

"I thought I did," grumbled Lisa. "I mean, once you understand what employers are interested in, I thought it would be easy to answer accordingly."

"Not exactly," replied the coach abruptly. "You need your own S's. I call them the three S's of an interviewee."

"Three more S's?"

"Yes, but remember, they're not for employers. These ones are for you. It's a secret trick that has done wonders for my clients over and over again."

"I'm all ears," Lisa replied.

The 1st S:

As usual, the coach remained silent for a while, which allowed Lisa to grab a pen and open a blank page in her notebook. And then he asked Lisa a question that surprised her.

"Lisa, do you love your job?"

"Which one?"

"Your career, the job of selling," elaborated the coach.

"I do. We've established that, haven't we?"

"We did. So why don't you sound like it during the interview?"

"Can you elaborate?" asked Lisa.

"A job interview is a sales meeting, Lisa. The one thing that sells is passion. And as an employer interviewing you, I didn't feel any passion," said the coach. "I'm not convinced that you actually like your job, let alone love it."

Lisa remained silent.

"From where I was, there was not much passion coming from you. Did you even smile once?" he asked.

"No, I mean, I don't know," Lisa stammered. "I wasn't really paying attention to that," she admitted.

Staring blankly at her notebook, she revisited all her interviews in her mind. "I was focusing on my answers." She was noticing a common thread.

"That's the problem," the coach said. "Your answers should be secondary. During an interview, employers are essentially looking for attitude."

"So, wait," said Lisa, "do my responsibilities and achievements not matter anymore?"

"Of course they do," said the coach. "That's what got you an interview in the first place," he explained. "But that's *not* what will get you hired. What makes people tick is emotion," declared the coach. "**People buy out of emotion and they justify it with logic.**"

Lisa was silent. She wanted to agree with the coach, but she was in sales herself, and she felt she knew a thing or two about the topic.

"I think that people buy if the solution and the price are the best fit," said Lisa.

"Wrong. People buy *you*. The way you are with them, the way you make them feel, your accent, your smile, your passion. Remember: **selling is a promise of a better tomorrow.**

"With no smile or passion at a time where employers know you would be at your best, the prospect of a better tomorrow doesn't look very promising, does it?"

"I've never seen it that way," confessed Lisa. "I think once my demotivation set in at *Cloudcom*, I found it much more difficult to sell to anyone," said Lisa, "and I thought it was just the market being more challenging and clients being more fussy," she continued.

"**People buy me because of the way I make them feel,**" she repeated as she wrote it in her notebook. "And now that we're talking about it, I don't think I made people feel amazing during my interviews," she admitted.

"In my years recruiting at an agency," the coach continued, "when I asked employers for feedback after my candidates had interviews with them, do you know the main reason they mentioned for rejection?"

"Lack of emotion?" Lisa guessed.

"No," chuckled the coach. "They would start their sentences with '*I didn't feel that...*' or '*I felt that...*' and regardless of what they would put at the end of these sentences, it was mission impossible to make them change their mind.

"The way people feel about you will trigger their decision. We are resolutely and inherently emotional. At the source of every decision, we do things out of fear, anger, love, passion, ambition, jealousy... And then we find reasons to justify our emotions."

"I understand that now, it makes sense," commented Lisa. "But what's the first S, then?"

"Your first S is for '*Smile.*'"

Lisa stared blankly at her computer for a moment. That didn't sound like it related to the conversation they had just had.

"I need to smile more?"

"Not exactly," said the coach, and Lisa frowned. "I'm not talking about a fake smile. You must truly *enjoy* the interview if you want it to go well."

"You mean that *the employer* must enjoy the interview, right?" she asked, almost certain it was a mistake.

"No, *you* must enjoy it. If you're truly passionate about your career, you will *love* talking about it," he explained. "Your smile shows your passion. A smile is attractive, and marketing is about attracting. It makes people feel comfortable.

"In fact, it makes people smile back; we're programmed like that. So if you want them to enjoy the interview, you better start enjoying it yourself, or your smile will be fake."

It was starting to make sense. Of all the things she thought about preparing, she would never have thought so much about her attitude.

"Passionate people radiate, they're contagious," the coach continued. "They trigger the release of dopamine, the brain's chemical for pleasure," he explained. "If you were to ask me to choose between experience and passion, I would choose passion.

"The passionate person I hire can become experienced, but I can't give passion to the experienced one if he doesn't have it already. It is passion that has often made history, not experience."

"So, the first S, Smile, is about... energy? Emotion?" Lisa wavered slightly.

"It's about both. The late Zig Ziglar used to say that *'Emotion is energy in motion.'* They're two sides of the same coin, and you can tell if someone is passionate about what he does by the smile he has on his face at every question."

Lisa felt as if someone was showing her a secret passage into people's hearts. It seemed too easy, and fear appeared almost from nowhere.

"Can you really smile and be passionate when you're stressed and anxious?"

"Stressed and anxious? You're talking as if a job interview is a chore that you have to endure."

"Oh, come *on,* coach, how else would you see a situation where people fire questions at you, analyze your every move, expressions, and answers, and where you risk failure at every word you say?"

The coach waited before answering, pointing out, "That's *your* paradigm.

"The way I see it, employers are so desperate to find new sources of energy that they spend countless hours searching for the person who can bring it. This is one of the most important activities of any company.

"Employers pay a recruitment team, job adverts, and sometimes recruitment fees, even, just for the chance to have an interview with the right person.

"On the other end, a job seeker has done the hardest part of the selection process: he was noticed and shortlisted for an interview because his profile seemed to fit.

"There's only that last step left: speaking to employers. And after all this, do you know what most job seekers do?"

Lisa remained silent, sensing it was a rhetorical question.

"They blow it! They shut down because they're afraid of failing, and fear or desperation becomes the main energy in that interview."

After a brief pause, the coach carried on, almost whispering as if he was going to deliver a secret.

"Lisa, you're either a thermometer or a thermostat," said the coach. "A thermometer only indicates the temperature. If the interviewers are cold, the interviewee becomes cold, and vice versa," explained the coach. "Most of your competitors are thermometers," he continued.

"What I'm suggesting is that you become a thermostat. *You* decide the emotional temperature you want in the room. Be yourself and enjoy every bit of the interview, even if you make mistakes. Laugh about them. Make it a point to enjoy yourself regardless of the temperature of the room. You'll soon find out that you'll set the temperature yourself."

"I like what you're saying, but how can I keep smiling if the employer asks a question I don't have an answer to?" she asked.

"You're still stuck in student mode," the coach sighed. "As students, we're programmed for years to see these events as tests where all that matters are your answers, which will dictate whether you'll pass or fail. That's how people are programmed since childhood," he argued.

"That mindset buries passion and brings out the most negative energy there could be: apathy," he concluded.

"You *must* enjoy your interviews if you want others to enjoy it, too.

"If you don't find yourself smiling and even laughing at times during your job interview, if you're not having a great time, then chances are your passion is buried ten feet down, leaving the outcome of your interviews and your career in the hands of the devastating force of anxiety, stress, or fear of failure."

"I understand what you're saying," Lisa sighed reluctantly, remembering Patrick Haddad at *The CRM Guys*. "But you have to admit, sometimes it's hard to enjoy the interview. It depends on who the interviewer is and how they are."

"How so, Miss Thermometer?" he teased.

Lisa ignored the ill-timed sarcasm.

"Sometimes people are very stern or harsh. Questions can be pressurizing, there could be several people conducting the interview, and sometimes they look concerned or even frustrated. I remember once, someone was even checking his phone while I was talking."

"So, let me summarize," said the coach after a moment of quiet. "What you're saying is that your success depends on how nice the people at the interview are?"

"I think they have a huge influence, yes."

"And I think you're back into victim mode." replied the coach. "You can't control how other people react to you. You can only control how you present yourself to them. You can't just tell yourself 'well, they weren't acting professionally to me, that's why I wasn't hired.'"

"I know, you're right," she groaned. "So, just... focus on enjoying the interview, regardless of who's in front of me."

"Employers want to interview you because they want to *feel* something from you. If they act like jerks, you won't work with them. Period. But during the interview, you either give them anxiety or passion. Smile and shine, Lisa.

"Enjoy yourself; you guys will be talking about an amazing human being. Rise to the occasion and prove it."

Lisa cleared her throat sheepishly. "I'm pretty sure you're overstating things a bit, but thanks."

"You're wrong," he replied with certainty. "There is only one like you. And as far as I know, nobody looks like you, smiles like you, speaks like you, or thinks like you. Nobody works like you and nobody writes like you.

"Nobody has your career, your results, your experience, even. You're unique and amazing in every way. We all are. But there's only one like you, and you're telling me that you want all this amazingness to come out only if the conditions are right?"

Lisa was silent as she processed the coach's words.

"Let your fears go," the coach urged. "Embrace how amazing you are, accept that the employer will *never* see anyone else like you. Smile and shine, Lisa, that's what employers want to see and feel. Don't make your success dependent upon their mood or personality that day."

A tear streamed down her right cheek. In an ocean of rejections and fears about her immediate future, the passionate plea from the Three Circles Coach re-ignited a spark she seemed to have lost for a while.

"Even if people make it clear that they're not interested?"

"It doesn't change a thing about your uniqueness. Plus, you don't know what's going on in someone's head, and you shouldn't care. Smile, regardless of where you are.

"Show how passionate you are about your job and career. Show them how everything was a *great* experience. Not once will they hear something negative coming out of your mouth, because light can't create darkness. Smile, because you're about to start enjoying job interviews like never before."

They remained silent as Lisa reached for her pen, but then a thought occurred to her.

"Coach, what about the questions I wouldn't know the answers to?"

"What about them?" asked the coach.

"Well, I'm a little worried that they would destabilize me and shift my energy and make me more nervous."

"I'll get to that," the coach assured her. "Just remember: your job is just to try to have fun and not stress about it."

The words were like thunder in Lisa's head.

"I think I'm starting to understand. I'll read out loud what I'm writing, alright?" she asked.

"Sure," replied the coach.

Lisa began reading.

"THERE ARE 2 ENERGIES DURING JOB INTERVIEWS: APATHY VERSUS PASSION.

→ I CONSCIOUSLY MAKE THE CHOICE OF ENJOYING MY INTERVIEW TO ALLOW MY PASSION FOR MY CAREER TO COME OUT.

→ I SHOULD FOCUS 100 PERCENT ON THE INTERVIEW, INSTEAD OF SECOND GUESSING WHAT EMPLOYERS WANT TO HEAR AND ANALYZING THEIR REACTION.

→ PASSION IS ATTRACTIVE AND CONTAGIOUS, AND TO PROTECT IT, I MUST ENJOY THE INTERVIEWS AND THE QUESTIONS AS IF THEY WERE A GAME, REGARDLESS OF HOW THE OTHER PLAYERS PLAY.

→ THERE IS ALWAYS A GAP BETWEEN MY PROFILE AND WHAT THE COMPANY WANTS.

→ FOR DIFFICULT QUESTIONS, I WON'T BE ABLE TO SCORE 100 PERCENT EVERYWHERE, SO THAT'S OK. I MUST CONTINUE TO ENJOY THE INTERVIEW.

→ IT'S BEST TO LET EVERYONE HAVE A GOOD TIME REGARDLESS OF THE OUTCOME."

She stopped to read what she wrote again before asking, "Is this correct?"

"It is," the coach replied. "The only indication that you have done well at an interview is if *you* have enjoyed it yourself!" he explained.

"But what if the employer doesn't enjoy it?" asked Lisa.

"Then trust me, you won't either," he replied. "Remember, there is always a gap between what the employer wants, and what the best job seeker has to offer. You can't answer all the questions the way they hope you do. There's nothing you can do about this fact," he stated.

"You must smile and shine. If you truly love your profession, then act like it and start enjoying these interviews, because I guarantee you that if you do enjoy them, employers will enjoy speaking to you, too."

"I think I get it now. I was putting so much pressure on myself securing the job that I focused on the answers, not the energy," she said. "But what about the anxiety before or during an interview?"

"That's not anxiety, it's the same emotion you have before a game takes place. What do you call that feeling?" he asked expectantly.

"It's *excitement!*" she exclaimed.

"Bravo, Lisa! It's okay to feel excited. The employer expects that. After all, something great might be about to happen. But don't call it anxiety."

"Thank you. Can I ask one last question?"

"Ask away."

"Sometimes I say things or I do things that I regret almost immediately, like when I stutter or realize I'm not really answering the question, or when I'm visibly confused. Is this just me or is this common?" asked Lisa.

"It's completely normal," the coach replied. "I suggest you laugh about it at the interview and regain control after that."

"Right. Enjoy it. Have *passion*," she reiterated. "So, would you say that passion is part of my marketing circle, then?"

"Absolutely, along with the way you dress, your actual smile, your eye contact, and everything else," said the coach, sounding pleased.

"Got it," she said. "So if my first S is smile, what's the second S?"

"'*Stories*'," answered the coach. "But what do you say if we have a five minute break? I have an important call I have to make."

"Sure," she agreed. "I'll be here."

As the two hung up, Lisa grabbed her phone and saw two missed calls from Sabrina and one from a landline number. She knew that the landline could mean another potential job interview. Since she wouldn't have enough time just then, she decided to call back once she was done with the three S's.

Glancing at her emails, she also noticed two new answers from her follow-up emails. The first email was an apology for not being able to interview her at the moment, as the role Lisa applied to was currently on hold.

'*At least now I know,*' she told herself.

The second was from another recruitment firm where the agent mentioned that she tried to call after Lisa sent her a second follow-up email. She asked Lisa to call her back, as Lisa's profile was apparently shortlisted by the recruiter's client for an interview. Her follow-up emails were starting to gain momentum.

A moment later, the Three Circles Coach called again. When Lisa told him what happened, he was pleased.

"That's great. Well done for actually following up. Most people shy away from doing that."

"Thank you. I think I need to make sure I always diversify my job search. I sometimes feel like I'm spending too much time on one or two things."

"Like what?"

"Well, the past few days for example, I've done mostly unsolicited job applications and follow-ups, but I haven't been to a networking event yet, and I haven't even started to connect with people on LinkedIn. I haven't done an online search for visible or hidden jobs in a while. Having lots of techniques is great, but it just feels overwhelming. Is this normal?"

"Of course. But let me tell you something *crucial*," the coach said. "You must see things from a distance. Always remember that the purpose of your marketing is to generate job interviews.

"Your work-in-progress spreadsheet will always show you the big picture of what you could do, of what works and what doesn't," he insisted. "That spreadsheet is your dashboard; you must monitor what works and what doesn't. Are you still filling it up as you go along?"

"I'm a little bit behind, actually."

"Then make it a priority to catch up," said the coach. "Step back from the steering wheel and keep an eye on your dashboard."

"I get it. Sometimes I just don't see the point."

"The point?" repeated the coach. "How many times has your resume been read this week?"

"I have no idea. I mean, I'm tracking my applications, but I haven't really made new ones this week apart from the unsolicited applications."

"And that's how people find themselves in the middle of nowhere with their job search," he sighed. "It's not about filling up the spreadsheet, it's about getting your resume read. The point of your marketing is to generate resume views," the coach reminded her.

"The only way for you to know if your job search is going well, or if one thing is working better than another is to track the number of times your resume is read. Whether through your emails opened, or online profile views.

"*That* is the fuel of your job search. You can't drive without keeping an eye on your dashboard, because if you run out of fuel and get stuck, then what?"

"Point taken," said Lisa. She suddenly remembered that tracking her own results ensured that she was in charge of her own motivation. And she knew this was important if she wanted to be in the right mindset during interviews.

"Otherwise, all of these techniques wouldn't be of much use, she reckoned. *"I need to remain focused on the match and track the score." she said to herself.* The thought that she might have been low on resume views and not even realize it made her heart race.

She knew she couldn't afford to waste even one day. In just a few days, her flight to New York would depart.

She had no clue whether she would let it go or get on it. It all depended on her results, which meant she had to keep track of them.

'*By now, I should know what works the best,*' she thought. '*I'm probably doing things that are not the best use of my time.*'

For the second time, she realized the importance of keeping an eye on her spreadsheet. It was her job search dashboard, and she couldn't afford driving her job search recklessly.

With the date of her return ticket approaching, she couldn't believe how careless she had been. Not wanting to delay the session any longer, she wrote in her notebook:

TRACK MY RESUME / PROFILE VIEWS DAILY AND ADAPT ACCORDINGLY.

→ A LOW RESUME VIEW RATE COULD MEAN THAT MY EMAILS ARE LANDING IN SPAM, PEOPLE ARE ON HOLIDAY, MY SUBJECT LINE NEEDS TO CHANGE, MY EMAILS ARE WRONG, ETC.

→ I SHOULD BE IN A POSITION TO WORK OUT THE MOST EFFICIENT JOB SEARCH METHODS FOR MY SECTOR/INDUSTRY AND FOCUS ON IT.

"I'll do that, I promise," said Lisa.

"Great!" replied the coach. "Where were we before we hang up?"

"You were about to introduce the second S."

The 2nd S:

"Oh yes, *Stories*..." he continued. "Most of your answers must be storified."

"Meaning...?" Lisa asked, probing for more.

"Employers are looking to verify your experience. What you gave me during our mock interview were factual answers. I already knew most of what you mentioned from your resume. Why would you repeat what's on your resume?"

"I thought I expanded on my resume, didn't I?"

"At times, but that's not experience."

Lisa groaned. "Why is it that every time I feel I'm advancing with you, the next minute I feel lost?"

The coach chuckled. "Because you're overriding your internal pro-gramming, and that's hard."

"Maybe, but I still don't know what you mean by '*storifying my answers.*'"

"Can you define the word 'experience' to me?"

"Okay..." Lisa thought for a moment. "For me, it's a skill or knowledge acquired by doing something long enough."

"And would you agree that this is already present on your resume?"

Lisa thought for a moment. "I guess so."

"So, your job during the interview is to share the process that led you to acquire these skills and knowledge. The *story* behind that experience," the coach stressed.

"Share how you acquired the skills, knowledge, and attitude you're trying to promote. Tell me the story of how it happened, not just a generic example or what's on your resume."

"How is that different than a regular example, though?"

"Instead of saying *what* you've done, or *what* you would do," he explained, "tell them *how* you've done what they're asking you, and walk them step-by-step through *how* things went."

Lisa wrote in her notebook:

IT'S NOT ABOUT <u>WHAT</u> I'VE DONE BUT <u>HOW</u> I'VE DONE IT.

THERE IS A DIFFERENCE BETWEEN GIVING EXAMPLES (FACTUAL) AND NARRATING STORIES (MORE VISUAL → SELL BETTER)

The best way to sell something is to attach a story to it," continued the coach. "You can sell me a pen, or you can sell me a pen that was used to sign a historical peace treaty. A story makes the product or a service special and unique. And do you know why it does that?"

"Not really," replied Lisa.

"A story is the most powerful way to activate someone's imagination. Your mind literally switches to story mode when you're hearing one. We feel more relaxed and reassured. And of course, we can imagine the entire story in our minds.

"It's like adding the images to the words. **With stories, you're no longer telling them, you're showing them.** Only stories do that, and that's why it's such a powerful selling tool."

Lisa immediately took note of what the coach was saying:

STORIES ALLOW ME TO SHOW THEM, INSTEAD OF JUST TELLING THEM.
THAT'S WHY STORIES SELL SO MUCH!

Although still unsure how she would actually tell stories during her interviews, she was starting to understand the power of storytelling.

"I always thought employers were asking for specific facts during job interviews…"

"They're looking for your stories," repeated the coach. "They're the only true gauge for your experience. Answers are just facts that trigger the analytical part of the brain, but that's already been done by the resume.

"If you're at the interview, you *already* have the right profile for them. They already analyzed that. Now, what employers are looking for are your stories."

Lisa was silent, mulling over the concept.

"Just remember this," the coach continued. "An employer is looking to be *reassured*, and stories can do that because they show him *how* you have come across and overcome similar situations."

"I think I get it," commented Lisa. "Just for my notes, can you list all the benefits of answering with storified examples, as opposed to factual answers?"

"Sure," replied the coach. "Telling relevant stories means that, firstly, you allow the listener to sit on your shoulder and watch *how* things went at the time, by activating their imagination.

"It's like adding images to the sound, where the listener can see you in action. It will help you *show* them *how* you did something, instead of just *telling* them *what* you did.

"Secondly," he carried on, "a story also allows the listener to observe your behavior or attitude in similar situations he might have, and that will reinforce their assessment of your soft skills.

"And finally, stories sell like nothing else because they induce trust, the main ingredient for anyone to be convinced. Listening to a story makes the brain naturally produce oxytocin, the trust chemical.

"Remember, **people buy out of emotion and they justify it with logic.** It's not the product or the service you have that sells, it's what others feel they can do with it."

"Dopamine, oxytocin…" Lisa mused. "That's quite a cocktail you're prescribing, coach," she chuckled. "I look forward to giving this a try tomorrow."

"Just remember, **you must prepare your stories in advance. Analyze each line of the job description and prepare relevant stories,**" instructed the coach.

"I will," agreed Lisa. "But how do you transition from an answer to the story?" she asked. "I mean, is there a method to bring up stories smoothly in conversation?"

"*That* would be the third S: *Structure*," the coach stated.

The 3rd S:

"You're right when you say you need to have a method for answering," he said.

"Before you begin with your stories, you need to start with a brief, quantifiable, and contextual answer, like, 'Oh, I've been doing this on a weekly basis for the last three years,' or, 'This is a situation I came across a few times while working at such-and-such company,'" said the coach.

"Once you do that, you then invite them to your story by using a transition phrase, like, '*I remember the last time I had to implement such-and-such,*' '*six months ago, I came across a similar situation and I did this,*' or, '*I just delivered a similar project actually, and this happened.*' Do you see what I mean?"

"I do," she replied. "But I'm a little worried that answering questions with stories might make each answer way too long."

"That's a fair point; I've seen many people drown their audience in too many details, and that's obviously not what you want to do. That's why the third and final S comes in handy," he explained.

"The final S is for *Structure*. Every great story has one. Having a structure in mind means that you will be guiding and in control of how quickly the story runs and where it's heading, while keeping the listener engaged."

"Is it similar to the E.E.S. structure?"

"That depends. What's E.E.S?

"It's a structure I found online to help answer the '*Tell me about yourself* question," explained Lisa. "It stands for Education—Experience—Strength."

"It sounds like you've been using a structure already. That's great," the coach commented. "How did that feel during the interview?" he asked.

"It was really reassuring; I felt much more in control," admitted Lisa. "The issue is that most of my other answers were absolutely not structured," she confessed.

"I noticed that. But let me tell you a secret, Lisa," said the coach. "There is one structure that works for three of the five types of S questions an employer will ask, which will constitute 90 percent of your interview, anyway. Which types of questions do you think will constitute 90 percent of your interview?"

"Let's see..." mused Lisa. "At a guess, they would be 'skills,' 'soft skills,' and 'success.'"

"Exactly," confirmed the coach. "'Stability' questions are a formality when you know what to say, and 'salary' questions are relevant only if you pass the 'skills,' 'soft skills,' and 'success' questions," he elaborated.

"So the structure that I teach all my clients for these 3 types of questions are: *Situation—Action—Results*, or S.A.R."

"Situation—Action—Results..." repeated Lisa. "I think I know what these mean, but can you elaborate?"

"'Situation' is the part of the story that introduces the challenge and its context," the coach began. "It obviously needs to be relevant to the question, but it also needs to hook your audience into wanting to know more.

"'Actions,'" he carried on, "is the part of the story that describes the actions you have taken. Showcase everything you have done to highlight your skill set *and* your soft skills.

"Mention the things you did, you said, you studied, you prepared, et cetera. If you've used any relevant tools, techniques, or methods, that's also where you should mention them.

"And finally, 'results,'" he concluded, "is the final part of your story. If you have done the previous steps correctly, you've piqued your interviewer's interest, but at this stage, your interviewer does not know how the story ends. This is where the 'results' part comes into play.

"**Whatever happens, your story *must* end positively for the employer in one way or another. So make sure you choose the right story.**"

"Situation—Action—Results," repeated Lisa. "Can you give me an example?"

"Sure thing," replied the coach. "Ask me a question."

Lisa thought for a moment. "Um..."

"Wait, as I reply, just remember what I told you. I will first give you a general answer, ideally that is quantifiable. Then I will use a transition sentence to tell you a relevant story. After that, I will follow the S.A.R. structure to narrate the story. Are you ready?" asked the coach.

"Sure," replied Lisa. She cleared her throat. *"Can you think of a time you made a mistake?"*

"Of course," began the coach. *"I made a few in the beginning, and I think this is one of the reasons I've progressed so quickly.*

"I remember once when I was at Cloudcom, I sent the wrong proposal to the client by mentioning a price that was ten times less than what I was supposed to. The client accepted it almost straight away, and that's how I realized my mistake."

'The situation,' Lisa made a mental note to herself.

"It was completely my fault," the coach continued. *"I used a template and had done it so many times at that point that I didn't review my proposal before sending it.*

"I immediately called the client to apologize, and thank God I always closed the client on the phone before sending him the proposal, so he wasn't too surprised by my call."

'Actions,' Lisa noted to herself. 'So results are next.'

"Luckily," the coach began wrapping up, *"he agreed to disregard my mistake this time, but it served me well; I made sure that I double-checked each proposal twice ever since then, and it never happened again."*

"Pretty smooth," Lisa acknowledged.

"Thank you, but how did you feel as an interviewer?"

"I thought I cornered you with my question, but you turned it into a great experience for you. All in all, you took full responsibility and you solved the problem. Plus, you learned from it. So that's three soft skills you highlighted, right?" Lisa asked rhetorically.

"But how did you feel?" he insisted.

"I felt convinced and reassured," replied Lisa. "I was visualizing the scene at the same time you were explaining it."

"Did I mention that *'I always take responsibility for my mistakes,'* that *'I'm a problem solver,'* or that *'I always learn from my mistakes?'"*

"Not outright, no. 'Show, don't tell,' right?"

"Correct. I showed you all this through the story, I didn't tell you. If I did, would you have believed me?"

"Not really. It's the sort of thing everyone says."

"I'm glad you understood all this," commented the coach. "This was a behavior-based question, though. Let's see how we could do it with a skill-based question," the coach suggested. "Would you like to ask me a competency question?"

"Sure," Lisa obliged. *"Suppose that this was your first day in your new role and you had to be autonomous, what would it look like?"*

"Great question," the coach began, which probably gave him time to think of an answer. *"I think that the best way I can answer this is by showing you what I did during my first day at Cloudcom."*

"Sure," replied Lisa, noticing the smooth transition towards the story.

"On my first day at Cloudcom," the coach began, *"my manager was not actually at the office, since he had an emergency to attend to. So I had to be productive despite not having previous training or experience in that industry.*

"So the first thing I wanted to do was understand the complete sales cycle, how we identified potential clients, how we contacted them, what happened after, et cetera. As I spoke to a couple of sales consultants, I was able to draw the whole process on paper.

"Now that I had the big picture, I started to listen and shadow people to try to learn some scripts that I could use during the selling process. That took me some time, as I also picked up a few common objections I would be facing, but it was a great learning experience.

"At around 3:00 PM, I had the entire process figured out, along with specific scripts that successful people were using at various stages, and how to handle common objections. That's when I decided that it was time to call a few clients.

"Just like that, I started creating a list of potential companies and identified the direct contacts of decision-makers. Before the end of the day, I actually had a list of 34 potential contacts that I would present to the following day.

"I came an hour early the following day, since the market that I gathered the contacts for was an hour ahead of us. By the time my manager came, not only was I on the phone and pretty much operational, but I actually already had one demo planned.

"I'd also sent him the document outlining my entire first day, with how I did it, step-by-step, along with all the processes I drew and the scripts I copied. This document was actually later used as a manual for any new joiner."

"That was amazing!" Lisa enthused. "This S.A.R. model is really versatile," she continued. "I saw how you piqued my interest with the situation, it was a great hook.

"The actions part shows not only the skills but really highlights the soft skills, too! And the way the whole story ended is great, too. I see what you meant when you said that it should end well for the employer!"

"I'm glad you like the method. Just remember your three S's. *'Smile—Stories—Structure.'* Did you also notice how I enjoyed talking about this?" asked the coach.

"It's contagious, you're right. All in all, it sounded like you were having a good time remembering it, and I enjoyed listening," commented Lisa.

"I'm glad you noticed," said the coach. "Let's have one last try with a 'success' question this time."

"Sure!" said Lisa, excited. *"What would you say is your greatest achievement?"*

"I think one of the achievements I'm most proud of is when I first joined Cloudcom. At the time, I was starting in a brand new market: the Saudi market. Since we had no customers over there, Cloudcom was not known at all and there were already several established competitors that covered a vast part of the market.

"This meant that two out of every three clients I had to contact were already using a competitor's conference call solution. I knew this would be a challenging market from the start, and that's why I devised a plan of attack that I was hoping would serve me well.

"I focused on only one thing: my KPIs. Since my manager simply gave me a target, I had to create daily achievables that would support me hitting this target, and I did.

"On a daily basis, I made it compulsory for myself to pitch to at least 25 new companies and organize a minimum of five online product demos per week. In order to achieve this, I had to make sure I had a new call list every day and be relentless with following up.

"I focused on my process, not on individual client outcomes. I knew for sure that if I had the stamina and self-discipline to stick to my daily and weekly KPIs, I would soon be able to hit my target.

"I actually broke the company's record on the fastest deal ever made by a new joiner, despite not having previous B2B sales experience at the time and having started in a brand new market. That, I think, is one of the achievements I am most proud of.

"On top of this, it taught me something invaluable: regardless of how challenging an economy or a market is, it all boils down to what we're able to produce on a daily basis.

"The numbers do add up at the end and will create momentum. That's something I continued to experience throughout my career at Cloudcom."

"How about you just go to the interview on my behalf?" Lisa teased.

The coach chuckled. "I think you'll be fine."

"Coach, I was wondering something..." she said. "As I browsed the net to prepare for my previous interviews, I came across the S.T.A.R. method of answering questions. Have you heard of it?"

"I did, yes."

"So what's the difference between *'Situation—Action—Results'* and the S.T.A.R. method? Other than the T for 'tasks,' I mean."

"It's similar, but with a few key differences. S.T.A.R. is a structure to answer behavioral questions, which are there to analyze how you would behave, or have behaved in specific situations.

"The questions usually sound like *'Tell me about a time you had to do such-and-such'* or *'Can you describe a situation where you had to do this?'*" explained the coach. "It's a way to analyze part of your soft skills, but it's not geared for stories and *only* works for behavioral questions," he continued.

"The structure I showed you will help you for three types of questions. I dropped the T because I find it useless and confusing," he added.

"The most basic structure of any story is 'Situation—Action—Results.' I think the 'tasks' was added because S.T.A.R. sounds catchier; 'tasks' adds no real value. S.A.R. is designed for stories, and that's the true difference."

"Right, got it."

Truth be told, Lisa wasn't sure she could reproduce what the coach did. He did it with such a disturbing ease that it was almost intimidating. She knew that she needed to write down a few stories before things would come naturally to her, too. Then something dawned on her.

Answering When You Do Not Have Any Experience in the Topic:

"Coach, what if I'm asked a question about something I've never done before?"

"Then you would need to switch to a different structure, but you'd stick to your three S's. *'Smile, Story, and Structure'* is something you want to keep throughout. But before I tell you which structure I would be using, can you tell me how *you* would answer if you were asked about something you've never been exposed to before?"

"I would say what I said to *The CRM Guys*: that I've never come across this situation but I can learn."

"That wouldn't be convincing," the coach replied. "Everyone says that. Remember, you always want to prove things with a story. If there is no story, then it's almost useless to say that you can learn."

"So what structure would you suggest here?" asked Lisa.

"Have you ever heard of an objection-handling technique used in sales called *'Feel—Felt—Found?'*"

"No," she replied.

"Alright. The first thing you should do is to answer the question as honestly as possible, and then start the *'feel, felt, found'* answer. *'Feel,'*" he explained, "is for showing empathy. If you're asked any question, it's probably important and a worry for the employer.

"So the first part is to acknowledge the importance of the topic for the employer. You can say something like *'No, I haven't been exposed to XYZ yet, but I appreciate how this is an important topic for the role,'*" said the coach.

"See how this disarms the person in front of you? Defenses are down here, because not only are you being honest, but you also empathize with his concern, so he feels understood and heard. Does this make sense so far?"

"So far so good," she confirmed.

"Now, *'felt'* is to give him an example of a situation where you didn't have the skills for a *similar* task, but it needs to be from an employer's or a manager's perspective.

"For example, it could sound something like, '*In fact, that's exactly how my previous manager **felt** when he asked me to do something I've never done before. He was hesitant and worried because this was critical to the business,*'" said the coach. "Now you see, I've just shifted the pressure away from the interviewer.

"He doesn't have to make a decision just yet, and he doesn't have to feel he has to defend his position because I'm not trying to convince him directly.

"Instead, I invited him to a story that I hope he will relate to, but this time with another employer I've worked with. Does it make sense?"

"Completely," replied Lisa.

"Great. Remember, your example during the 'felt' part must be relevant to the topic," he explained. "So if his hesitations are due to the fact you've never used a specific software, then find a similar example about a software you had to learn quickly without previous experience.

"If it's your lack of exposure to a specific market, then find a similar situation of a brand new market you had to tackle, like when you started at *Cloudcom*. What's important here is that your example is in a similar field so that your interviewer can identify with it."

"It needs to be relevant or he won't feel reassured," Lisa paraphrased.

"That's right," confirmed the coach. "And you can do that because your career is filled with situations you had to face for the first time and learn as you go.

"**All you have to remember is to choose a story of another employer who was in the same shoes as your interviewer, and that had to make a decision on whether to trust you or not for a similar task.**"

"Come to think of it, I have a lot of examples of things I had to learn on the spot or of first time tasks I had to complete on time."

"I'm glad you can see that. Everyone has these types of experiences," agreed the coach. "And if you made sure the challenge you're about to narrate is relevant to the question that was asked, then your interviewer is about to see what could happen if he were to trust you. Ready?"

"Ready," Lisa confirmed.

"Next is '*found*,' which will highlight the result your previous employer experienced. It would sound something like this, starting from the beginning: '*No I haven't had a chance to be exposed to XYZ market yet, but I appreciate how me not having this experience might be a risk for you.*

"In fact, I remember my previous employer felt exactly the same way when he first decided to put me on the Saudi Market. I was a woman who doesn't speak Arabic, in a very competitive market, with no previous experience in the field.

"At the time, my manager saw my resolve and decided to give me a chance nevertheless. *After only one month, he actually found that I was able to quickly exceed his expectations and targets. That's when I also secured the fastest deal in the company's history.'* Did you see what I did?"

"It ended with a compelling result for the employer that trusted me, so my interviewer can hopefully relate to him and project himself if he was to trust me, too."

"Exactly!" exclaimed the coach. "That's why the story is narrated from the employer's perspective," said the coach. "But remember, your answers should always respect the *'Smile—Story—Structure'* model.

"The only thing that might change is the structure, even though most of the time, it would be *'Situation—Actions—Results.'* This time the structure we're discussing is *'Feel—Felt—Found.'*"

"Got it. Can you ask me something like this, and I'll try to answer on my own?"

"Sure," said the coach. He paused for a moment, before asking, *"It looks like you've never sold any CRM solutions in the past, is this correct?"*

Lisa took a long breath before answering. *"That's correct. I haven't been exposed to the CRM market yet, and I appreciate how this point is important for the role.*

"My previous manager had exactly the same concern when he hired me; he felt that coming from a retail background, I would struggle to sell on the phone in a B2B environment, and in a fairly technical market.

"At the time my manager saw my resolve and decided to give me a chance nevertheless. After only three weeks, not only was I comfortable with that sector, but I was also able to secure my first deal, which eventually became the fastest first deal in the company's history." She was on a roll by then.

"So I know I do not have any experience in the CRM sector yet, but having come across similar situations in the past, I don't think it would take me long to get the ball rolling. My career has been built on first time opportuni-

ties like this one, and I hope you will take into consideration my consistent track record in similar situations."

Once Lisa finished, she was pulled out of the moment by the sound of hands clapping.

"That was amazing!" the coach enthused. "'*Smile, Story, Structure.*' You're doing it, well done!"

"Thank you."

"You're welcome," replied the coach. "And I loved your conclusion."

"Yes, I got a little carried away with the exercise."

"How did you feel while you were answering?"

Lisa thought about it for a moment. "In control," she decided. "I was in the moment, completely present. Following a structure helped. And I enjoyed it; the story made me proud."

"I certainly felt it from where I was," said the coach. "You were talking from the heart, and as an employer, I felt reassured."

"I understand the method," Lisa volunteered, "but I don't understand why it works."

"Which circle are you in during job interviews?" he asked, in lieu of an answer.

"The sales circle."

"And what is the number one condition for a sale to occur?"

"The number one condition is..." Lisa trailed off before offering, "Trust?"

"Correct," replied the coach. "Like in most sales opportunities, there are two forces at play: fear and trust. If you want, you can picture a spectrum with *fear* on one end and *recklessness* on the other," the coach proposed.

"For every job interview, you will begin somewhere on the left side of the spectrum, with fear or anxiety being much more prevalent than trust amongst most employers."

"How come?"

"You're a complete stranger to him and he's probably seen several candidates lying on their resumes or exaggerating. Maybe he's hired candidates who looked good on paper, sounded good during the interview, but showcased a poor attitude or poor performance when he hired them.

"So his defenses are up, but he won't show you," explained the coach. "In fact, have I ever shared with you my definition of a job interview?"

"Not yet," replied Lisa.

The coach obliged. *"A job interview is a verbal exchange in which the employer will be casually digging for problems."*

Lisa thought back to interviews she'd had in the past. Each one really was *'casually digging for problems'* once she thought about it. The coach continued.

"Remember the cocktail your three S's make: dopamine and oxytocin. With the three S's as the backbone for your interview, the more they'll be *'casually digging for problems,'* the more they will appreciate your passion and feel reassured by your stories."

For the first time in her job search, Lisa felt at peace, as if everything was suddenly making sense.

As they agreed that it was enough for one day, Lisa wanted to spend the rest of the day preparing for her interview. The role was not what she was after, but she was glad to have a chance to practice what she learned with the coach.

As usual, she grabbed her notebook to recap what she had learned:

EVERY JOB INTERVIEW WILL GO THROUGH 5 TYPES OF QUESTIONS
(THE EMPLOYER'S 5 S'S):

→ STABILITY—SKILLS—SOFT SKILLS—SUCCESS—SALARY

HOWEVER SMILE—STORY—STRUCTURE MUST MAKE UP MOST OF MY ANSWERS

→ FIND RELEVANT STORIES AHEAD OF EACH INTERVIEW
(SEE REQUIREMENTS ON THE JOB DESCRIPTION)

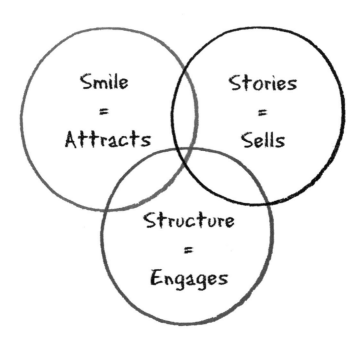

SHOW, DON'T TELL

→ STORIES SELL MORE THAN ANYTHING ELSE!

<u>DIFFERENT STRUCTURES TO ANSWER MOST QUESTIONS</u>:

FOR S1 (STABILITY): → E. E. S—EDUCATION, EXPERIENCE, STRENGTH.
FOR S2, S3, S4 (SKILLS, SOFT SKILLS AND SUCCESS QUESTIONS):
→ SITUATION—ACTIONS—RESULTS.

FOR THINGS I'VE NEVER DONE BEFORE: → FEEL—FELT—FOUND.

The only part of the interview she didn't go through with the coach was the salary negotiation. She made a mental note to remember it next time she spoke to him.

Lisa spent the rest of the day preparing stories for the job interview. She was convinced she wouldn't go for the role, but the opportunity to put into practice what she learned with the coach was too great to miss.

She reviewed every line of the job description, preparing stories for the skills and attitude required for the role. The five S's of employers helped her anticipate standard questions and the three S's helped her design her storified answers.

The following day, Lisa wasn't as anxious as she was for the other interviews. The fact that she didn't want the role she was going for, combined with the fact that she had her stories ready, made her feel more serene.

With only nine days before her flight, she knew it would be an impossible choice to make.

Her car was going to be sold that day and she would soon be free of debt, as she would use the extra cash she would get to reimburse Sabrina. With what remained from her final pay from *Cloudcom*, she could perhaps afford an extra month of rent in a shared accommodation.

But after that, nothing. Nothing would be left for a possible flight back, nothing would be left to start afresh in New York, nothing would be left for anything. It was beginning to dawn on her, just how precarious her situation was.

"And I still have a weekend to deal with," she mused to herself. Two days where she knew she would get no offers or replies.

Taking a deep breath, she refocused her mind on the immediate task of getting relaxed and preparing for her interview in an hour and a half.

Taking her car for the last time, she realized how she was, little by little, being stripped of her belongings. It was her first car and it had represented a step forward in her life, and soon it would be gone.

Lisa listened to the soothing sound of her engine, feeling her heart calming in her chest. '*I'll buy another one soon*,' she thought. After she gave her car to the valet service of the Emirates Towers, Lisa proceeded to the sixteenth floor, where *Louis Vuittel's* offices were located.

After announcing her arrival, Lisa was shown to the waiting area, where she found several people there already. Almost mechanically, she took her phone out to check her emails. The coach had apparently sent her an email 40 minutes ago:

Enjoy your interview, smile and shine, Lisa!

Once her turn came, she was escorted by someone who seemed to be the secretary or the coordinator of the HR department, accompanying candidates into various meeting rooms.

As Lisa's interviewer entered the room, she remembered how she switched into 'thermostat' mode. She told herself right there and then that this interview was going to be fun and she was going to enjoy it.

Lisa made sure she held onto her smile and stories despite her interviewer's poker face in the first few minutes. But amazingly, as the interview progressed, she noticed that her interviewer was smiling a bit, too.

At times, Lisa noticed how he was almost captivated by her stories. The smiles even turned to reserved but nevertheless clear laughter from both sides on a few occasions. If Lisa still had any doubts that her interview was going well, a question towards the end cleared up that doubt for good.

"And when can you start, if you were selected?"

Taken by surprise, Lisa blanked here for a few seconds. She had been hoping an employer would ask her this question at every interview she'd had. But it only manifested when she actually did not want the job... That's when she truly realized the power of not being needy.

"I could start in as early as one week, but I have to be transparent with you; I'm in the process of securing more job interviews for this week that I would like to attend as well."

"Of course," the interviewer replied. "Do you have any questions?"

This was the moment Lisa was actually waiting for. She didn't want to work in a store again, and she wanted to leverage the feeling she created.

"As you now know my profile better, my background and track record are a combination of both office- and store-based sales practices. I was wondering if you could see an opportunity internally that would combine both sides?"

He thought for a while. "Not at the moment," he answered, "but this is something we can consider later on as an internal move. Career progression is something that is very important to us, and based on individual performance and attitude in our stores, we do select a few employees every year for internal roles at the corporate level."

"Okay," replied Lisa. "Thank you very much."

With that, the interviewer stood up and accompanied Lisa to the elevator. After mentioning that he should be in touch in two weeks at most, the elevator arrived and Lisa bid the interviewer goodbye.

As she waited for the valet to return her car, Lisa felt good for the first time after an interview. She still wasn't interested in going back to the retail side, but she was pleased with her performance.

Her smile and her stories really made the difference, although she realized that it was impossible to answer all of the questions with stories. Some answers had to be factual, but every time she brought up a storified example, she noticed how her interviewer was more captivated, and the fact he was taking notes was a very positive sign, too.

The valet arrived and Lisa jumped into her car. She had nine days left before her flight, and pretty soon she wouldn't have a car.

The previous day, a buyer agreed to pick up the car and pay Lisa. He had already left a deposit when he came to inspect it, so Lisa knew this was certainly the last time she would drive her car. Her appointment with him was in 30 minutes: just enough time to empty her car of her personal belongings. Once she arrived, she proceeded to do that, and an hour later her car was sold.

With the extra cash, she sent a text to Sabrina, asking for her bank details to settle the debt. After that, Lisa was finally debt-free, but with almost nothing left. She had hoped that she could get more from her car, but there hadn't been time to wait for the perfect deal.

And with the landlord having kept her deposit, things were not looking good for her chances to avoid her flight to New York. The fines that she would have to pay if she overstayed her VISA were also a concern.

Back on her laptop, she vowed to spend the day sending new job applications and following up on the existing ones. She was determined to do anything in her power to try to get an acceptable employment offer before her flight was due.

As she opened her inbox, an email from the Three Circles Coach was sitting there. The subject line read as follows:

How did it go, Lisa?

And the body was fairly brief:

Hi Lisa, how was it? Let's catch up when you're online...

Before you do, here's a thank you email template you can send to your interviewer, or ask the recruiter to forward it to the client if you've been through an agency.

1st paragraph: Say thank you.

2nd paragraph: Re-establish how your background is a fit for the role, and how it would help the employer.

3rd paragraph: Invite them to get back to you anytime for more info.

4th paragraph: Reconfirm when they would get back to you at the latest, which you should have gotten from the interview, and commit to let them also know when your other interviews are progressing as well. This hints that you are in demand and paving the way for subsequent follow-ups.

Let me know when you're done.

The Three Circles Coach.

PS: Make sure you send a LinkedIn request to anyone you interview with. The more you do that, and the more you'll be able to message them directly, and have access to a larger network on LinkedIn.

Lisa quickly customized the coach's template and sent it to her interviewer:

Dear John,

I wanted to take a moment to thank you for the time you have spent with me during our interview earlier. Thanks to your generosity, I now know a lot more about the role and the culture at *Louis Vuittel*, which clearly matches with my personality and career background.

I'm confident that my consistent track record in generating revenue and exceeding targets in both B2C and B2B environments will play a big part in my future success, and will help me get the ball rolling in no time.

Should there be any further information you might require, please do not hesitate to ask, and I will promptly provide it.

You mentioned that you would have a response within the next 2 weeks. On my end, I will keep you up to date on my progress with the other roles I'm interviewing for.

Thank you once again for your time and generosity,

Sincerely,
Lisa Dutoit.
05X XXX XXXX

To download this template for free, please go to:
www.nameyourcareer.com/jobsearchtemplates

With that done, Lisa sent a quick message to the coach through Skype chat, to let him know she was ready.

Bridging the Gap

When the call connected, Lisa told the coach about what she thought was the best interview she had ever had.

"I'm glad to hear that, Lisa, but did *you* have fun?" the coach asked, and Lisa already knew why he was asking that.

"I have to say, I really enjoyed it. It flowed; I was in the moment, smiling and even laughing at times. We both had a good time, I think," she replied.

"That's great," commented the coach. "And what questions did you ask at the end?"

"Oh, I asked him what other roles he might have that would be more in line with my background."

"What did he say?"

"Not much. The same old, actually; that there will be opportunities internally, blablabla..."

"Did you ask him anything else?"

"No, that's it, I think."

"So how do you know if you'll be selected?"

"Well, I think he liked me," replied Lisa. "What you said about having fun, smiles, stories, structures, everything was there."

"That's excellent, Lisa, but do you know if you're the one they will select?"

"To be frank, I don't really want to be selected for this role," Lisa mused. "It's another sales role in a store, and I'm not planning on returning to that field."

"I know, we've established that already. But that wasn't my question," the coach insisted. "Regardless of whether you would take the role or not, I'm asking you if you are in a position to know that you'll be the one selected for the role," he explained. "Do you see what I mean?"

"I do," Lisa confirmed, "but apart from the strong feeling I had throughout the interview, I don't have any other clue that I'll be the one selected. Although I think I will, to be honest."

"OK," acknowledged the coach. "I don't think you will, Lisa," he declared bluntly.

"Sorry, you what?" asked Lisa, positive she had misheard him.

"I don't think they will select you," the coach repeated.

"What makes you say that?" she demanded, already digging in her heels.

It was by far the best interview she has ever had, and she was certain the coach had to be wrong.

"Well, for one, if you were to tell me that you wanted to do something different than the role I had on hand, I would suspect that you would be leaving us soon. And stability is non-negotiable when deciding whether to hire someone," explained the coach.

"But you said I could ask him if he had any other role than this one."

"I sure did," confirmed the coach, "because you made your decision beforehand that this would not be a role you would accept. Since you were going, you might as well ask for what you want."

"So, I'm confused; was it the right thing to do?"

"Of course it was," the coach assured her. "You didn't want this role and you were ready to reject their invitation for an interview. Instead, you went there, practiced the three S's, and planted the seed about the type of role that would make you stable at their company," he explained.

"Plus, you've met someone who could think about you for future roles. You didn't waste your time at all," he continued. "But it's not just doing well at an interview that will get you an employment offer."

"I think I see what you mean," Lisa said thoughtfully. "That's actually depressing, to be honest."

"Why is that?"

"Well, I'm nine days away from my flight to New York, and the only thing that would keep me off the flight would be if I get a serious opportunity for an employment offer," Lisa pointed out. "And what you're saying is that *even if I do well at an interview*, I still might not get an offer."

Lisa held her head in her hand as she spoke. Despite all the techniques and methods she was learning, the tunnel still seemed to go on forever.

After a brief pause, the coach finally delivered his conclusion in a soft voice. "That's because you haven't identified and bridged the gap between you and the employer."

After a moment, Lisa felt tears wetting her hands, still covering her face.

"Identify and bridge the gap..." she repeated slowly. "It sounds like yet another thing I need to learn," she scoffed sarcastically. "When will this end?" she sighed, tacking on, "I'm sorry..." in a tearful voice she couldn't bring herself to hide.

"You don't have to be," the coach assured her gently. "It's a good question."

Lisa looked up at the screen waiting to hear more.

"When will this ever end?" he repeated. "Lisa, the only reason our work together has been so emotionally and intellectually demanding for you is because we're trying to run a marathon at peak performance.

"That's already demanding, but imagine how dreadful it becomes if the person who's running the marathon is not actually trained," he pointed out. "Your mind is awakening to a whole new realm: a reality that makes your success predictable.

"But to reach that, first we have to get you through a marathon job search, with every technique and method making your stride longer and your pace faster. Because I'm sure you've noticed, we are timed, so we have no choice but to work on these techniques and methods."

The coach paused as Lisa remained silent.

"I know it's exhausting, Lisa, and you probably want this marathon to end now; that's normal. That's because you've done 90 percent of the job search already, and your mind is starting to play tricks on you, like in a real race.

"But the truth is, you are almost there, and more importantly, you will use these techniques for the rest of your career, not just now."

"Thank you, coach," Lisa sighed, calmer. "I just wish I knew all this before. It should be a compulsory topic in any field of study. Nothing would have been more useful than knowing all this in advance."

"That I agree with," agreed the coach.

"Anyway..." She trailed off, distracted. "What did you mean by identifying and bridging the gap?"

"Lisa, listen carefully," the coach instructed. "**There will always be a gap between you and the employer. Your job during the interview is to identify it and bridge it.**"

He let the words sink in for a few seconds. "The employer has an ideal candidate in mind that doesn't really exist. And every candidate is compared to that fantasy candidate. That's your gap," he explained.

"I see..." Lisa grabbed a pen, discouragement slowly shifting to intrigue.

"Question for you, Lisa," continued the coach. "In sales, if a client raises an objection, is it a good thing or a bad thing?"

"Well, bad, of course," she answered; it felt so obvious. "I'd rather he doesn't have any objections."

"That's where most people are wrong," he corrected her. "In sales, an objection is probably one of the best things that can happen to you."

"Why do you say that?" she asked skeptically.

"Because an objection is a doubt or a fear, not a decision just yet. Remember how I said that people make decisions based on emotions?"

"Yes."

"Well, an objection is only an emotion at this stage. If you allow that emotion to settle in, it will become a decision.

"If your prospect fears or is worried that your services might not be the right ones, your job is to identify that and tackle it before that emotion turns into a decision. Fail to identify objections during your job interviews, and you'll fail to reassure the employer. The decision will seldom be in your favor."

"But what if the employer doesn't have an objection?" she wondered.

"Employers always have doubts, Lisa. The perfect candidate doesn't exist."

"How would you uncover their fears, then?"

"Simple," said the coach. "By asking questions. You usually have an opportunity at the end of each interview where your interviewer will give you space to ask questions."

"What type of questions would you ask, then?" Lisa returned.

"Let me start by telling you what type of questions I would *not* ask," the coach countered. "The only questions you can't ask are selfish questions," he declared.

"What counts as 'selfish' questions, then?"

"I mean questions that are about what *you* can get from the employer," he explained. "Can you see which ones I'm talking about?"

Lisa thought for a moment.

"Do you mean that I can't ask about the package for the role?"

"That's one selfish question, yes. There are more," the coach continued, "such as asking about your holiday allowance, benefits, working hours, et cetera, is not appropriate, either."

"But some interviewers don't mention these, and I think they are important questions as well, aren't they?"

"No they are not. They're selfish," he rebuked her. "Remember, an interview is a sales opportunity, and selling is a promise of a better tomorrow," he continued.

"Your questions should be about them and how you can help them, not about what you can get in terms of package or what time you can get home," argued the coach. "It sends the wrong signal to the employer. Do you see what I mean?"

Lisa held her forehead with her left hand as her heart raced faster. Unbidden, she remembered all the times she had asked about the working hours and the package.

"It does," sighed Lisa. "But what if these points are not mentioned during the interview?"

"They'll be mentioned in due time if you're selected for the role. You won't be asked to make any decision without knowing these elements," the coach reminded her.

"Okay, I understand," replied Lisa. "So what questions do you think are more relevant?"

"First understand this, Lisa," the coach began. "Your questions reflect your level of intelligence, and asking good questions will also make the employer realize how smart you are."

"Really?" she asked, incredulous.

"Yep," the coach replied. "And your questions must be used to build bridges between an employer and yourself."

"Bridges?"

"Yes. Remember how we said that there will *always* be a gap between you and an employer?"

"Of course, yes, the gap between me and his ideal candidate," Lisa remembered out loud.

"Exactly. There are two types of gaps you need to identify and bridge: the culture gap and the profile gap. First, **understand their company culture and see how you fit.** Next, **identify the profile gap and bridge it.**"

"I'm not sure what you mean with the first step, coach. Why would understanding their company's culture be important?"

"The cultural fit is one of the most important selection criteria, Lisa."

"Okay, but to be honest, I'm not sure I understand the concept of culture at a company level."

"That's okay. A company culture is the way things are done in that company. Think about all the unspoken and unwritten rules that govern everyone's behavior.

"Think about the way they conduct their meetings, their management style, the way they hire, the values they promote, the way they behave with one another, what success means for employees in the same company, what they celebrate, or how an individual's performance is measured.

"All of these things are very different from one company to another, even if you compare the cultures of two competitors in the same field," the coach explained.

"In fact, you'll find that the two main reasons people resign are either because they do not feel the culture is the right one for them, or their manager isn't the right one for them," he continued.

"Think of yourself as a seed, and a company culture is the soil. You won't grow in just any soil. Some soil is made for you, some isn't. And good companies are very much aware of what seed they're planting if they want to see the fruits one day. Does it make sense?"

"It does. So the first type of question is to identify any culture gap in advance?"

"Yes, but it's more than that. It's also to make sure that the employer doesn't see a gap where there isn't."

"You lost me again, coach, sorry. What do you mean?"

"Well, the whole point of identifying and bridging the gap is to seek alignment. Sometimes, the employer might see a gap when there isn't one. Once you understand what the employer sees as a gap, you'll have the opportunity to either agree with it, or bridge it."

"I see," said Lisa. "So would the first question be something like *'How would you describe your company's culture?'*"

"It could be, yes, although I think that we could phrase it in a way that doesn't sound like you're interviewing them," he replied ruefully.

"How about: *'For you, what's the best thing about working at ABC Company?'* or *'For you, what would you say is unique about ABC Company's work environment?'* or *'What is the typical career path for someone in this role?'*"

"These are great questions," commented Lisa. "They sound very casual. Not sure how the third one relates to the company's culture, though..."

"That's a fair point. For one, the last question shows how you project yourself in the long run. Stability is still very much one of their top concerns at this stage of the interview," he pointed out.

"But the way a company grows their employees is also a direct consequence of its culture. On top of this, these three questions put the employer into a situation where he has to 'sell you' the job at his company. There is also a bit of reverse psychology going on here, if you think about it."

"Impressive," Lisa mused. "The employer will be selling me the job and his company's culture. Great way to understand how they see things."

"But remember that the point of all this is to highlight how you're aligned with their company's culture, so make sure you comment everytime you appreciate something they describe or every time you find similarities with your previous environments," instructed the coach. "They need to know if you fit with their culture."

Lisa had never really thought about how a company's culture could affect the outcome of a job interview. In fact, the more time she spent with the coach, the more she realized how little she knew about how companies operated when they recruited for people.

"Thank you, coach. Are there some other gap-revealing questions that I can include?"

"Sure," the coach obliged. "You've got to also try to identify any gap between your actual profile and the role itself: that's step number two that I mentioned earlier."

"How do you suppose I do that?" asked Lisa.

"Questions, Lisa, questions. It's all about asking the right questions," the coach returned.

"There are three typical questions I recommend: '*Now that you know me a little better, how do you see my experience fitting with the role or the team?*' or

'*What's the biggest challenge you have right now that you would like me to tackle?*' or

'*What are your expectations for this role during the first 30 to 90 days? How about twelve months from now?*'"

Lisa was writing down every word in her notebook.

"They sound like I'm taking charge of the interview, though. Is this normal?"

"Yes," replied the coach. "Each question gives the employer an opportunity to unveil a gap. How you fit with the role or the team, the biggest challenge he has at the moment, and the short- to mid-term outcome he's expecting."

"But what if he doesn't want to answer these questions?"

"It happens, but I don't think he'll avoid all three questions. Besides, your job is to ask the questions, not to get the answers. Just follow the process and don't you stress yourself with the results.

"And remember," the coach added, "your questions reflect your level of intelligence, and I think that these questions do a great job of that."

"Thank you," she replied.

After Lisa finished jotting down the questions, she felt strangely empowered. Finally, she would know what was going on in their heads.

"I must tell you about a common mistake people make, though," the coach cautioned.

"Sure," she agreed.

"The key to getting answers for these questions is in how you ask them. If you do not learn them by heart, you'll be coming up with slightly different questions.

"It's all about the words you will be using. The real power behind these questions is in how you phrase them; I highly recommend you learn these scripted questions by heart."

"Sure," she repeated, before moving on. "So, suppose that I actually identify a gap. How do you propose I bridge it?"

"Well, you have two possible scenarios here," he explained. "Either this is something the employer misunderstood or you neglected to mention, in which case, use *Smile—Stories—Structure* to bridge that gap.

"Or, it is something that you haven't done before that the employer feels is important for the role? In which case, you will use *Feel—Felt—Found* to bring to his attention a similar situation where you did not have previous experience and where you managed to perform greatly nevertheless.

"Whatever the case, make sure you answer with a storified example," summarized the coach.

Lisa continued taking notes.

ASKING SPECIFIC QUESTIONS WILL ALLOW ME TO IDENTIFY CULTURAL
AND/OR PROFILE GAPS.

FOR EACH GAP I FIND, I SHOULD BRIDGE THAT GAP WITH A
SMILE—STORY—STRUCTURE, OR A FEEL—FELT—FOUND
IF I DO NOT HAVE THE EXPERIENCE HE'S LOOKING FOR.

Then something occurred to her.

"So, am I right to assume that with the gap-finding section of a job interview, I would literally be in a position to know in advance the outcome of an interview?"

"Smart girl!" crowed the coach. "Yes, the idea is that you will free yourself from some of the anxiety that follows an interview."

"Based on the gaps I find, I will be in a position to know—or at least to have an educated guess—whether they will call me back or not, since I will know the 'size' of the gap. Right?"

"Pretty much, yes."

"I think this is so important, coach. Thank you."

"You're welcome. Just don't forget to try to close the sale before the interview ends."

"Wow, I almost forgot that a job interview is a sales meeting..." she mused. "But how would you go for the close at a job interview?"

"Before you close the interview, it's important that you review four of the five employer's S's: *Stability—Skills—Soft Skills—Success.*

"If there's anything you'd like to add that you feel could strengthen any of the other four S's—another relevant achievement, for example, a certification you're about to acquire, or even a skill or an industry exposure you feel would matter for the role—now is the time to mention these points.

"Sometimes, interviewers themselves forget to ask some very important questions, but it's your job to make sure you're not forgetting anything that is relevant. Don't just count on their questions."

"Got it, coach."

"And remember, you must end the interview with a closing question, like '*What would be the next step in the interview process?*'"

"I do ask this question sometimes, actually," said Lisa. "It helps me see if they really are including me in the next interview stages or not. I found that when they don't want to answer this question, it's usually a bad sign for me."

"No, Lisa," the coach corrected, "next time they won't answer this question, remember that it only means there is still a gap between you, and you need to bridge it."

"Oh yes, you're right," agreed Lisa, reading on her notebook the list of questions she would now include at each job interview:

1. IDENTIFYING CULTURE GAPS:

   – 'FOR YOU, WHAT'S THE BEST THING ABOUT WORKING AT ABC COMPANY?' OR

   – 'WHAT WOULD YOU SAY IS UNIQUE ABOUT ABC COMPANY'S WORK ENVIRONMENT?' OR

   – 'WHAT IS THE TYPICAL CAREER PATH FOR SOMEONE IN THIS ROLE?'

2. IDENTIFYING PROFILE GAPS:

   – 'NOW THAT YOU KNOW ME A LITTLE BETTER, HOW DO YOU SEE MY EXPERIENCE FITTING WITH THE ROLE OR THE TEAM?' OR

   – 'WHAT'S THE BIGGEST CHALLENGE YOU HAVE RIGHT NOW THAT YOU WOULD LIKE ME TO TACKLE?' OR

   – 'WHAT ARE YOUR EXPECTATIONS FOR THIS ROLE DURING THE FIRST 30 TO 90 DAYS? HOW ABOUT TWELVE MONTHS FROM NOW?'

3. CLOSING QUESTION:

   – 'WHAT WOULD BE THE NEXT STEP IN THE INTERVIEW PROCESS?'

Lisa felt like the questions were brand new toys she would soon be testing. But with only nine days to go before her departure date, she wished she had more time to make the most of them.

"Coach, do you think I'm going to make it?"

The coach remained silent for a moment, as if he needed to choose his words carefully.

"I don't know, Lisa. I really don't know."

As shivers raced down her spine, Lisa regretted asking. The coach's answer hadn't reassured her at all.

"I have nine days to find a job, and I'm not even expecting any positive answers from previous job interviews. Sounds to me that this is a long shot."

"Your challenge is not time, it's efficiency. You can't control time, but you can control your ability to push through everything we've covered so far at the same time, without creating any gaps in your process."

"What do you mean by 'gaps in my process?'"

"Well, when job seekers get interviews, they tend to apply less, as they are focusing on job interviews. Once they no longer have job interviews, they go through gaps because they realize that they stopped what got them job interviews in the first place.

"In my experience, if you stop trying to generate interviews for one week, you'll be creating a gap of two to three weeks for job interviews."

"I see..." Lisa's anxiety only increased as she realized that her recent interview preparations had made her slow down on some of the elements that got her job interviews in the first place.

"Lisa, if you're able to keep the momentum of job interviews, regardless of how busy you get, then your job search will go quickly.

"So always keep these five activities in check: first, sending direct and unsolicited job applications; second, constantly networking; third, constantly following up on your applications; fourth, rehearsing all the elements of a job interview, including every scripted question or answer; and finally, most of all, **keeping yourself motivated.**"

He stressed the last point like a drill sergeant giving orders. "To be frank with you, Lisa, it's the last point that has caused more people to fail than anything else. When the battle is lost inside, the outside can't work out," explained the coach.

"Maybe," interrupted Lisa, "but the fact is, you can't find a job in nine days."

"So how long would you need?" he asked.

"With the right techniques? An extra month, maybe."

"You're wrong, Lisa," retorted the coach. "That's a trick your mind is playing on you. We talked about this, remember?"

"Right, I remember," she sighed. "Measure in interviews, not time. So, in your opinion, how many job interviews are necessary to find a job?"

"Well, if you follow the job interview techniques that we have been discussing, while practicing beforehand with a friend and recording yourself..." He paused for a moment of thought. "I think you can make it with three to five job interviews."

"In nine days," she gasped, incredulous. "And I suppose that would need to be three to five interviews with different companies, correct?" she asked, still trying to gauge her chances.

"Oh yes, we're only counting the first stage interviews you would have with one specific company," confirmed the coach.

Although the coach's method to measure the length of a job search with the number of job interviews made sense, Lisa couldn't fathom a way she could secure three to five job interviews in less than two weeks. Not wanting to sound negative, she decided to write down that session's lesson.

REMINDER: THE LENGTH OF A JOB SEARCH IS CALCULATED IN NUMBER OF JOB INTERVIEWS (WITH DIFFERENT COMPANIES).

TIME HAS NO EFFECT BY ITSELF.

I SHOULD NEVER STOP TRYING TO GENERATE JOB INTERVIEWS (EVEN IF I'M BUSY PREPARING FOR JOB INTERVIEWS). THAT IS MY LIFE LINE.

THE MORE CHALLENGING A JOB MARKET IS,
THE MORE JOB INTERVIEWS ONE WILL NEED.

That final line she wrote prompted her to verify it with the coach.

"So, would it be fair to assume that when the job market is good, one will need an average of three job interviews to find a job, but if the market is a little more challenging, then one can aim for five job interviews, and if the market is even more difficult, then one will need... what? Seven to ten job interviews?"

"That's the idea, yes, but these numbers only work with the right job interview techniques," the coach explained. "The more challenging a market is, the fewer new jobs are available, which increases the competition for one job. This means that you'll need to show up more times at job interviews, that's all."

"And so, if you were to advise someone in this market, providing he has done his resume right and uses the right tools and methods to get job interviews faster, how many job interviews do you think are necessary for him to find work?"

"It varies but I usually ask him to shoot for five. If his sector is not recruiting much, I will ask him to aim for seven to ten."

"But you said three to five for me..."

"I did. That's because you've been already practicing the three S's during previous interviews and you're starting to really get it."

Lisa did not say a word for a while, letting the idea of securing three job interviews in the next nine days settle in. She wanted to write things down:

IT TAKES AN AVERAGE OF 5 TO 10 WELL PREPARED JOB INTERVIEWS WITH DIFFERENT COMPANIES TO FIND A JOB.

→ THE MORE I PRACTICE AND RECORD MYSELF (AND LISTEN), THE MORE MY CONVERSION INCREASES.

→ BY THE TIME I REACH THE 3RD OR THE 4TH INTERVIEW, I'M HOPING TO START RECEIVING CALLS FOR 2ND STAGE JOB INTERVIEWS.

"OK, thank you. It will be tight, but I think I still have a chance," Lisa sighed, thinking about all the pending applications she could follow up with, one networking event she could go to, and all the people she could still send her resume to.

"I think you can do it, Lisa," the coach assured her. "Besides, you only need one job interview to be selected for a second round. You can literally make it any day now."

"I can do this," she whispered, invigorated by the coach's words.

"I only need *one* great job interview." She cleared her throat.

"Coach, what's left of our sessions together?"

"Not exactly sure," the coach answered. "I think we have one hour left together."

That was in line with what Lisa thought as well, so she continued. "Okay, and in terms of training, what else do I need to learn?"

"Salary negotiation, my dear. Salary negotiation," he replied. "We can do this now, or next time. It's up to you."

Lisa thought it over, and for the moment, her priority was to make sure she would get extra job interviews. Glancing at her phone, she noticed that it was already 12:05 PM and she had several missed calls that she was curious to call back, including one from Sabrina.

"I think we'll have to keep it for next time, coach," she decided.

"I would have done the same," agreed the coach. "I think you have enough on your plate now."

As the two disconnected, Lisa dove straight into her missed calls. The first two were from the same landline number, which Lisa hoped would be a company trying to reach her for an interview.

The last one was from Sabrina. Checking her emails, she found a reply from an unsolicited application she sent to Mai Ebrahim, a recruitment agent from *HR Connectors* specialized in the IT & Telco sector.

Opening Mai's email, Lisa found in her signature the same number as the one from the missed calls.

Mai wanted to discuss a role in Abu Dhabi, located approximately one hour and fifteen minutes from Dubai by car, which Lisa no longer had. The role was with a mid-size IT consultancy called *Abu Dhabi Systems Technologies*, as Business Development Manager for the GCC Countries.

It would entail a lot of traveling, especially to Saudi Arabia, Bahrain, Kuwait, Qatar and Oman, but Lisa didn't mind traveling. Salaries in Abu Dhabi were usually higher than in Dubai, and the role seemed promising. After calling Mai back, Lisa secured more information about the role as the coach instructed her to do.

Since Mai was confident her client would shortlist Lisa's profile for an interview, 1 PM was proposed as the likely time for a face-to-face interview tomorrow. Lisa pursued by asking questions about her interviewers and their role in the company.

After the two hung up, a few minutes passed and Lisa received an email confirming her interview with *Abu Dhabi Systems Technologies'* headquarters.

As she was getting ready to reply to Mai's email, another email popped up out of the blue. It was an event company located in Dubai, which she followed up with the day before. Her departure date approaching, she figured that her follow up process was gaining momentum.

The event company, *Eventia*, also wanted to interview Lisa, at 9:30 AM the following day.

Which meant that after her 9:30 AM interview with *Eventia*, she would need to travel to Abu Dhabi for her second interview. As Lisa was thinking whether she should rent a car for the day or get a taxi, Sabrina called again.

"Hey, hun," Lisa greeted.

"Hey, Lisa, how have you been?"

"I know," Lisa sighed, jumping the gun, "we haven't spoken in a few days, I'm sorry. With the moving, selling my car, the sessions with the coach, and the job search, things have been hectic," she explained.

"Don't worry, I understand. I just wanted to have some news and see how you've been."

"Thank you so much. I'm good, all things considered."

After Lisa updated her friend, the topic shifted towards whether or not she would be flying back to New York.

"I'm not sure," Lisa answered. "I think it will all depend on the next few days. I have two interviews tomorrow, and one of them is in Abu Dhabi, so let's see how these go, first," she explained. "I was actually trying to figure out how I was going to get there without a car."

"You can take mine if you want," Sabrina volunteered.

"Don't be silly," Lisa scoffed. "How would you get to work?"

"With Youssef's car; he doesn't use it much, since he's working from home these days."

"Oh, that would be great," Lisa gushed. "And there's one more thing I've been meaning to tell you." She paused and gathered her thoughts. "Whatever happens, I will never forget everything you did for me, Sabrina. If it wasn't for you, I think I would have fallen into a depression."

"Pffft!" Sabrina scoffed cheerfully. "That's nothing at all; you would have done the same for me!"

Lisa supposed they both knew how draining a job search could be. The constant uncertainty, the financial worries, the shame of not having found a job when everyone else seemed to have one, the feeling of being unwanted and rejected...

"And honestly, I wish I could do more," Sabrina carried on. "In fact, if there is anything I can help you with, please don't hesitate to ask. You're almost there!"

"Thank you, Sabrina," said Lisa, and she suddenly thought of her coach and everything she had learned. "You know what? Maybe I need your help."

"Sure!" agreed Sabrina.

"OK, I'd like you to interview me so I can practice. I will probably download an app on my phone to record our mock interview. Would that be okay?"

"Sure. We can do this in the evening, after work, but... I'm not sure I'll know which questions to ask."

"That's completely fine. I'm going to send you an email with a job description, along with the five S's that an interview should include..."

Lisa guessed Sabrina didn't know what the five S's were, but she agreed.

After the two hung up, Lisa went back to her job search.

Strangely, she wasn't that worried about the interviews. The techniques she learned with the coach and her last performance with *Louis Vuittel* made her feel more confident. Her focus was centered on securing more job interviews. She had two already for tomorrow, and her aim was at least three.

For the moment, Lisa continued sending her follow-up emails for applications that were still under process.

Her dashboard was priceless, as she knew exactly which email to send to which employer and when.

She even had a name for her follow-up email series: THE COUNT-DOWN.

Not so long ago, Lisa would never have sent those emails; she would have been terrified that they would upset potential employers. But the emails she was sending were actually serving the employers by keeping them up-to-date with her situation so they could organize accordingly.

Sometimes, her old program would briefly sneak in and attempt a comeback just before she hit the 'send' button. '

"What if my previous email upset them?' 'What if they're about to call me already, maybe I should wait...' or her most consistent worry, 'If they didn't get back to me before, my application was probably not successful. Maybe I should move on.'

But she knew now that these thoughts were based on her imagination. Nothing bad would really happen.

Helped by the fact that she no longer had anything to lose, Lisa was determined to get a reply for every job application, or at least until her last follow-up email, where she would expose the unresponsiveness of some employers by addressing it to their bosses, and Cc'ing the unresponsive people once again for full transparency.

'*If they want me to stop, they'll just have to tell me,*' she thought. '*From where I'm standing, my emails could be landing in their spam folders.*'

That was enough to unplug the old program and push on with her follow up process.

On top of it, she was able to find some new hidden jobs using the various techniques she discovered with the coach. Finding direct decision-makers' email addresses was time-consuming sometimes, but she knew that this was her best chance, even if she also sent her application via the 'apply now' button.

After all this, she also found time to send more unsolicited job applications to companies within the same sector as *Cloudcom*.

She knew that her mock interview with Sabrina would help her prepare better by rehearsing and re-listening to the recording to fine tune anything that would need to be fine-tuned.

She was ready to rock this.

Interview Day

The following morning, Lisa was anxious as she got ready. These two interviews were perhaps the last ones she would have before her flight.

A Skype message popped up on her mobile as she was putting her makeup on. It was the coach, who wrote:

> You're ready, Lisa. Smile and Shine.

Lisa smiled. Her most important focus for the interview was having fun: truly enjoying both interviews.

Two hours later, Lisa had been in an interview with Philip, *Eventia's* founder, for 40 minutes already. Though the mood was great, she was strangely destabilized by one question her interviewer asked.

"So, when would you be able to start if we were to make you an offer?"

Lisa was taken back. Was he really going to make her an offer?

He had explained before how the role was urgent, and thanks to Lisa's *'feel, felt, found'* method, he didn't seem bothered with her lack of experience in the event industry.

Philip was clearly a veteran in the event sector, having founded the company some 25 years ago in Dubai.

"I can start as early as next week," Lisa answered, waiting for his next question.

"And what's your salary expectation?" he asked.

Lisa's heart began to race. She wished, more than anything, that she had prepared the salary negotiation with the coach.

"In my previous role, I was earning 8,000 AED per month, plus commissions," she offered.

"Okay, Lisa, so here's the thing..." Philip began. "I think you have a great profile, and in the event that you're selected for the role, I wanted to share with you our package for it," he continued.

"Since you are yet to gain some experience in our field, we can/ offer you a monthly salary of 9,000 AED per month, plus commissions. We will re-evaluate your performance after six months and, based on that, decide where your salary should be reviewed.

"Either way, should you hit your targets, the commissions would take you to an extra 20,000 to 30,000 AED per month. Do you have any questions?"

Lisa couldn't believe it. Was he really hinting at offering her the job? He did say that this was 'in the event' she would be selected for the job. She was confused. 'It's time to find and bridge the gap.'

"I do have a couple of questions, if that's okay."

"Sure thing. Go ahead."

"For you, what's the best thing about working at *Eventia*?"

Philip seemed pleased with the question and proudly explained some of the great things, like the company's family-like culture.

"Thank you. It sounds like you've built a great company and a great workplace," Lisa commented, smiling sincerely. "And what is the typical career path for someone in this role?" she pursued.

"Well, that's up to you, Lisa. The fact that we're a fairly small company means that there's a lot of room for growth, and that means various career avenues for our people, too.

"We could grow internationally and positions of country managers could be created, for example, with dedicated teams under the top performers. Everything is up for grabs right now," he said with a smile.

"Thank you," said Lisa. "Is it okay if I ask you some more questions?"

"Sure, fire away," he agreed.

"Now that you know me a little better, how do you see my experience fitting with the team?"

Philip pursued with his analysis of Lisa's strong points and the energy he thought she could bring to the existing team. Her track record of achieving results and her ability to think outside the box and find solutions were mentioned, too.

Finally, Philip tempered his feedback by mentioning that the only question he was still struggling with was whether Lisa would commit to the role and to the event industry in the long run.

Lisa recognized the gap: he was worried she would leave.

"Well, I appreciate your concern, Philip, and here's what I can promise you: I will not take this role if I am not going to commit fully for the foreseeable future," she replied.

"As far as I'm concerned, I'm not in love with any industry, product, or service, but I'm certainly passionate about selling," she continued. "And if the company is great, then these are the two ingredients I'll need to succeed in the long run."

Philip was listening carefully, trying to foresee any risk for his company.

"I actually have another question, if that's okay," said Philip. "For you, what makes a job fulfilling?"

"That's easy," she answered. "Helping others. I'm in sales because I believe that I can help people get what they want.

"At first, I might help them identify what they want exactly, but at the end, the thrill of selling happens not so much when I earn commissions, although that definitely is a great feeling," she chuckled, "but when my clients genuinely feel like they've found a solution for a pressing need or a problem they have. I think that every single job should be about helping others if we want to be fulfilled."

"Thank you, Lisa." He smiled, and Lisa hoped she wasn't just imagining that he sounded impressed. "If you have more questions, go ahead."

"Sure. What's the biggest challenge you have right now that you would like me to tackle?"

"Good question," commented Philip. "One of our challenges now would be to acquire clients in the technology and financial sector."

Again, Lisa identified another potential gap. She knew that Philip would trust her for the technology sector, since she was part of that sector at *Cloudcom*, but she wasn't sure if he was equally confident for the financial sector.

"Funny you say that, actually." She smiled and pursued with a '*situation—action—result*' structure.

"When I joined *Cloudcom*, they didn't have any clients in the financial sector, and although I did develop a couple of clients in the Telco, I really wanted to be the first person to secure a client in the banking sector.

"So what I did was list all the banking institutions across the country, and I identified key decision-makers via LinkedIn. I knew it was only a question of time and perseverance for me to secure meetings with them. So I kept calling and emailing that target audience for several months, until one of them agreed to have a meeting demo with us.

"They confirmed a big order only a week after my visit to their offices. From that point, since we already had a client in the banking sector, we used him as a reference to promote our solutions to other banks. Now, *Cloudcom* has eight clients in the banking sector, and two of them are some of their biggest clients."

"Thank you for sharing this," commented Philip.

"Most welcome," she replied, before continuing. "Philip, what are your expectations for this role during the first 30 to 90 days?"

Philip thought about the question for a moment.

"Ideally, I'd like you to sign your first project within the first three months. Of course, we'll train you and give you all the support for that to happen."

"How about twelve months from now?" she pushed. "What would be your expectations?"

"Well, if you can bring in around ten projects a year, you would be hitting your targets and earning really good commissions."

Lisa knew it was time to end the interview. Hesitantly, she was pleased with her questions. It had always seemed so awkward before, but now she was positive she had bridged every gap.

"Thank you so much for answering my questions, Philip," she enthused. "What would be the next step in the interview process?"

"Please let me think about our conversation today, and if I have any question, I'll get back to you within 24 to 48 hours," he reported. "Do you have other interviews planned?"

The fact that Philip enquired about Lisa's other interviews was a dead giveaway that he liked her profile.

"I have an interview today in Abu Dhabi, and I'm hoping to have two more this week," she answered.

Philip smiled and stood up to indicate the end of their interview.

"Well, good luck then, Lisa," he said, extending his hand for Lisa to shake. "I'll get back to you very soon."

"It was a pleasure, Philip. Thank you so much for your time," said Lisa.

Philip's secretary accompanied Lisa to the door, and as soon as she was alone, Lisa clenched her fists with excitement and thrust them into the air. "YES!" she said out loud in the elevator leading to the car park.

Salary Negotiation

Lisa's mind was racing, and she needed to share what just happened with someone. As she pulled her smartphone from her handbag, her thoughts immediately jumped to Sabrina.

But as she unlocked her phone, she found a message from the coach on Skype, asking her to call him after her first interview. She called as soon as she got into Sabrina's car, connecting her phone to the handsfree Bluetooth system.

"Hey, coach!" she greeted, deciding to wait before starting her journey to Abu Dhabi.

"Oh, hello, Lisa. How did it go?"

"A-MA-ZING!" she exclaimed.

"Oh," the coach chuckled. "How so?"

"It's like I was putting all the pieces of the puzzle together, question after question. I knew exactly what I was doing and every answer made me more and more confident. I even found two potential gaps at the end, and I'm so glad I did."

"Good to hear that," commented the coach, clearly pleased. "Do you have any questions for me before your next interview?"

"Actually, I'm a bit shaky on salary negotiation still."

"Okay," agreed the coach. "Do you still have time before your next interview?"

Lisa's interview was in three hours, and her plan was to take the road to Abu Dhabi straight away and have lunch in the capital before her interview so she could get a feel for the city.

"I have plenty of time, but I'm going to be driving, so I won't be able to take notes."

"That's fine, I will record our Skype call. This way, you'll be able to write down the scripts once you listen to it after you arrive."

"Sure thing," she said. She started the recorder, turned the GPS on, and made her way out of the car park. "Alright, I've started the recording."

"Perfect, thank you."

"Oh, by the way," Lisa interjected hastily. "I think I already have an offer from the event company I met this morning."

"That's wonderful. Did he give it to you in writing while you were there?"

"No, it was verbal."

"Then sorry to say this, but you don't have an offer at all. It's either in writing or it's nothing."

Lisa wasn't happy to hear it, but she remembered how many clients at *Cloudcom* promised they would sign a contract during her meetings and ended up not doing so.

Sighing, Lisa conceded, "Alright, I get it."

"Besides, did you try to negotiate the package he told you about?" asked the coach.

"No. Because the package he presented was actually higher than my last one at *Cloudcom*, and the interview went so well that I didn't want to spoil it by negotiating," explained Lisa.

"Hmm..." the coach hummed, without saying anything else.

"Hello?" coaxed Lisa, trying to make sure the coach was still online.

"Listen, a good salary negotiation is the best financial investment you could ever make. Think about it; with just a few minutes of negotiation, you could be earning much more money every month indefinitely.

"When all this is over and you start somewhere in a new job, you might heavily regret not having negotiated, because getting salary raises once you're working is much harder."

"It hasn't really been a priority," admitted Lisa. "I'm more concerned with finding a job, period."

"It shouldn't be a priority, I agree. But this is part of your job search process; it's as important as any other part. Do you remember the true purpose of a quality job search?"

"To find work, of course," said Lisa easily.

"Wrong," replied the coach. "Please never forget this, Lisa: **the purpose of a job search is to generate career choices.**"

"Yes, of course," Lisa returned quickly, recalling a similar conversation. "That's why we should always look for several jobs, not just one."

"Exactly! And along the way, you should try to generate the best choices for you. So how important is salary negotiation through this angle?"

"Very," replied Lisa "I need to make sure that I have the best choices on the table, because that will affect any decision and I will be bearing the consequences of that later."

"So Lisa, what is the purpose of a salary negotiation?"

"To earn more money?"

"Wrong again, sorry," said the coach.

Lisa cocked her head quizzically to one side, sliding her phone a bemused glance.

The purpose of a salary negotiation is not to earn more, but to give you the assurance that you're getting the best possible offer," the coach elaborated.

"If you start a negotiation trying to get more, you'll add more tension to the conversation around the salary. And since you'll be expecting more, you'll be disappointed if you can't get more," he explained. "All this tension and perhaps disappointment will create the wrong energy during an interview, and your interviewers will feel it," he continued.

"Your role is to just see how much more you could possibly earn. If you get nothing, then you know this was the best you could have gotten anyway. **A successful negotiation is when you know for sure that whatever you got was the best you could have gotten, even if you got nothing more."**

"There's less pressure when I think about it like that," Lisa mused as the concept began to make sense.

"There is," said the coach. "But at the same time, here's the first rule of salary negotiation: **Always negotiate any offer that is made to you,"** he emphasized.

"Since your goal is not to earn more, but to see if you already have the best offer an employer can give you, negotiating is here to make sure you're not leaving money on the table."

"I find it hard to negotiate because I'm afraid that if I do, I'll damage the relationship I'm trying to build with the employer," Lisa explained. "What happens if, when I negotiate with them, they decide that they won't offer me the role after all?"

"Is this fear talking Lisa, or logic?"

"I'm not sure. It sounds logical in my head."

"It's not," the coach replied. "If you reach the salary negotiation stage, it's a signal that you might already be the person they're looking for, so the worst thing that can happen during a professional salary negotiation is that they tell you to take it or leave it."

Lacking her usual means of taking notes, Lisa instead simply repeated the important points out loud, speaking more to herself than to the coach.

"IF I REACH THE SALARY NEGOTIATION STAGE, IT'S A SIGNAL THAT I MIGHT ALREADY BE THE PERSON THEY'RE LOOKING FOR.

"THE WORST THING THAT CAN HAPPEN DURING A PROFESSIONAL SALARY NEGOTIATION IS THAT THEY TELL ME TO TAKE IT OR LEAVE IT, BUT THEY WON'T PULL THE OFFER."

"Exactly," confirmed the coach, startling her. "Most people shy away from negotiating because they're afraid they could lose the opportunity.

"That's leaving money on the table, and the vast majority of professionals do that. In fact, in my experience, 99 percent of people either don't negotiate or negotiate poorly."

"What if the employer already gives you his best offer?"

"The vast majority of employers will *never* give you their best offer first. Why would they? They always need to have some wiggle room, in the event you need a tiny bit more.

"They can't afford to lose the right candidate for just a tiny bit more, so in most cases you will never get their best offer immediately. It's your job to see how much more they can afford."

"It makes sense," said Lisa, rethinking her interview with Philip.

"The first rule of salary negotiation is that you should never bring up the topic of salary first," the coach offered. "Wait until your interviewer brings it up. We've covered that, do you remember?"

"Yes, I do," she answered.

"The second rule of salary negotiation is that even if the employer brings up the topic of salary first, you should avoid answering salary questions before you've had a chance to sell yourself."

"How do I do that?" asked Lisa.

"By deflecting the question to a later stage. This has been inspired by the work of two great negotiators: Jim Hopkin-son, in his book 'Salary Tutor,' and Ramit Sethi's many videos on YouTube where he shares priceless tips, my favorite one being his role play with Justin Wilson." he said.

"If an employer asks you about your salary expectations too early, just say, '*I don't mind answering this question, of course, but can we leave the topic of salary for when you are confident I am the right person for the role?*'"

Lisa was glad she was recording that script because she knew she would need to deliver it exactly like that to avoid making the employer feel rejected.

"Try to leave this topic for as far into the interview process as possible," added the coach.

"I'll try, but what if they insist?" asked Lisa.

"I'll give you a three-step approach in a minute, but please understand this: **when it comes to salary negotiation, the one who mentions a figure last will have the upper hand.** You must do your best to not give a figure before they share one with you."

"Why is that?"

"If you mention a figure first, how do you know they didn't have more for you?"

Of course. It made sense once she thought about it.

"If you mention a figure first, you might give them a huge discount, or they might use the figure you give them as a starting point for the negotiation. Either way, you lose."

"But if they ask me about my salary expectation and they really insist, how can I *not* give them a figure first?" Lisa insisted.

The coach obliged. "As I was saying earlier, there are three steps to a quality salary negotiation.

"Before your interview, make sure you do some research about what the market is offering for profiles like yours. If you go on Google and type in something like '*salary guide report <<the city you're targeting>>*' you'll find tons of information from recruitment companies, job portals, or specialized sites like payscale.com or salary.com.

"You must know in advance what the market offers for your skill set. And as you're gathering this info, make sure you capture the figures and their sources on a proper document.

"If the employer disputes your findings, you'll be glad to show him your sources, instead of making it your word against his. Does this make sense so far?"

"It does," she confirmed, slightly distracted. In the past, Lisa had always thought that her past salary was a good indicator of what the market offered, but she was now curious to find out what it really was, especially at the top of the bracket. "So then what? What do I say if they really insist on knowing my salary expectations?"

"OK Lisa, just follow this 3-step methodology: I call it O.M.G.—short for Obtain-Mark Time-Gravitate. Let's begin with 'Obtain'"...

STEP 1: "Obtain" a figure from them first.

"Since they will insist on knowing your salary expectations, give them the range you have found in your research and turn the question back to them.

"Just say something like, '*Based on my research, the salary for this role ranges from X AED per month for someone very junior to Y AED per month for someone more senior.*

"*How does your budget compare to this?*' The key is to finish with that question, that's very important," added the coach

"I understand," said Lisa. "This way, I'm trying to get them to throw a number first."

"Right," he confirmed. "Try to see what cards they have in their hand before you show yours. Avoid answering their question about your expectations for as long as you can," continued the coach. "Question for you," he added. "What if they challenge your findings about the salary range you just mentioned?"

"Then I could show them my sources. I would have put together all my findings into a separate document."

"Well done. Sometimes HR personnel will want to challenge you on that range, especially if their salary is on the lower end of that bracket and they thought that they were closer to the middle or the upper end," explained the coach.

"I got it coach. Sorry to insist again, what if they don't fall for this and keep insisting on knowing my salary expectations?"

"Then shoot for the moon; ask for the top of that range," the coach replied. "Just say, '*I think that based on my solid track record and my X years of experience in the field, my aspirations for this role would be [top of that range] AED per month.*'

"Then hold your tongue and allow some sort of blank in the conversation. This will force them to reply on the spot, without giving them time to put together a good counter strike."

"I think I'd be too scared of making a bad impression," Lisa admitted.

"That's what they're counting on," said the coach. "They're hoping you'll be afraid and intimidated. But that will cost you money," he insisted. "These minutes of discomfort and tension can make you a lot of money every month.

"Perhaps the best return on investment you could ever make, Lisa. Name me one investment where you invest for a few minutes, and where you can get indefinite monthly returns."

"Maybe," she conceded slowly, "but if they don't like my attitude, I might just not get the job at all."

"Wrong. Your attitude up to this point is extremely professional. Remember, the worst thing that could happen during a negotiation is that they say 'take it or leave it.' Nobody is going to say, *'What?! How dare you negotiate?! Let's disqualify her!'*" said the coach.

Lisa laughed despite the anxiety still sending shivers down her spine.

"If they insist on knowing your salary expectations, they like you. In my years of experience, I can tell you this: employers expect that top performers will be harder to secure than the average Joe.

"They expect to enter into some sort of negotiation, trust me. This is all just a game where each person has to play his role the best he can."

Lisa remained silent, letting the thought sink in. The road between Dubai and Abu Dhabi was a straight six-lane motorway. She glanced at the GPS; she still had 48 minutes before arriving at her destination.

"Okay," said Lisa, "so let's say that I shoot for the top of that range and they get shocked by my salary expectations?"

"Then you've brought them exactly to the place you wanted them to be," replied the coach. "There are only three scenarios:

	Interviewer	You	Interviewer	You
Scenario 1: You gave the range and asked how their budget compared.	*Well, our budget is on the lower end of that range.*	Oh... how far are we?	*Well, the maximum we could afford is...* Or *Well, our bracket is between XX and YY per month.*	Repeat the top of that range, while acting thoughtful and go to step 2: "Mark Time"
Scenario 2: You gave the range and asked how their budget compared.	*You didn't give me your expectations yet.*	Based on my track record and my solid experience, my aspirations would be around XYZ (top of the range).	**"No, that's way above our budget. Are you flexible?"**	**"How much did you have in mind for this role?"**
Scenario 3: You gave the highest number in that range.	**"No, the maximum we can offer is XXX AED per month."**			

Either way, you'll get a number from them during this stage."

"And then?"

"Step two."

STEP 2: 'Mark time' and create discomfort.

"They will mention a figure, and after a short pause to show that you're a little disturbed, you just need to say, *'Listen, I really like the role and I love what I heard about your company, I do.*

But I think that [the figure they mentioned] does not reflect the value I can bring to this role.'

"Make sure you add nothing after that; you need to create some discomfort. This sentence is your anchor point, and from this point the wind is going to blow from four different directions."

"Do you mean four types of objections?" Lisa asked after a moment of puzzling over the statement.

"I do, well done," the coach replied. "Can you try to guess the four objections employers always come up with?" asked the coach. "They're always the same," he added. "Employers are really predictable in that regard."

Lisa pondered the question briefly.

"They'll probably say that their budget can't accommodate that. That's something I heard so many times."

"That's correct. What else have you been told?"

Lisa thought about it for a moment.

"I've been told in the past that the company policy didn't allow for any negotiation and that they wouldn't want to make any exceptions because they preferred to treat everyone fairly."

"Okay," said the coach. "What would you call that?"

"Exposing a gap between what I ask for and what their employees earn?"

"Yes, let's call it 'benchmarking your salary expectation with what others are earning, to make you feel out of sync.' This is a great strategy because it puts the employer into the moral position of guaranteeing quote, unquote "fairness" between employees.

"Hence the company's policy," explained the coach. "Don't worry, we'll tackle this in a moment, but for now we have two tricks that employers use to challenge your expectations: their budget and misalignment with others. What other objections do you think employers will use?" he asked.

While the coach was talking, she remembered another objection she was confronted with during an interview she had for an internship.

"One time, an employer told me that he couldn't give me more because the market wasn't great at the moment."

"Excellent!" said the coach. "Employers use the economy to avoid salary negotiations. So we have three out of four excuses that employers will use: the budget, their policy, the economy... What would be the last excuse they could come up with?"

Lisa couldn't think of anything else. She had only been confronted with those three in the past.

"That's all I have. What's the fourth one?"

"Delaying tactics," replied the coach. "When employers say that your salary will be reviewed at a later stage, like after a probation period or based on some sort of performance."

"Oh, right. I got that in the interview I just had, actually," remembered Lisa.

"These four objections are really standard," commented the coach. "Now, please remember this: these objections act like the wind on a boat in the middle of a flowing river.

"In order to remain anchored and in position for a salary negotiation, you must make sure that your sail is not facing the wind, and since it could be blowing from four different directions, you must make sure your sail is actually not opened."

"I'm a bit lost in the metaphor," interrupted Lisa.

"If you argue and confront their objections, they will win. You must ignore them. That's what I mean by keeping your sail closed, so the wind doesn't move your boat.

"Because right now, the interviewer wants you to keep moving and to not stop at the salary, but you have dropped your anchor in the river. Do you remember your anchor point?"

"I need to say 'it's not in line with my expectations,' or something like that."

"It can't be 'something like that.' Everything is in the words you're going to use. This is a delicate surgery for which you want to be a qualified surgeon, not a butcher. Use these exact words: '*I think that X amount does not reflect the value I can bring to this role.*'"

"Right, that's it," said Lisa. "Can I summarize what we have so far? I want to be sure we're on the same page before we move on."

"Go ahead."

"So, the interview flows like a river so far, but after getting a figure from the employer, we are in a situation where we want to pause and see what else is possible; that's why you said that we drop the anchor.

"My anchor point is to say: '*I think that X amount does not reflect the true value I can bring to this role.*'

"The employer will throw four types of objections at us to get us moving towards *his* agenda.

"He'll say his budget doesn't allow room for negotiation. He'll say they have a company policy and they can't offer more. He'll point at the economy or the market to justify not being able to negotiate further. Or he'll use delaying tactics, stating that a review will be conducted at a later stage.

"Did I get that right?"

"I couldn't have explained it better!" the coach assured her. "Your job now is to brush off each of these objections and get back to your anchor point."

"And how would you *'brush off'* these objections?" asked Lisa, worried about the little time she had to prepare before her next interview.

The coach pursued by explaining what he meant.

STEP 3: Gravitate—Brush off objections and strengthen your position.

"Lisa, you must not debate the objections that are thrown at you. That's a trap; they are a diversionary tactic. If you dwell on their objections, your boat will be moving in the direction of the wind. Bring your sail down and stick to your anchor point."

Lisa felt good with the coach's approach. She didn't have to get into a drawn out debate, after all.

"So I just need to stick to my anchor point?"

"Yep," replied the coach. "But step three is really about justifying why you feel you deserve more. That's the time you remind your interviewer of your track record, your experience in a specific industry, the fact that he won't have to train you much, or anything else that would really add value to your application," he explained.

Objection	Brush Off	Gravitate around your anchor point
I'm sorry, that's really the maximum budget.	I understand and it wouldn't be my place to comment/debate on your budget.	However, I don't think that XXX reflects the value I can bring to this role, especially based on the fact that...
That's our company policy; everyone in the company starts at this level.	I appreciate that, and it wouldn't be my place to discuss your company policy.	In regards to the figure you have mentioned, however, I don't think that XXX is commensurate with the value I can bring to this role, especially taking into consideration that...
Unfortunately, the economy is not great at the moment. That's the best we can offer you.	I understand that, and my experience with the economy is that it will always be going up and down.	And I wouldn't want my salary to be calculated in relation to the economy. I think my compensation should be in line with the true value I can bring to this role, and I don't think that XXX reflects that, especially if you take into consideration that...
That is actually only the starting salary, it will be reviewed again after six months.	I'm really glad that we can have a salary review in six month.,	But for now, I don't think that XXX as a starting salary reflects the true value I can bring to this role, especially considering my experience/track record in...

"I get it," Lisa assured him. It seemed fairly simple, up to that point.

"I hope so," said the coach. "But you need to be careful."

"What do you mean?" she asked, bemused.

"Professionals make one mistake that derails everything," he answered, before pausing for emphasis. "They *talk too much*. During this stage, emotions will soar and stress will make you talk too much. It's normal. But if you forget everything else, remember this: **Silence will make you money if you apply it fearlessly.**"

"So when should I remain silent, then?"

"When you've made your point. If you continue trying to justify things, afraid to create a blank, they'll be able to tell that you're afraid," explained the coach. "If you want to measure the quality of your salary negotiation, measure how many blanks in the conversation you created."

"Isn't this going to create more tension?" Lisa asked, concerned.

"You bet it is!" laughed the coach. "It's a game of poker, and creating blanks makes you sound confident," he added. "No one likes blanks, and you'll find that one of you will want to break the silence, because it's uncomfortable.

"Be the one that creates a blank, and don't fill it. You'll find that they will, and they will concede some ground just to stop the discomfort. Force them to fill it up."

"I'll try my best," Lisa promised, though she couldn't deny that the idea made her nervous.

"I'm sure you will," said the coach. "Do you have any questions?"

"What if they ask about my current salary or my last salary?"

"Pardon?" asked the coach, sounding bewildered.

"In job applications, they sometimes ask for my last salary, and it's a compulsory field," Lisa elaborated.

"You should *never* mention your last salary, under no circumstance," he replied urgently. "If you do that, you will leave money on the table and give the employer the upper hand for any salary negotiation."

"So what should I put in the application form?"

"Put a crazy number, like *2,500,000,000* per month. They'll think it's a mistake and will process your application anyway."

"But what if they call or ask for my last salary during the interview?"

"It would be highly unethical. Your last salary is none of their business. I'm sure only a handful of people around you know your real salary; how can a perfect stranger ask you about it?"

"It happens a lot, and I feel that if I don't answer, I might get disqualified or something."

"You won't. They're just using your fear to squeeze this information out of you."

"So how do I answer, then?"

"Give them something they can't fight: the law."

"What do you mean? There is no law that forbids them from asking this question."

"You're right," replied the coach. "But are you really allowed to divulge such company information?"

"I don't see the problem, legally speaking. It's my salary, so what's the issue?"

"Every company makes sure that they make you sign something that says you can't reveal confidential company information. Are you saying that the salary an employer paid you is public information?"

"No, I see your point..." mused Lisa. "But how should I respond?"

"Just remember this script," replied the coach, his tone turning cheeky. **"That's none of your business!"**

The two burst into laughter.

"Any alternative script?" asked Lisa once she regained her composure.

"Of course," the coach chuckled. "Just say, '**Unfortunately I won't be able to answer that, as the employment contract that I've signed specifically stipulates that I am not allowed to share such company information with the public. That would be a breach of my employment contract, so I wouldn't be comfortable answering this question.**'"

"But what if they say it's part of the recruitment process?"

"Brush it off," the coach instructed. "Say '**I respect your process, but allow me to ask my employer when the time comes for an offer, if it is okay to share this information. I wouldn't want to breach my contract without at least his verbal permission.**'"

"I've never heard of this before," Lisa admitted. "I'm not sure we can move forward without that information."

"Don't fall for that," he chided. "Just say '**I understand that this is part of your process. If you want, I can give you my employer's contact details and you can ask him directly. If he doesn't mind, then I'm completely fine as well. But for legal reasons, I wouldn't do it without his permission.**' This shows that you'd love to cooperate with them but not at the expense of your previous employer. You're offering a solution that they won't be able to act on, because they know your previous employer will probably keep this information confidential as well. Remember, this is none of their business, Lisa. Their job is to give you an offer if they're interested in hiring you, your job is to negotiate and see what else is possible."

Lisa was quiet for a moment, before sighing glumly, "I never knew any of this. I've probably missed out on so much money over my career."

"Most likely," the coach agreed sympathetically. "But that won't happen again. Remember, no matter the results, you now have a fighting chance to fast track your finances and your career."

"Well, we'll see," said Lisa. All the hope in the world didn't change the fact that she was unemployed still.

"I've seen this before, Lisa. You're ready."

It sounded like the session was drawing to a close, and she was fairly sure it was once again the end of her package.

"Is this another goodbye?"

"Well, I do have to let you go; you'll need to listen to the recording and write down some scripts. Whatever happens, just have fun. Your situation is temporary. Everything is."

"Thank you so much, coach. I'll stop at a coffee shop near my interview and do some final preparation."

"Good luck, Lisa. You're amazing beyond your limitations. Don't let fear dictate your future. This is your story; you're the writer, no one else."

"So... I'm guessing we won't talk after the interview?" she wondered, knowing the answer but dreading it all the same.

"This was our last session, but I'm here if there's something you feel we haven't covered."

"I'll never be able to thank you enough."

"Good luck out there. Whatever the outcome, make sure they'll never forget you. Smile and shine!"

"I will," she promised quietly. She couldn't get emotional; it would ruin her makeup.

Taking a deep breath, she hung up and glanced at the GPS. She would be arriving in seven minutes, with ample time to listen to the recording and prepare in case of a salary negotiation.

Her interview would be conducted at *Abu Dhabi Systems Technologies'* headquarters, in the iconic round building, nicknamed the 'Dirham' building, where many technology firms in Abu Dhabi were located.

As she drove towards the company's headquarters, Lisa felt that Abu Dhabi would be a good place to work and live. The UAE's capital city was an oil rich Emirate in the UAE, often seen as Dubai's big brother.

For a time, Abu Dhabi was behind Dubai in terms of tourism, new construction projects, and innovation and entrepreneurship. But this had been changing and Abu Dhabi was catching up on Dubai's attractiveness as one of the best places to live for expats.

After parking her car not far from the company, she found a coffee shop nearby, where she settled in and ordered a salad.

As she was waiting for her order to arrive, she pulled out her notebook to take notes while she listened to her conversation with the coach.

As her salad arrived, she continued listening to the session while she was eating, pausing the recording from time to time when she needed to write something down.

Once her lunch was over, Lisa went to the bathroom to make sure she was refreshed and presentable. She still had 50 minutes before her interview, so she opted for a latte and began some research about the company and the salary range for similar positions in Abu Dhabi.

Once done, she tried to summarize what she understood from the coach's 3-step salary negotiation method—O.M.G.

O: OBTAIN – I MUST OBTAIN A FIGURE FIRST.

WHEN AN EMPLOYER ASKS WHAT MY SALARY EXPECTATION IS, I MUST FIRST ANSWER WITH THE RANGE THAT I FOUND DURING MY RESEARCH.

I SHOULD THEN ASK THEM HOW THE RANGE COMPARES TO THEIR BUDGET. IF THEY DO NOT WANT TO ANSWER AND INSIST ON KNOWING MY EXPECTATION, I'LL SHOOT FOR THE TOP OF THE RANGE I GAVE THEM, JUST TO CREATE A REACTION. *(ONCE THEY SAY IT IS TOO MUCH, I CAN ASK THEM WHAT THEY HAD IN MIND, OR HOW FAR WE ARE... AND THUS GET A FIGURE FROM THEM FIRST.)*

IN THE EVENT THAT THE EMPLOYER CHOSES TO GIVE ME A RANGE INSTEAD OF A FIGURE, IGNORE THE LOWER PART OF THAT RANGE AND REPEAT OUT LOUD THE HIGHER END OF HIS BRACKET *(ACTING LIKE THIS COULD BE AN ISSUE...).*

M: MARK TIME – I MUST CREATE SOME SORT OF DISCOMFORT USING SILENCE AND MY ANCHOR POINT:

'JOHN, I REALLY LIKE THE ROLE AND THE COMPANY, I DO. BUT I DO NOT THINK THAT XXXX *(THE FIGURE THEY MENTIONED)* REFLECTS THE TRUE VALUE I CAN BRING TO THIS ROLE. *(THEN REMAIN SILENT UNTIL THE EMPLOYER SPEAKS...)*

G: GRAVITATE – I MUST STATION AROUND MY ANCHOR POINT AND SOLIDIFY MY POSITION.

1. BRUSH OFF ANY OBJECTIONS STATING IT IS NOT MY PLACE TO COMMENT ON XXX.

2. GO BACK TO MY ANCHOR POINT

3. SOLIDIFY MY ANCHOR POINT BY MENTIONING VARIOUS STRENGTHS FOR THE ROLE.

I SHOULD KEEP GRAVITATING AROUND MY ANCHOR POINT UNTIL THEY RUN OUT OF OBJECTIONS.

That's when it occurred to her that in order for an employer to send an offer in writing, she should not accept anything verbally.

REGARDLESS OF THE OUTCOME *(EVEN IF THEY DO NOT BUDGE AND REACH A 'TAKE IT OR LEAVE IT' SITUATION)*, OFFER TO GIVE THEM AN ANSWER WITHIN 48 HOURS ONCE I RECEIVE ALL THE DETAILS VIA EMAIL. THIS WILL FORCE THEM TO SEND THINGS IN WRITING AND COMMIT TO THEIR BEST OFFER BEFORE I AGREE TO ANYTHING. IT WILL ALSO MAKE THEM THINK CAREFULLY ABOUT THE OFFER SINCE SO FAR, I HAVE NOT ACCEPTED.

Abu Dhabi Systems Technologies, ADST for short, was a company similar to *Cloudcom*, in the sense that they were selling conference call solutions, but were much bigger in the region. Lisa often came across ADST while speaking to clients who were using their solutions instead of *Cloudcom's*.

The company was a merger between a local semi-government company and a large IT software manufacturer. Strangely, she learned to see them negatively, since everytime Lisa or a member of her team lost the contract, they figured it was for the benefit of ADST.

But this was before. Today, Lisa knew that she needed to reset her thoughts, clearing her head of any negativity or imaginary fears. *'They just really need to find the right person for their business,'* she thought. *'That's all they want.'*

She figured the interview would be brutal. They would want to know her KPIs, the monthly revenue she generated at *Cloudcom*, and above all why her role was terminated.

Lisa was prepared to answer these questions. She resolved to be as honest as she was with Andy about her termination, while making sure everything else would highlight how she had matured.

Like a real athlete, she was reviewing scenarios in her head, where she answered questions using the *smile—story—structure* technique and truly enjoyed her interview. She knew that was the key, and she was ready. Or at least she was pretty sure she was.

The Last Interview of the Day

The time passed by and despite trying to think positively, Lisa was anxious. The fact that she was in Abu Dhabi, an environment she did not know well, was adding to that stress.

After paying for the bill, Lisa made her way to the building where ADST was located. Arriving on the 18th floor, she asked to see Ahmed, the managing director of the firm, who happened to be an Emirati National.

Before long, a tall Emirati dressed in a traditional white Kandoura came to greet her with a warm smile.

"Hello, Lisa. I'm Ahmed. Follow me, please," he offered.

"Nice to meet you," replied Lisa, surprised that the managing director himself would actually come to greet her.

As they entered a meeting room, Ahmed gestured for Lisa to have a seat and dialed an extension, still standing up.

"Rahma, Lisa is here," he stated. "Would you like to drink something, Lisa?"

"Water, please," requested Lisa with a smile.

"With pleasure," he replied as he took a bottle of water and a glass from the stand. "Did you find us easily?" he asked as he sat across from Lisa, next to two empty chairs.

"I did, thank you."

Lisa was surprised with Ahmed's immaculate English accent. She figured he must have studied or lived in the US. He had a pleasant vibe, and Lisa guessed he would be in his late thirties.

A sophisticated Emirati woman dressed in Abaya came in at that moment, accompanied by a grey haired Englishman.

Shaking Lisa's hand, Rahma and Tom introduced themselves respectively as the HR Manager and the Head of Sales for ADST.

Much to Lisa's surprise, Ahmed stood up and headed towards the door.

"I'll let you three discuss. Please let me know if my presence is necessary." He glanced at the HR Manager, who nodded, evidently understanding what he was alluding to.

As Ahmed closed the door behind him, Tom spoke first. "So, Lisa," he began, looking at her resume, "would you like to tell us a little bit about yourself?"

The interview went on for around 45 minutes, where Lisa was grilled by Tom on numbers, sales methodologies, and clients, while Rahma asked more behavioral-based questions.

Despite the length of the interview, Lisa was pleased with all of her answers, making sure she brought in as many stories to her answers as she could. The mood of the interview warmed up after only a few minutes, despite having to tackle the question about why Lisa left *Cloudcom*.

After covering the first four S's of an interview, the pair decided it was time to tackle the fifth S: salary.

"Can you tell us what your salary expectations are?" asked Rahma.

"I don't mind answering this question of course, but would it be okay to leave the topic of salary for when you're confident I'm the right profile for the role?" answered Lisa, trying to delay that discussion as far as she could. She wasn't sure she was ready to implement the coach's techniques in front of two interviewers.

"Well, before making a decision about that we would like to have all the information, if that's okay. What are your salary expectations?" Tom repeated.

"Sure," said Lisa. "Based on my research and my experience with *Cloudcom*, I know the range for this type of role varies between AED 8,000 plus commissions for someone fairly junior to AED 20,000 plus commissions for someone much more senior. How does your budget compare to that?"

"That's a fairly broad range," Tom pointed out, clearly unfazed. "What would you expect exactly?"

Lisa made a conscious effort to remain calm, despite the negotiation not going the way the coach and her rehearsed. She decided to stick to the process nevertheless. She knew she had to get a number from them first. After a deep breath, she summoned all the courage she had and decided to shoot for the moon, like the coach taught her.

"I understand." She paused, collecting her thoughts. "Based on my solid track record and my five years of experience in sales, my aspirations for this role would be 20,000 AED per month."

Lisa couldn't believe she'd said that, and her heart pounded in her chest. The pair of ADST executives shared a brief look at each other, creating the first awkward moment in the conversation. Lisa remembered the coach's teachings; she remained calm and refused to give in to the tension created by the ongoing silence.

Instead, she focused on her posture, making sure her two feet were firmly planted on the ground and her back was relaxed. She needed to channel her anxiety, as she was starting to doubt that she was ready for the conversation. After what seemed to be an eternity, Tom asked, "Would you like to respond to that, Rahma, or should I?"

"You go ahead," replied Rahma with a poker face.

Tom turned towards Lisa.

"Listen, Lisa. Frankly, I don't think that you're quite at that level yet. I mean, don't get me wrong, I think you have a great profile and you definitely have the right energy, but 20,000 AED..." Tom trailed off, raising his eyebrows as if to say *'come on!'*

That's when Lisa came to an epiphany. *'It's a game, Lisa. It's just a game,'* she said to herself, and she smiled. She made a decision to follow the coach's process, regardless of what Tom or Rahma would throw at her.

"How much did you have in mind?" she asked with an intrigued look.

Tom pretended to ponder the question for a while, glancing at her resume.

"If we were to offer you the role..." He paused. "The maximum budget we have is 12,000 AED, and that figure *will* go up with your performance and your tenure," he explained.

'Two objections in one,' Lisa mused to herself. Marking her first silence in the conversation, she was able to get a figure from Tom. *'I now know your cards,'* she thought.

"Thank you, Tom, I understand what you're saying," she began. "In all honesty, I do like the role and your company sounds really great.

However, I don't think that AED 12,000 truly reflects the value I can bring to this role, especially based on my track record," she finished, marking a second voluntary pause.

This time, it was Rahma's turn to talk.

"We have a salary grade for this role," she explained, "and to be frank, AED 12,000 is already at the top of that range."

"I understand, and it wouldn't be my place to comment on your grading system. But I don't think that AED 12,000 is commensurate with the value I can bring to this role, especially based on the network of potential clients I can bring with me," said Lisa, noticing Tom's expression shifting. She must have pushed the right button.

"We really appreciate that, and we've taken this into consideration as well, trust me," argued Tom. "That's why we're speaking to you about the top of that range.

That's really the maximum we can go to, considering the uncertainty of the market. And like I said, you really shouldn't worry about your starting salary with us, because it will be reviewed after six months against your performance."

"It's good to know there is a salary review, and this definitely increases my interest in the role," said Lisa, determined to stick to her anchor point. "But the starting salary you have mentioned is just not in line with what I feel I can bring to the role," she argued, brushing off Tom's delaying tactic and holding tight to her anchor point.

Rahma looked at Tom, as if to say that she was out of answers and it was his decision. But Tom was a veteran sales person whose resilience got him to his current position.

"Lisa, what's really important for us is to hire someone who isn't going to be interested solely in the money, but would want to grow with us. And like I said, the economy is not on our side, can you at least think about it?"

"I appreciate the market is a little slow right now, but to be frank with you the market is always going to go up and down, and you know this better than me.

"What's important to me for my next move is that my salary is calculated based on the value I can bring to this role, not on the state of the economy," said Lisa, finding it much easier to stop talking and leave her blanks as she felt more in control.

Silence stretched on after that, with Lisa feeling determined to stick to her guns no matter what the interviewers next move would be.

Finally, Tom looked to Rahma before looking at Lisa again.

"We'll speak to Ahmed to see if he can give us special authorization to go beyond the maximum grade, but let me tell you now, it won't go beyond thirteen or fourteen thousand, and that's if he accepts," said Tom.

Lisa thought for a moment, marking that purposeful pause. She decided to ignore the lower number Tom had suggested, focusing on the highest one.

"14,000..." She paused again, taking her time to ponder on the topic, drawing out the discomfort.

It was Tom who gave in to the awkward silence.

"I'll tell you what, Lisa: Rahma and I will push for 15,000 to try to at least get 14,000, but we're not guaranteeing anything here."

Lisa couldn't believe it. In just a couple of minutes, she was able to get the equivalent of half of her studio apartment rent covered by the employer. Taking a deep breath, she stuck to her guns and refused to give in just yet.

"Listen, I really appreciate that you're willing to take a step in my direction," she said. "Since we still have a gap between us, can we discuss the benefits that go along with the package?"

Rahma was able to answer that question, reading her notes.

"You'll also receive full medical coverage, a yearly return flight to your home country paid by the company, and 30 calendar days of vacation time," she said, before adding, "But there's really nothing more we can do in that regard."

Lisa wanted to be sure she would be getting the maximum they could afford, and figured it would be best to keep the tension a little longer.

"Thank you, Rahma," said Lisa, before pausing briefly. "Is it ok if I think about this once I receive the official offer?"

"Of course," said Rahma.

Tom decided to let the topic rest for now. Apparently, he was tired of being out-argued.

Taking a deep breath, he asked, "Before we finish this interview, do you have any questions?" He smiled.

For Lisa, it was a great time to ask some gap questions. The next question would bring the temperature back to Lisa's comfort level.

"Sure," she began. "For you, what's the best thing about working at ADST?"

The tension evaporated as Tom and Rahma tried to sell ADST to Lisa as best they could.

After a few questions, Lisa identified a gap around her non-compete clause on her contract with Cloudcom, which would not allow her to approach her past clients for the benefit of ADST.

According to UAE laws, this clause could only apply to a restricted geographical area, like Dubai, and a specific industry or sector, to allow job seekers to find work as well.

After explaining that her contract was in line with the UAE law and that the clause solely applied to competitors in Dubai, Tom seemed satisfied and reassured.

Much to Lisa's surprise, as she was preparing for the interview to end, Rahma explained that she would like to see if Ahmed would want to speak to her before she goes.

As she left the room to speak to Ahmed, Tom smiled and asked her if she had other interviews planned.

"Well, I'm expecting an offer with another company in Dubai," she answered.

"Good for you," replied Tom with a smile that seemed like it was trying a little too hard to be genuine. As Ahmed made his entrance into the meeting room, Tom stood up and extended his hand to Lisa. "Thanks for your time today, Lisa. It was nice to meet you."

"Likewise," replied Lisa with a genuine smile, feeling like she was shaking hands with a fierce but respectful adversary at the end of a fair match.

As Tom closed the door behind him, Ahmed spoke first. "So... you're still alive?" he joked.

"I am," laughed Lisa. "They've been really professional."

"I'm sure they were," said Ahmed before continuing. "Lisa, why would you think our company is an environment where you could grow?" insisted Ahmed.

Lisa pondered on the question. It's not that it was a difficult question, but she needed to refocus after the interview she had with Tom and Rahma.

"You know, Ahmed, I'm not looking for a job. I'm looking for fulfillment. And for me, there are only two ingredients: knowing that my work means something for others, and the company's culture."

"Can you clarify your first point for me?"

"I think that fulfillment happens when I serve others, and sales is an area where we provide solutions for clients' issues and needs. If the culture of the company is great, then I think I will grow inevitably."

"Thank you. Tell me about you, do you have parents here, are you married?"

Although this was a personal question, Lisa took it as an attempt to know her better, rather than being nosy. She knew that in the U.S. questions about family status were illegal in job interviews, but the UAE had no laws preventing them.

"No, I came to the UAE alone."

"And where do you see yourself five years from now?"

"Oh, I don't know," said Lisa candidly. "But I know this: I will be successful and probably one of the best sales people you have ever met."

Ahmed smiled.

"And would you prefer to live in Dubai and commute to work, or would you move to Abu Dhabi?"

"I think I would move to Abu Dhabi. I'm not keen on commuting an hour and a half back and forth every day."

"Fair enough," he agreed. "That's all I wanted to know for now."

Standing up to indicate the end of their short exchange, Lisa followed Ahmed back to the reception area. "I'll have Rahma get back to you this week," he informed her.

Lisa's head was spinning as she smiled, unable to say a word for what seemed an eternity.

"With pleasure," she managed, losing every ounce of articulation she had used during the interview. "And thank you so much for the opportunity and the time you've spent with me," she added.

"Our pleasure," replied Ahmed, holding the main door towards the elevator. "Have a safe trip back."

"Thank you, have a great rest of the day."

"Bye, Lisa," replied Ahmed with a smile.

The elevator was packed with people and Lisa was shaking. Was she going to get an offer? And if yes, how much would it be? Either way, she knew that she made an impression because she enjoyed the meeting, recounting the laughter and the general mood.

Exiting the elevator, Lisa had to restrain herself and slow her pace, as the adrenaline was pumping into her heart, pounding against her ribs. Running towards her car, she covered her head with her hands as tears flowed down her face. She had come a long way.

As she grabbed her phone, she noticed a missed call from a familiar landline number. "Could it be *Eventia* wanting to have a second round of interviews?" she wondered aloud.

She tried to call Philip back, but she couldn't get through.

As Philip's phone was ringing, she thought she would also check her email, in case he sent her a message, which was the case.

Her eyes read the email scanning quickly for the word 'interview' or a date, but to no avail. Instead, it was the phrase '... *please find our employment offer attached...*' that jumped off the screen.

Opening the attached document, the offer showed 9,000 AED plus commissions, along with similar benefits that ADST told her about.

In a strange way, she wasn't as happy as she thought she would be. She knew that she did great at her interview, but she was frustrated that she didn't have a chance to negotiate with Philip.

Confident about her ability to do so, she decided that she wouldn't accept the offer before seeing what was possible with Philip, despite her eagerness to end the agony of her job search.

After reading the details of the offer, she replied to Philip's email on her smartphone.

Dear Philip,

Thank you so much for your email, and I'm honored to have been selected for the role.

I do have a couple of questions in regards to the offer, and would welcome a time to discuss on the phone.

Would you be able to call me back at your convenience?

Thank you in advance,
Lisa.

PS: I purposely did not include my questions to this email as one answer might trigger another question. Hence why a brief conversation would be more effective.

To download this template for free, please go to:
www.nameyourcareer.com/jobsearchtemplates

As she started the engine, a voice in Sabrina's car notified Lisa that she was connected to the handsfree system, as Lisa's heart was still racing from the recent developments.

She didn't know when or if Philip was going to call her back. The email she sent him was vague to not raise any defenses from him. But Philip could be asking her to put her questions in an email, and she knew that there was no way she could conduct a proper salary negotiation by email.

She vowed to not do that and keep pushing for a time to speak if Philip wanted her to communicate via email.

Approximately five minutes later, her phone rang; it was Philip calling her back already, and her heart skipped a beat. Taking a deep breath, she answered the call and rolled out the script she had just practiced with ADST.

After about ten minutes, Philip, being the owner of the company, agreed to send her a new offer in the morning for 12,000 AED plus commission and benefits.

After hanging up, Lisa brought her phone to her chest and sighed with relief, "AlhamduliLlah." 'All thanks and praises to God' in Arabic, an expression she had adopted since coming to Dubai, and that everyone would say from time to time regardless to their religious background.

Not only did she get more than what she was earning at *Cloudcom*, but the extra 3,000 AED meant that in the event she bought a new car, the monthly payment would be covered by her employer.

As Lisa hit the road back to Dubai, her makeup clearly spoiled by her crying, she called her mom to give her the good news. She was already awake despite being early morning in Virginia.

"Which one will you choose, Lisa?"

"I don't know, I only have one offer officially, but if ADST does come back with an offer, it's a great problem to have, Mom. In fact, the true purpose of a job search is to generate career choices, not find a job," commented Lisa, somehow willing to also reassure herself with this fact.

Sharing and Reaching Others

Because of rush hour, Lisa reached Sabrina's house at 4:35 PM.

As she rang her friend to indicate she was parked outside her house, Sabrina was already at home. Lisa assumed that she probably left early to be there for her when she arrived. She couldn't wait to tell Sabrina about the events that unfolded that day.

Lisa rang the bell and after a few seconds, she heard Hanaa running to the door, hardly managing to pull the handle down due to her small size.

Welcoming her with a big hug, Hanaa immediately asked, "Did you bring me something?"

Lisa burst into laughter as Sabrina came to join them, sweeping Lisa into a hug.

"How did it go, sweetie?"

"It went *great!*" said Lisa. "Thank you so much for the car." Lisa handed the keys over.

They went inside and had tea. Lisa told her about what an amazing day it was, leaving out no detail.

But as the conversation neared the end, Sabrina looked like she was daydreaming.

"I'm sorry, I'm talking too much," Lisa sighed sheepishly.

"No, no... Sorry, it's just that I had a difficult day at work."

"Oh come on, Sabrina, nothing's difficult for you." The attempt to lighten the mood didn't quite work out. Taking a closer look at Sabrina's face, she looked like she had been crying not long ago. "Are you okay?" Lisa asked, toning herself down as the mood shifted.

Taking a deep breath, Sabrina tried to not cry as she announced the fateful news to her friend.

"I've just been made redundant," she said bluntly.

"You what? Why?" asked Lisa, in shock.

"The COO decided to merge my department with the operations department due to a reorganization." She held back her tears. "And my boss and I were made redundant, effective today."

"Oh my God, Sabrina, I'm so sorry," Lisa gasped, at a loss for what else to say.

It wasn't exactly how she had predicted the day would end.

"Youssef is really stressed, obviously, and so am I. It's like we're going to live that nightmare all over again." Sabrina burst into tears.

Lisa remembered what ordeal her friend went through last time she was looking for work. Sabrina still had a mortgage and a car loan. And along with Youssef being a freelancer and Hanaa's school fees, her redundancy package would melt like snow under the sun.

Taking a deep breath, Lisa grabbed her friend's hand and drew her face nearer to hers, with a look that would be referred to later as The Look.

"Listen carefully, Sabrina. You will not live that nightmare again, I promise you that. You're going to find work at the speed of light. I have the recipe, and it works, Sabrina, trust me," said Lisa.

"I hope so, but I'm not in sales. If it worked for you, it might not apply to other profiles."

"Nonsense! It worked for my cousin Leonard after a nine-year unemployment period, and he has no degrees at all."

"Maybe it works in Virginia, but Dubai is different."

Lisa could relate to that mindset, of course. Fear had already taken root in her friend's mind, and it was trying to sap away any hope or rational thinking.

"Employers are the same; they all want the same thing."

Sabrina didn't seem as confident as Lisa, of course, but dredged up a smile.

"I'm sorry, tell me more about your day. I'd like to know everything," she said with a trembling voice.

"I will," said Lisa, "but for now, we have a resume to work on."

Sabrina nodded and took a deep breath, tears still flowing. "Thank you, Lisa."

After a brief pause, Lisa said something she never thought she could say just a couple weeks ago.

"Listen, Sabrina, you might think I'm crazy right now, but you're about to have the time of your life. You will never forget what's about to unfold."

They worked on Sabrina's resume that evening, the mood lifting as Sabrina regained confidence in her ability to find work. Lisa helped her make her resume shine in a way that Sabrina never thought possible.

Strangely, the feeling of helping a friend was better than any employment offer Lisa could get. She vowed to always share the Three Circles Coach's methods with anyone who would need it.

What she didn't realize was that by teaching the coach's methods to others, Lisa was going to become more and more comfortable with her future job searches, which in turn would help her secure outstanding positions with different companies and fast track her career.

Later that day, Lisa went back to the flat she still was sharing with three other flatmates. Finally allowing herself to dream of a bigger flat and a better financial future, Lisa would never forget her fateful job search.

As she sat at her desk to send a thank you email to ADST, her notebook was open on the first page from the Three Circles Coach's sessions. A phrase circled in red caught her attention:

I CHOOSE WHETHER A SITUATION HAPPENS TO ME OR FOR ME.

It was at that moment that she decided to save money more aggressively, so she could be prepared for the many bumps that she knew she would face in her career.

The words of the coach were still echoing in Lisa's head, as she turned the pages of her notebook.

Coming to the end of it, she realized that she never finished drawing the three circles with what she thought were the elements that made each circle cross with one another.

After a deep breath, she drew the three circles, almost as if it were the conclusion of her notes. She couldn't put everything she learned and many aspects had their place in more than one circle, now that they were all crossing. After a few minutes, she added what she thought were the most important elements of a job search:

POWERFUL RESUME: Keywords + Acton Verbs + Quantities + Results

Finding hidden jobs online with less competition

Job Application Emails that get resume opened!

Sending Job Applications directly to Decision makers (not HR)

The art of Networking

The following-up process

Help others first and build a powerful network

Never ever lie, but don't shoot yourself in the foot!

Smile and shine

Marketing = Attracting

Selling = Convincing

OPPORTUNITIES

YOUR BRAND

FULFILMENT

Serve Others Never be needy

The 5 S's of every interview

Smile, Stories & Structure

Feel, Felt, Found

Bridging the Gap

3 steps of salary negotiation

Career Fulfillment is about serving others

Serve employers through outstanding resume formatting and E-mail communications

Think like an employer in everything you do

Lisa went to bed earlier than usual that night, still anxious to hear from ADST and make a final decision.

Although she had to wait for two days before an employment offer from ADST came through, Lisa was relieved when she finally received it: AED 14,700 per month, plus commissions and benefits, almost twice what she had at *Cloudcom*.

Lisa was amazed that she had managed to get herself a choice between two companies.

After carefully weighing each career path, Lisa opted for the role at ADST, which Tom, Rahma, and Ahmed were very pleased with.

Tom and Rahma told Ahmed about Lisa's performance during her interview, and Lisa quickly became one of the top performers at ADST.

She vowed to never let herself down again.

The End

A FINAL MESSAGE FROM THE AUTHOR

Thank you ever so much for reading this book. My hope is that you have not only enjoyed it, but also found it useful for your future job searches.

I strongly believe that a job search is one of the most career-defining moments in your life. Although it may be uncomfortable right now, you will soon find that it is the best thing that happened to you in a while.

If you conduct it well, a job search could generate choices for you. Mastering these techniques will allow you to have an active role in choosing the people, the company, the industry that you'd like to work with.

I can't possibly let you go without sharing with you one more piece of advice. Although the vast majority of job seekers are willing to put aside their fears or assumptions and apply the tools, methods, and scripts available in this book, there is always someone who would contact me to say that he has applied *"all"* of the techniques mentioned in this book, but *"it doesn't work."*

Please do not fall for this. The job search formula recipe works. Every single time I have tackled these claims and analyzed someone's job search (the way he wrote his resume, his job search dashboard, the way he conducted interviews, etc.), I found critical gaps in the person's job search process that prevented him from gaining momentum and from securing great jobs.

The step-by-step formula outlined in this book must be applied properly in order to work. If things don't work out just yet, don't blame the formula. You just need to review it. As Lisa realized, not taking responsibility for her own job search is perhaps the most dangerous thing that could happen.

It's not the formula (or the market or whatever) that doesn't work. It's what you do. Any new approach needs time and dedication to learn and apply.

Review your process: if your phone is not ringing, then your number one suspect is your resume. Your number two suspect is the search itself. The way you send your applications, your ability to find jobs with less competition, the quality of your follow up process, etc.

Finally, if you're not able to pass first stage job interviews, then I would suspect your three S's should be reviewed. *(A good idea would be to record yourself having an interview and re-listen to the recording.)*

Like anything worthwhile, the three circles job search formula takes some time and practice to learn, and I hope that narrating it in the form of a story has helped you in that process.

But if you truly want to master the *'three circles job search formula'*, **then teach it.**

You do not have to become a coach, of course, but you can definitely try to mentor someone in his or her job search. The person would surely benefit, yes, but you would benefit more than him. I guarantee it.

The more difficult the case might look to you, the faster the formula will work for the person. Why? Because, as with Leonard's example, the bigger the employment gap, the more impactful the formula becomes.

So if you're passing by a homeless person every day, then today, stop by him or her and say: *'Hi, I'd like to help you find work, is this something you might be interested in?'* Remember, no case is hopeless; just make sure the person's three circles are in sync with one another.

Maybe I sound naive. I'm not. Please remember, these homeless or long-term unemployed people were not born this way, they had an accident that brought them to where they are today. Allow them to one day tell the story of this perfect stranger who changed their life without asking for anything in return.

Finding a great job is a game changer for people and their families. And the more you teach this formula, the more you will master it for yourself. The more people you help receive phone calls, regain hopes, and secure jobs, the more fulfilled you will be.

So reach out to others.

Present the three circles job search formula at gatherings, career fairs, or networking events. Offer this book to someone. Please spread the word in some way, as everyone deserves to smile and shine.

Back to you. I have added an index section in the next page to allow you to locate any specific scripts, message templates, or tools without having to search through the pages.

Finally, among all the things that can influence the success of a book, reviews surely rank at the top. If you have enjoyed this book, please consider spending 30 seconds to write a review.

Thank you so much for giving me a chance to serve you.

Hamza Zaouali.

ABOUT THE AUTHOR

Hamza Zaouali is the owner and founder of Name Your Career, a training & coaching firm helping professionals excel in their careers and companies grow to their full potential.

Hamza has lived and worked in Paris, London, and Dubai, where he served as a headhunter, an employer / manager, and a career coach. Over the years, he has recruited, coached, or trained thousands of professionals from all walks of life and seniority levels in countries around the world.

He is also a business trainer and a keynote speaker, helping companies recruit better, manage smarter, and sell more. His clients range from SMEs to large multinationals.

To learn more about Hamza Zaouali and Name Your Career, please visit: www.nameyourcareer.com.